Professionalism Under Stress

Dedicated to…
our families, teachers, students,
and those with commitment and courage
strong enough to prepare and act to fulfill their callings.

A book for …
Corporate, Combat, Collegiate, and Church Professionals
Champions of People and Organizational Development
Gunfighters and Others Working with Intense Stress
Leaders and Emerging Leaders in Organizations
People with Callings to Live a Legacy
Parents, Teachers, and Mentors
Pragmatic Optimists

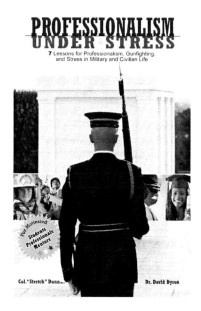

PROFESSIONALISM
UNDER STRESS

7 Lessons for Professionalism, Gunfighting, and Stress in Military and Civilian Life

For Motivated
Students
Professionals
Mentors

Col."Stretch" Dunn   Dr. David Dyson

At any moment in history the world is in the hands of two percent of the people, the excited and the committed.
-Winston Churchill-

An estimated 1-5% of people
prepare and take action to do their best
to PLAN and LEAD in LIFE as true professionals.
If you are among or desire to expand the ranks of those
those dedicated to serve and fulfill their callings,
this book is for you and those you serve.

For the Preparation, Action, and Library
of

_____

Professionalism Under Stress

7 Lessons for
Professionalism, Stress, and Gunfighting
In Military and Civilian Life

Col. "Stretch" Dunn   Dr. David Dyson

LEAVE A LEGACY PUBLISHING

Reader Results and Responses

Journalists

The authors show executives how to use military discipline in the workplace.... Army Col. (retired) Stretch Dunn and executive business coach Dr. David Dyson break down in an easy-to-understand manner how stressed-out workers and managers can achieve better balance in their lives.... Stretch's military background and Dyson's business savvy derived from training corporate executives make this book a must-have.

Roy Williams
Business Writer, *The Birmingham News*
Author, *911*, God Help Us

Military Professionals and Veterans

If I had to limit my library to two books, one would be The Bible and the other would be your work. I have been refining the leadership skills I learned in the military, and I must tell you that my journey would have been much easier if your book had been in my hands earlier in my evolution.

Gerry Casey
UAB Medical Center
Navy Veteran

"The unexamined life is not worth living." So writes Socrates. More than anything else, Professionalism Under Stress is a handbook, a practical guide for a reflective life, accessible to anyone who aspires to be a leader....

Richard M. Swain, COL USA (Ret.)
Professor of Officership, U.S. Military Academy

As a combat leader in today's Army I have learned many things. One of these is to use every asset available.... This book.... provides effective tools to assist a leader in being more progressive, caring, and efficient.

Sergeant Major Victor Legloahec
United States Army Sergeants Major Academy

It was very inspiring and applicable to all—for cadets to enlisted cadre to commissioned officers and even civilians.

LTC John L. Salvetti
Tank Battalion Commander, Korea

Your book is hard-hitting, factual and absolutely a must-read for those of us who aspire to be true professionals. I sent a copy to my son Mike, who is serving in Baghdad. I use the concepts and actions daily as a career manager working with clients to help them with stressful career transitions.

Col. Bob Barfield (U.S. Army Retired)
Chairman, Personal Leadership Association

Leadership and discipline have been keys to survival on the battlefield and in the corporate world. When and how to react, based on proper training, has been the answer in situations that could have had serious results. The lessons provided through this book are essential to the advancement of both individuals and institutions.

Col. Bill Voigt (USAFR Retired)
President, Veterans Day, Birmingham

Your book can help working professionals enhance their leadership capabilities.

Dr. Byron Chew
Monaghan Professor, Birmingham-Southern College
Marine Corps Veteran

This is great. Successful leaders possess both strong integrity and determined will. These principles are verified by the experience of the authors. I intend to give a copy of the book to my son as a source of guidance in his business career.

William A. Jackson
Major General, AUS Retired, Retired Judge

As an author, trainer, and motivational speaker, I have found Professionalism Under Stress *a cornucopia of insight on how to take command of one's destiny….this book establishes proven standards for mental, physical, and spiritual development. As a former U.S. Marine, I especially relate to the underlying esprit de corps throughout this valuable resource for personal growth and fulfillment. The solid principles of military leadership and engagement morph into inspirational examples of professionalism….the authors have outlined essential parameters for balancing success with life-long happiness….*

John O'Malley
Marine Veteran
President, Strategic Visions

I hope everyone in our company reads this book.

> Hack Sain
> Founder and Retired CEO, Sain Associates
> WWII Veteran

Civilian Professionals

Professionalism Under Stress is a thought-provoking experience that asks and answers many questions we have in life. A quote from the book that hit my core, perked my attention, and encouraged me to listen more carefully is: "Seasoned veterans help you move from book smarts to street smarts.... They are the bridge to learning the meaning of caring for others." Finding a mentor and teacher is essential for one's growth. To become "this" seasoned veteran should be everyone's goal, to give back to life what you have learned.

> Simon Coulls
> Vice President/Director of Golf, Limestone Springs

I highly recommend the lessons and actions on writing a plan for life with a professional plan that helps you focus and communicate intent and expectations with others on your team.

> Hayes Parnell, III
> President and CEO, Covenant Bank

Stretch and David have taken a complex subject and made it manageable for me to take action while we face changes to excel in an increasingly competitive global market.

> Bo Gilbert
> Vice President, BE&K Engineering

...a practical guide to implement lessons for personal leadership and true professionalism in the seven areas of life!

> Dwight Wiggins
> President, Concord Financial Group

I found your book stimulating, encouraging, and insightful and have implemented some of your leadership principles.

> Mark Miller
> Sr. Vice President, Miller Wealth Management

Attending your seminar [based on the book] made me realize that going through college and a MBA I was not taught about how to be a professional under stress, which affects me everyday.

> Bob Cornelius
> Superior Bank

Many thanks to you...for presenting the workshop on professionalism under stress. We appreciate your commitment to veterans and to those who care for them.

> Dr. Susan Laing
> Associate Chief of Staff for Education
> VA Medical Center Birmingham

Faculty and Students

How I wish that the adult "guide to life" that you set forth in Professionalism Under Stress had been available when I was in my youth.... You have managed to crystallize in this volume so many things that it took me decades of trial and a lot of error to understand and apply in my life and career.... Now at 85, I am thrilled to see what you have made available to adults of all ages from the neophyte level on up to the end of one's days.

> LTC C.A. "Ole" Olsen (USA Retired)
> Professor Emeritus, U.S. Military Academy

...the manner in which it is written appeals to both military and non-military personnel....Your advice was well received by our future leaders.

> Master Sergeant Marcus G. Merritt
> Senior Military Instructor, Auburn University

...delivered a powerfully insightful, gripping, and educationally useful account of leadership lessons, while challenging us....

> Bonnie Cannon
> Ph.D. candidate, Auburn University

My friend has a brother fighting in Iraq. You helped us understand better what he is going through and how his family and friends can support him.

> Michelle Morrisey
> Coordinator, UAB International Training

Classifications and Publishing

Title: *Professionalism Under Stress: 7 Lessons for Professionalism, Stress, and Gunfighting in Military and Civilian Life*

Authors: Col. C.H. "Stretch" Dunn, Jr. (U.S. Army Retired) and Dr. David Dyson.

Publishing and Copyright

15th edition 2006, November, Leave a Legacy Publishing.
Copyright 2003-2006 Dyson Leadership Institute.
U.S. Copyright Registration number TX 6-037-368.
ISBN number 0-87121-014-2. $15 suggested donation/price.
Printed by Banner Press, Birmingham, Alabama U.S.A.
Cover design by Brady Parks. Layout consulting by Kyle Crider.

We continue to add ideas and make improvements as we move toward our goal to create a distinctive resource that merits your reading and advocacy to others.

Communications and Purchasing

Teachers, trainers, professors, journalists, and others who use this material, please cite the authors as your source and inform Dyson Institute of your uses. We seek to serve as a resource for those who write and teach ideas to serve others. You may purchase books and other resources listed at the back by contacting:

Dyson Leadership Institute
www.ProfessionalismUnderStress.com; www.DysonInstitute.org
Bookstore@DysonInstitute.org
Leave a Legacy Publishing
Legacy@DysonInstitute.org
205.969.Dyson (3976), 968.Fax1 (3291)

By the Authors

Patriotism In Action:
Guide to Veterans Day in Birmingham
Saluting National Veterans Award Honoree Lt. General Hal Moore
Dr. David Dyson and Col. Stretch Dunn (Retired)
(2006)

Professionalism Under Stress:
7 Lessons for Professionalism, Stress, and Gunfighting
In Military and Civilian Life
Col. Stretch Dunn (Retired) and Dr. David Dyson
(2003-2006)

Patriotism In Action:
Guide to Veterans Day in Birmingham
Dr. David Dyson and Col. Stretch Dunn (Retired)
(2004-2005)

Patriotism and Professionalism In Action:
Remembrances and Roots of Honor
Dr. David Dyson and Col. Stretch Dunn (Retired)
(2003)

Ethical Decisions and Actions:
Choosing "The Harder Right"
[seminar workbook]
Col. Stretch Dunn (Retired) and Dr. David Dyson
(2005)

Suggestions for Successful Living:
Positive Ideas for the 7 Areas of Life
David Hilton Dyson
(1994)

The Career Planner
David Hilton Dyson
(1978-1982)

Contents

Pages

Preface and Purpose 1

Author and Reader Favorites 14

Second Chance to Leave a Legacy 16

Creation of a Calling 18

Meaning of the Title and Cover 20

Mission and Executive Summary 22

Preparation for Professionalism Lessons 24

Definitions 25

Our Approach to Helping You 26

Process of Learning and Development 28

Sources of Character, Competence, and Trust 30

7 Lessons for True Professionals 33

1. Prepare character and competence... 34

2. Earn empowerment... 46

3. Practice no excuses accountability... 54

4. Develop ethical fitness... 60

5. Think with positive expectancy... 76

6. Fulfill your callings and live a legacy... 80

7. Be a champion for your callings and colleagues... 96

Preparation for Stress Lessons 106

7 Lessons for Stress 111

1. Develop your *Fitness Package*... 112

2. Identify sources of stress... 126

3. Distinguish between good and bad stress... 136

4. Develop a strategy for normal and intense stress... 140

5. Use stress to help achieve peak performance... 154

6. Practice *safe stress* in advance... 158

7. Create structures, habits...to leverage stress... 162

Preparation for Gunfighting Lessons 166

Definitions 167

Early Lessons Learned from Combat Experience 168

Military Terms Used 175

7 Lessons for Gunfighting Professionals   **177**
   1. Develop a "soldier's heart"…   178
   2. Anticipate fear and prepare your instincts…   184
   3. Find seasoned Noncommissioned Officer mentors…   188
   4. Be tough…experience extreme stress safely…   192
   5. Prepare to choose the *least-worst* option…   198
   6. Be decisive, aggressive—even audacious…   202
   7. Put your personal affairs in order…   210
7 Lessons for Gunfighting Leaders   **215**
   1. Make gunfighting a last resort…   216
   2. Make sure the best leaders do the leading…   220
   3. State intent, expectations…simply and clearly…   226
   4. Lead by actions, not just position…   232
   5. Prepare for suffering and death…   236
   6. Keep the memory of loss alive…   240
   7. Persevere—resolve to succeed…   244
Summary of Lessons   **255**
Call to Action   **264**
Assessment and Action Plan Tools   265
   1. Professionalism Assessment and Action Plan   266
   2. Professional Life Plan Templates   268
   3. Personal Life Plan Templates   270
   4. Wheel of Balance and Action Plan   274
   5. Fitness Package Assessment and Action Plan   276
   6. Time, Inspiration, Money, Energy (T.I.M.E.) Checkup   278
   7. Gunfighting Assessment and Action Plan   280
   Abstracts of Capstone Workbook and Patriotism Book   282
Closing   284
Appendices   **286**
   Glossary   287
   References and Recommended Reading   304
   Genesis of our Book   312
   Appreciation   314
   Dyson Leadership Institute   316
   Resources   318
   Author Biographical Summaries   320

Author and Reader Favorites

Models, concepts, and ideas embedded in the lessons:

Definition of a True Professional, Master Professional	25
Aristotle	29
Iceberg/Sources of Character and Competence	31
The Army Leadership Model	37
Be, Know, and Do	38
The Seven Areas of Life	41
Seven Best Practices for Life Leadership	41
Seven Levels of Leadership	43
Developing as a Diamond	44
Ralph Waldo Emerson	45
Dyson Empowerment Model	48
Seven Levels of Empowerment from Leaders	49
Seven Components of Attitude/Character	50
Seven Components of Ability/Competence	51
Earning Empowerment	52
Dunn-Donnithorne Be a Pro Leadership Model	61
Beliefs That Lead to Good and Bad Behavior	63
Right Versus Right	66
Seven Step Guide to Ethical Decision-making	69
Dyson Hierarchy of Seven Motivating Values	71
Seven Levels of Decision-making Options	74
General George Patton/If Not Bliss, Then Bounce	79
The Purpose of Life/Seven Core Values/Life Mission	82
Professional Mission and Vision	84
Legacy	86
The Sentinels' Creed	89
Rotary and Civitan	90
Kiwanis and Exchange Club	92
Optimist	93
Boy and Girl Scouts	94
Engineers and Family Physicians	95
Research Results Assessing Trust in Attitude	99
Pragmatic Optimist	108

Dyson Life Leadership Model 113
Professional Fitness for a Soldier 118
Time, Inspiration, Money, and Energy (T.I.M.E.) 130
Wheel of Balance 132
View from Gabbratha 139
Stress Junkies 142
Dealing with Disappointment 144
Satisficing 146
Performance Anxiety 146
Time and TV 148
Stress Home Remedies 149
Peak Performance Research 156
Battle Drills 159
The Path of Least Resistance 163
3X Rule 163
Prime Time Management 164
Warrior Ethos/General of the Army Douglas MacArthur 179
General of the Army George C. Marshall 183
Least-worst Option 198
General Robert E. Lee 199
Shoot me! Shoot me! 201
Audacious Action 205
Albert Einstein 207
Flight Requires Both Wings/The Kiss 213
Leadership As a Calling 225
General Colin Powell 229
President George Washington 235
The Wall 241
President Calvin Coolidge 245
Leadership Glue Factory 251
Jihadist Playbook 251
Sun Tzu 252
Call to Action: Summary of Seven Suggested Actions 264
Seven Steps to Achieve a Priority Resolution 271
President Ronald Reagan 285
Leadership Definitions 293

Second Chance to Live a Legacy

In Vietnam, 1968, I was company commander leading a convoy of soldiers and heavy equipment returning from the Plei Me Special Forces camp to our base camp when enemy soldiers ambushed us from the tree line with rocket-propelled grenades and automatic weapons. Bullets hit my backpack radio—probably saving my life. Instincts took over as my troops returned fire, eventually defeating the assailants.

Several seeds were planted that day that led over three decades later to a desire to contribute lessons learned through this book:

1. Advance preparation through planning, battle drills, and practice had saved my life—and the lives of other soldiers—because we knew what to do under intense combat stress and the "fog of war."

2. The realization was that, for whatever reason, I had been given a second chance to make my life make a difference. That fueled my desire to be all I could be and give back for some who did not make it home.

Over the next several months, I experienced more close calls as my unit had several engagements with the enemy. Over the years I collected keepsakes, wrote in journals, and learned from my share of wrong turns in a personal search for lessons with no shelf life. Many soldiers and students of the military art have more combat experience than I. Standing on their proverbial shoulders and drawing from lessons that go as far back as Sun Tzu (circa 300 B.C.), I collaborated with Dr. David Dyson to write our version of lessons to help on life's journey.

My primary aim has been to put into words lessons for my two grown children and their families that I trust will help them know what I have learned that they might find useful—and "what made me tick"—as a part of my legacy to them.

Compounding my drive to write this book is a lasting memory of Captain Tom Hayes and Sergeant David Brown. My long-time gifted friend, Tom, was killed in combat just before I left for Vietnam. Sergeant Brown, one of my best squad leaders, was the first of my soldiers killed. They were two of the Army's finest who lost their lives in spite of preparation and professionalism under stress. As one of those blessed to survive, I hope to pass on to patriots who serve our country — whether military or civilian—lessons that can help them prepare to be all they can be and live an enriched legacy.

My ten years in the private sector after my Army career led me to conclude that military lessons apply quite well to achieve business results. The Army's BE, KNOW, DO Leadership Model works well in both venues. The major difference in military and civilian professionalism and leadership is a matter of degree not kind. Because the stakes are so high (potential loss of life and freedom) in the military—and in some civilian professions like law enforcement or first responders—selected behaviors are more "enforced" than in civilian organizations, such as higher levels of obedience and self-sacrifice.

David Dyson and I crossed paths in 1993 at a seminar he led that featured Stephen Covey and *The 7 Habits of Highly Effective People*. Our friendship grew through participation in Dyson Institute programs, and along the way we discovered the compatibility of our beliefs, values, and lessons learned. After retiring from corporate life, I joined Dyson Leadership Institute to write, teach, and help motivated people be all they can be.

David's sense of calling came from civilian experiences, and the lessons he adds also have applications for soldiers and others in our society. We hope the organization of lessons learned and original concepts presented in this work help you serve as a true professional, whether in combat or civilian life.

-Stretch-

Creation of a Calling

Burdens can become blessings. Written choices create clarity for callings. Persisting through pressure can help you develop into a *diamond* of a person—stronger and more valuable.

As a student at Auburn, I had to admit the reality that if I kept doing the same jobs as I had been doing in the summer, I would not earn enough money to complete school—and I still did not own a car! I did the math. Income from working as a construction laborer during the week plus weekend work as a lifeguard, golf course laborer, or cutting lawns would not be enough.

Another motivation was stirring. Neither of my parents had a chance to go to college. I felt grateful for their support of my education, though I had no first-hand knowledge of whether a college education would help me succeed. I had seen graduates with good grades fall short of success. Deep down, I wanted to prove to myself I could "make it" on my own.

Doing something "outside the box" seemed necessary. I sought a job selling Bibles because it seemed meaningful and I had heard you could earn much more than with hourly wages. Plus, I figured, if I could follow the program of working 70 hours per week running my own business selling to strangers, I likely could do most anything else needed to survive—and hopefully succeed.

With my first bank loan, I bought my first car. After leaving home in Birmingham, I drove to Nashville for five days of school with The Varsity Company of Thomas Nelson Publishers. The last day, we were assigned roommates and instructed to drive to a territory 500 miles away from home, find a place to live, and work 12 hours per day knocking on doors to sell or take orders for Bibles. The guy with the greatest potential of anyone in the school was assigned as my roommate. We drove all day to Virginia and rented a room in a boarding house. The first day we went to our territories charged to work 12 hours and make 20 presentations. The second night, my roommate, the guy with the greatest potential, came home and said, "This is too hard; I am going back to Florida!"

After the summer, when the Top 20 in the nation were invited back to Nashville, I noticed faces of people who had not stood out at the school. The experience of seeing *great potential* fail to try long enough to succeed and seeing ordinary people do extraordinary things internalized for me that *plans and persistence are more powerful than personality. We have to be willing to be bad at something long enough to have a chance to get good at it.* I failed for days, though by the end of two weeks I was succeeding. *Writing goals and making promises to prove something to ourselves and others helps us persist through adversity and rejection.* [In defense of *potential who quit*, the job was tough: 12 hours per day, 6 days per week, making 100+ presentations per week to strangers. Like an Olympic athlete, success required dedication and dealing with paradoxes. Some people slammed doors in my face, others invited me to church. Sales school did not tell us about threats. One Saturday night, after my last presentation, a group of "drunk" men surrounded me wanting to fight; another time a man in the "hills of Kentucky" put a pistol to my forehead. Ambushes come in civilian life, too!]

A blessing that summer came from reading books by or about Andrew Carnegie and Napoleon Hill, *The Law of Success* and *Think and Grow Rich*, which advocate a common denominator set of "success formula" principles that should be taught in every home and school. Realizing that most homes, schools, and churches do not teach or act to help people write plans for life and learn key life leadership lessons, a sense of calling grew that I should help make that happen. After completing college, I learned many professional organizations need teachings and systems in place to help people plan and lead in life as good stewards of their callings and talents. Without plans, we can succeed though not at our best.

This book includes principles and best practices of personal leadership that apply to us regardless of academic, professional, or other life choice. Our purpose is to help you learn and act to develop higher level intention in your life with habits leading to positive instincts and results.

-David-

Meaning of the Title

Professionalism: A true professional is a person who seeks to master work and life through developing trust in his character and competence through habits for ethical behavior, even when under stress. Professionalism applies to any situation where someone depends on us—in a family as well as a professional environment. Professionalism helps define ourselves and our behavior whenever we are accountable to others. Commitment to development as a true professional should precede serving as a leader of others.

Stress: a given in life, stress brings out the best or worst in people. In high-pressure professions such as military or first-responders, the ability to function well even under intense stress can be a matter of life and death. Almost everyone endures strain, pressure, and tension daily. Learning how to combat negative effects while taking advantage of the energizing qualities of good stress is an art to which we seek to contribute in these lessons.

Gunfighting: a necessary skill for those who help defend our people. We use gunfighting as a metaphor for acute stress situations, when life and death are at stake, or when unforeseen ambushes take place requiring honed reflexes and instincts to respond appropriately.

Leadership: Our gunfighting leadership lessons apply whether the leader is in military units, in organizations engaged in "corporate combat" with those using unethical practices, or any other setting where one seeks to influence others and achieve victory in a meaningful cause.

Preparation and Action in Military and Civilian Life: we believe the best lessons from military and civilian life help dedicated professionals, particularly when internalized and applied with persistence.

Meaning of the Cover

Soldier at the Tomb of the Unknown Soldiers: a symbol for our concept of professionalism, also represented by civilians dedicated to preparation and action to fulfill their callings. The soldiers from the 3rd Infantry Regiment known as "The Old Guard" have provided uninterrupted protection at the Tomb 24 hours a day, seven days a week, since 1930, even when no one is watching. [Learn more about them in our companion book, *Patriotism in Action.*]

Color pictures: representative of those in civilian and military professions who aspire to earn trust in their character and competence to be true professionals. On the front cover from left to right are a female firefighter representing first responders, engineers at a project site, a physician ready for surgery, and a proud student graduate. Shown on the back are Dr. Dyson representing scholars and adult learners, a coach with two of his athletes, a father schooling his daughter, a mother raising a son, and two corporate executives developing a plan together. Collectively, they symbolize those interested in being their best-selves and serving the greater good.

Diamond: the symbol for the Dyson Leadership Institute logo and one used by the military. It represents the models for life leadership and empowerment as well as the process or preparation and action that, like a diamond, develops people under pressure over time to "be all they can be."

Mission and Executive Summary

Mission of the Book

To help professionals, soldiers, leaders, homemakers, parents, coaches—anyone serious about serving with significance—to learn, internalize, and act as their best-selves.

Here, we list the core of the lessons in one sentence each. In the body of the book, we illuminate the lessons and applications. Then, in the Executive Summary of Lessons and Call to Action near the end of the book, we provide an expanded summary of these lessons that will help you use and teach them.

7 Lessons for True Professionals

1. Prepare character and competence to develop disciplined habits and instincts so they can do the right things well, even under stress, thus earning trust in self and from others.
2. Earn empowerment rather than wait for it.
3. Practice "no excuses" accountability.
4. Develop ethical fitness and decision-making from the start.
5. Decide to think with positive expectancy and make the best of situations.
6. Fulfill your calling and live a legacy to find meaning.
7. Be a champion for your calling, your profession, people you serve, and your organization.

7 Lessons for Stress

1. Develop your *fitness package* for the 7 areas of life.
2. Identify sources of stress.
3. Distinguish between good and bad stress.
4. Develop a strategy for normal and intense stress.
5. Use stress to help you achieve peak performance.
6. Practice *safe stress* in advance.
7. Create structures, rituals, and habits to proactively leverage positive stress and mitigate negative stress.

7 Lessons for Gunfighting Professionals

1. Develop a soldier's heart through spiritual centeredness.
2. Anticipate feeling absolute fear under stress and prepare your instincts so you can trust them.
3. Find seasoned Noncommissioned Officers (NCOs) to serve as mentors and teachers.
4. Be tough. Experience the extreme physical stressors of hunger and sleep deprivation to develop habits and instincts to function effectively for long periods.
5. Prepare for paradoxes and having to choose the *least-worst* option.
6. Be decisive, aggressive—even audacious—indecisiveness is a fatal flaw.
7. Put your personal affairs in order.

7 Lessons for Gunfighting Leaders

1. Make gunfighting a last resort. When conflict is a necessity, make it a part of our nation's fiber.
2. Make sure the best leaders do the leading while troublesome "leaders" are removed.
3. State intent, expectations, and parameters directly and simply to encourage clarity and initiative.
4. Lead by actions, not just position or personality; demonstrate humility with character and competence.
5. Prepare yourself and your unit for suffering, disfigurement, and death; carry out death notification with dignity.
6. Keep the memory of loss and sacrifice alive; memorials and remembrances matter.
7. Persevere—resolve to succeed.

Lesson: an experience, example, or observation that imparts beneficial knowledge or wisdom and leads to action.

Preparation for Professionalism Lessons

Professionalism: professional status, character, or standards.

The general public seems to add the label "professional" to someone who has chosen a profession and has experience. We advocate a higher-level expectation for the *true professional*.

True Professional: person who seeks mastery and *earned empowerment* through *trust in character and competence*, preparing and persisting to develop fitness and habits to do *the harder right well—instinctively*—even under stress.

True professionals are members of a family, group, unit, team or organization where others count on them. Independence merges into interdependence. Accountability expands beyond personal integrity to trust from others.

Master Professional: professional who knows and does the right things instinctively, with excellence.

Like an Olympic athlete, the master professional develops fitness, capabilities, and instincts through preparation and practice over time until excellence comes naturally.

Character: keeping promises; doing what you say you will; displaying an attitude of commitment, courage, confidence; developing and demonstrating ethical fitness, moral strength, integrity...even after initial inspiration has waned.

Competence: adequate fitness or ability; suitable; capable; fit for the purpose.

Trust: firm reliance on the integrity, ability, or character of a person or thing. Something committed into the care of another; the condition and resulting obligation of having confidence placed in one; reliance on something; belief in integrity.

Our Approach to Helping You

Our core lessons aim at developing knowledge, habits, and instincts to do the right things well, instinctively, even under stress. We offer action-oriented lessons seeking to help those who desire to be conditioned, successful professional athletes in the sport of living—where success means achievement of one's calling and a sense of being in the flow of life. We further define such people as pragmatic optimists, who take a hopeful view and "look at the bright side" in a practical way that can be applied.

The ability to reach and maintain true professionalism requires preparation and conditioning. It is an arduous journey with few quick fixes. Rather, it is a process that requires rituals, habits, and instincts be formed that will enable you to confront both the normal stress of daily life and the occasional, typically unexpected, acute stressful situation. However challenging the process, there is great opportunity for joy and satisfaction along the way as you make progress.

Only a few will take such a journey. The few will identify their callings, then make choices to pursue those callings with persistent passion. With preparation and conditioning, habits will emerge that build fitness for living with a sense of fulfillment.

The gunfighting lessons apply both literally (for military or law enforcement) and metaphorically as a representation of intensely stressful situations. The domain of stress most readers will encounter is not the extreme of Victor Frankl in a Nazi concentration camp or Jeremiah Denton as a Vietnam prisoner of war in Hoa Lo Prison, the "Hanoi Hilton." Such men are true heroes of living with acute, prolonged stress. Surely, the test of time will reveal the courage of many other women and men who demonstrate true professionalism under prolonged, intense stress.

Many of the rest of us live in the dynamic tension of stressful environments featuring intense levels of activity. Many face the challenge of attempting to complete more activities each day than often is possible. Some are restless, born of the knowledge that too much time and energy often get spent on the urgent and seemingly precious little on the important. Then amid the normal chaos of life, we get *ambushed*; an unexpected crisis emerges—loss of a loved one, a serious accident, illness, loss of a job—and acute stress sets in.

For those who seriously want to get in sync with life, we offer our thoughts on how and why the reader should:

♦ embrace the concept of seeking to be a true professional in one's chosen field and other important roles in the seven areas of life;

♦ study and internalize those lessons that resonate with you and act upon them;

♦ follow through with consistent behaviors and rituals until reinforcing habits are ingrained that not only support daily living but also hone instincts to serve you well in intensely stressful situations.

In the Call to Action section we provide a set of assessment tools and plan templates to help those with whom our message resonates to move forward. We purposely repeated some thoughts in the text and tools. We do this to reinforce those ideas and help the chapter or tool stand on its own when studied or used separately. This book is one of a set that reflect the Dyson Institute's approach to professionalism, patriotism, and leadership in life. Abstracts of the companion book and stress strategy booklet are included in the Call to Action section.

Process for Learning and Development

People can change in a moment of calling and choice. However, most lasting improvement, especially transformation, comes after proactive, persistent efforts over time. For many, improvement occurs incrementally until critical mass helps with a breakthrough to a new level of belief and behavior. For most long-term lasting change, the Dyson Institute learning process is recommended:

Preparation →
Callings/Choices →
Beliefs/Values →
Knowledge/Skills →
Thinking and Decision-making →
Plans →
Actions →
Focus on Results →
Rituals, Habits, and Instincts

Our process is simple and effective. The successful and satisfied reader embraces a desire for improving as a professional and leader. He serves with significance and is willing to prepare and act to earn the trust needed in character and competence. Our concepts are best embraced by those who value stewardship and service to others.

These steps will help you develop as your best-self.
Read the lessons and applications in this book →
Hear lessons and applications in seminars →
See them in action through examples →
Write lessons to implement →
Plan what you will do →
Act on your plans →
Internalize →
Adjust →

Example of the Learning Process Using Goals

A simple example of applying the learning process follows using the skill of setting goals, a key part of a plan for professional life or any other area.

Read what respected authors have to say about setting goals—make them short, attainable with effort, measurable....
Hear speakers on goal setting at conferences and seminars.
See examples of goals and plans set by your mentors.
Write your goals and plans; studies show that those who write goals and plans accomplish as much as 10 times more than those who do not.
Plan by setting schedules with deadlines to keep moving forward.
Act by following through to get started, build momentum, and make reaching your goals possible.
Internalize the standard that writing goals and plans is a requirement of true professionals and get to the point that stating intent through goals is a habit.
Adjust goals and deadlines as circumstances dictate, but stay focused on desired end results.

We are what we repeatedly do.
Excellence, then, is not an act, but a habit.
-Aristotle-

Sources of Character, Competence, and Trust

Sources of Competence

- **knowledge** (information you use to know what to do)
- **skills** (ability to do something well)

Sources of Character

- **callings and choices** (what we discern as our highest purposes combined with what we decide are priorities)
- **beliefs and values** (strongly held opinions we hold as true, which filter our thinking and motivate us)
- **personal vision** (self-concept, expectations, affirmations)
- **attitude and attributes** (outlook and characteristics)
- **habits and instincts** (thoughts and acts that are automatic; reactions without conscious forethought).

Sources of Trust

- **Trust** in self develops based on internal beliefs and confidence in actions. Trust from others comes from actions, results, and perceptions that you have the **character** to do the right thing and the **competence** to do it well.

Many people wish for improvement. In professional life, many discuss during performance evaluations how they can improve. Most seem to focus on things to do—or do better.

We advocate a portion of time and effort get invested in developing sources of competence so you can increase your capacity to do better. This can come through education, training, coaching, and other learning and experiences. Many people think of character as integrity; it is that—and more. We use character and attitude as virtually synonymous and include the components of choice, commitment, character, courage, confidence, connection, and charisma in our components of attitude.

Where Character and Competence Develop

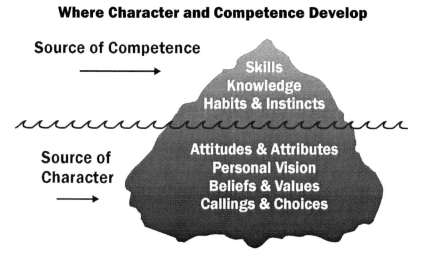

Source of Competence →

Skills
Knowledge
Habits & Instincts

Source of Character →

Attitudes & Attributes
Personal Vision
Beliefs & Values
Callings & Choices

Development beneath the surface provides the foundation.

Most of an iceberg's mass is below the surface. Similarly, our deepest development— to strengthen our foundation through choices, beliefs, and attitudes—occurs below the surface though manifests above the surface through our behavior as demonstrated by the skills, actions, and habits others observe. Development above the surface builds competence, below the surface forges character. Together, they forge trust in self and with others. [Dr. Joyce Shields and the Hay Group have a model, which influenced our thinking and model.]

Callings and choices are arguably the strongest source of inspiration for character development and competence. When a person commits to finding and fulfilling his highest purposes, his belief in and value for doing his best escalates. Our personal vision for the life we are called to lead becomes focused and internalized. Attitudes and attributes get honed and improved. Our improved thought process and behavior guides us to develop desired skills and habits. This develops our instincts to increasingly do the right things automatically.

The lessons offered develop these three cornerstones of a true professional—character, competence, and trust.

Lessons for True Professionals

7 Lessons for True Professionals

1. Prepare character and competence to develop disciplined habits so you can do the right things well, instinctively, even under stress.

2. Earn empowerment rather than wait for it.

3. Practice "no excuses" accountability.

4. Develop ethical fitness and decision-making from the start.

5. Decide to think with positive expectancy and make the best of situations.

6. Fulfill your callings and live a legacy to find meaning.

7. Be a champion for your calling, your profession, people you serve, and your organization.

Professionalism
Lesson 1

Prepare character and competence to develop disciplined habits and instincts so we can do the right things well, even under stress, thus earning trust in self and from others. Identify areas of improvement as priorities in plans and invest in lifelong learning and development. True leaders develop personal leadership and serve others first, then lead where they can do the most good.

True professionalism is a vital mindset for personal leadership and the foundation for all other levels and types of leadership. True leaders commit to becoming true professionals first, then they seek to serve and lead others.

Professionalism in Action

"Ears" — Vietnam 1968

One example of doing the right thing well under pressure is a young soldier in my Vietnam unit nicknamed "Ears" because of his talent and dedication for detecting mines. Those who followed him on mine sweeps trusted his competence to detect explosive devices, and thus prevent a detonation that could cost lives. Even at age 19, he had to take his job seriously and seek mastery of it to save him and others.

True professionalism is a lifelong commitment. Even after George Patton earned the rank of General, he continued to prepare through study of maps and history of warfare. His example is one of decisive action honed from a lifetime of learning. Napoleon Hill, who studied Andrew Carnegie's "success formula" and hundreds of the world's distinctively prolific people like Thomas Edison, reported they invested an average of 30 minutes daily in learning their profession and developing themselves. He concluded, these people developed themselves over time so as they matured wisdom and instincts they benefited from unexplained "hunches."

We should commit ourselves to stewardship and excellence in the important areas of life, performing beyond merely acceptable standards. While some students do the minimum required to secure a diploma, a true professional works to a

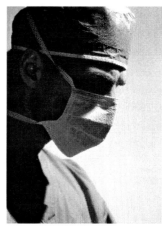

higher standard to be ready when his services are needed. The next time you hear a student or "professional" joke about getting by with minimal efforts and results, consider the impact if "Ears" had such an attitude and lack of passion for competence. Apply that standard to the medical student who will become a surgeon who operates on vital organs, the engineer who designs critical infrastructures, the teacher who influences society through the knowledge and values of her students. True professionals prepare anticipating they will be called to serve.

The antithesis of the true professional is the person who does only what will serve him, who does not take his work seriously, attends professional conferences for social purposes, or has the attitude, "I will be motivated to work hard after I find a job I like."

In our companion book, *Patriotism in Action*, we showcase soldiers in "The Old Guard" because of their professionalism when no one is watching. Whether guarding the Tomb of the Unknowns twenty-four hours per day even in the worst of weather or laying to rest a warrior who will not ride again, these soldiers consider their jobs noble even when laboring at routine, seemingly unappreciated tasks. They have internalized their purpose, which propels them to professionalism.

Whatever calling you choose as a profession can be a means for providing noble service. Prepare to serve and succeed, even before you are called to lead, even when no one is watching. Following is a brief look at two models that provide a foundation for our concept of professionalism and leadership.

The Army Leadership Model

Model: a schematic description of a system, theory…

The Army presents a superb, time-tested model for identifying areas of character and competence to develop that lead to professionalism and leadership. Our diagram, adapted to summarize the Army Model in Field Manual (FM) 22-100, lists 23 dimensions of **Be, Know,** and **Do** related to **values, attributes, skills,** and **actions** for developing competencies and characteristics.

U.S. ARMY LEADERSHIP AREAS/DIMENSIONS

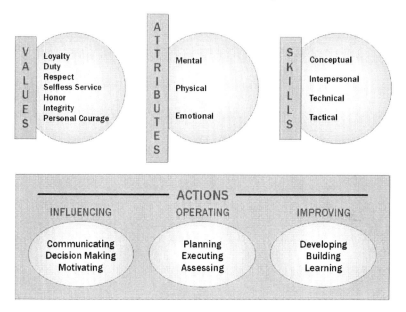

All aspects of the model are interrelated. Other branches of the U.S. Armed Forces have effective leadership models, and we present the Army model as a representative of the Military. The model provides a good example of applying our lesson, *State intent, expectations, and parameters directly and simply to encourage initiative* because it provides a unifying doctrine of principles by which all military leaders should act to accomplish missions and care for soldiers. The model applies at all levels of military leadership: *direct* (first line leaders, face-to-face), *organizational* (heads of units at brigade to corps levels, and *strategic* (senior officers and policy makers at major command through Department of Defense who consider societal concerns nationally and globally).

Be

Development of the values and attributes help you "**Be** all you can be." The *values*—loyalty, duty, respect, selfless service, honor, integrity, and personal courage—provide the foundation of soldiers' professionalism. The Army's *attributes* —physical, mental, and emotional—include fundamental characteristics—those born with and others developed.

Know

Honing skills with people, things, ideas, and techniques of the profession comprise the **Know** part of the Army model. *Skills* are abilities a person must have to carry out tasks competently. Skills include those acquired from training to master technical subjects and tactical operations, education to conceptualize for planning and problem solving, and interpersonal skills—all helpful in dealing with the ambiguity and fog of battle. Leadership skills differ in degree but not kind as one progresses from direct to organizational to strategic leadership levels. The skill areas continue to apply, but leaders at the higher levels must deal with greater complexity, uncertainty, risk of unintended consequences, and delay between action and effects.

Do

Translating Be and Know into *actions* is the **Do** component. At the direct level of *influencing*, leaders are close enough to quickly see the impact of their actions. Influencing people to do what is needed includes communicating a reason to do the mission and making sure people understand the standard— and are motivated to accomplish the mission to that standard.

At the organizational and strategic levels, the leader adds influence through policies and systems. As leaders rise in level of leadership, decisions must take into account wider circles of influence, even to the point that the impact from their decisions and actions may come to fruition years after their watch.

Operating involves actions to plan, execute, and then assess achievement of goals. Because organizational and strategic leaders work primarily through those they lead, empowerment and delegation are indispensable for operating at those levels. At all leadership levels, empowered soldiers and staff have both the responsibility and authority to get the job done in the way they see fit, limited only by the intent, expectations, and parameters communicated by the commander and moral values of the military services. In times of combat, the mental state of leaders and followers takes on greater significance and can complicate the ability to perform. Therefore, it is sometimes necessary to be more direct and lower the level of empowerment. Previously earned trust helps stakeholders understand the good intent behind the more directive style.

Assessment yields the means to *improve* to do it better the next time using tools such as in-process and after-action reviews as well as leader and subordinate assessments. The task is not complete without an evaluation of the performance that leads to improved actions and enables the individuals, teams, and organizations to learn and change. Actions to improve make sure the unit or organization remains capable of accomplishing future missions. Such actions as developing the next generation of leaders, fostering an ethical climate, and championing constructive change are embraced in this dimension.

We simplified the model and applications for this summary from hundreds of pages in the manual. You can find the Army model by entering Army+FM22-100 in a major Internet search program. For an excellent list of performance indicators for each dimension of the Army Model, see Appendix B in the FM.

Dyson Life Leadership and Empowerment Model

The Dyson Life Leadership and Empowerment Model focuses on developing life leadership and earning empowerment useful in personal, interpersonal, and team leadership—and provides a foundation for the other levels of leadership. The upper pyramid represents *Life Leadership*, the lower pyramid *Empowerment—earning and delegating it*. The two pyramids form a diamond, symbolizing that we become stronger and more valuable as we persist through pressure to develop enduring character and competence. A summary description follows.

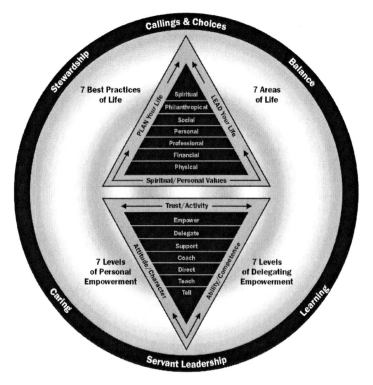

This model complements the U.S. Army model by giving greater depth to the levels of personal leadership. Further, this model strengthens the military model, which advocates empowerment of soldiers, by adding advanced levels for knowing how to prepare people for empowerment, plus knowing when to direct and when to delegate.

Callings and Choices

Life leadership begins with *callings and choices* (top of the circle). We seek *stewardship* to do our best with our callings, gifts, and talents by planning and leading our lives. We also seek *balance* with people and priorities in the seven areas of life.

7 Areas of Life

The *Seven Areas of Life* include all we do. The value of *balance* drives us to plan to invest in what provides impact in our priorities with time, inspiration, money, and energy (T.I.M.E.).

1. Physical—eat, sleep, bathe, groom, exercise...
2. Financial—budget, purchase, invest...
3. Professional—work, learn, train, plan and prepare...
4. Personal—plan for life, develop yourself, interests...
5. Social—share and do with and for others...
6. Philanthropical—contribute service and resources...
7. Spiritual—pray, study, worship, give and serve God....

7 Best Practices for Life Leadership

The *Seven Best Practices for Life Leadership* provide an answer for "what strategy do I follow to live as my best-self?" Be prepared for the question whether it comes from an associate, a child, or from within. This is a summary:

1. Lead my life—choose to seek and fulfill your callings...
2. Plan for life—discern your callings, write your choices...
3. Have an IMPACT—focus on IMPortant ACTions...
4. Balance life—time priorities for the 168 hours per week...
5. Live my priorities—calendar reflects what matters most...
6. Assess and adjust—compare desired to actual, adapt...
7. Renew and improve—invest 5-20% of your time developing mind, body, spirit, service capacity (professional development), and planned stewardship of callings (plan for life)....

7 Levels of Empowerment

The lower pyramid identifies the *Seven Levels of Empowerment* listed below from the personal perspective:

1. **Tell**—wait to be told…
2. Teach—learn how and why, though ask before acting…
3. Direct—recommend action for approval…
4. **Coach**—plan and share strategy, seek coaching…
5. Support—take more initiative though gain approval…
6. **Delegate**—take the lead for action, report…
7. Empower—own accountability and communicate…

The bottom of the outer circle shows core values of the team leader. The value of *caring* from a leader influences attitude for developing character and competence to earn higher levels of empowerment. The value of *learning* drives the leader to inspire through example and encouragement for developing ability in core competencies. *Servant leadership* means internalizing and exhibiting commitment to preparation and action to serve the people and the organization.

Terms and Meanings

Personal Empowerment: The level of trust for autonomy earned that influences the level of empowerment delegated by a leader.

Delegating Empowerment: The level of empowerment merited in supervising and mentoring another in a particular role determined by your trust in his attitude and ability.

[Learn more about using the model in earning empowerment as well as hiring and coaching in the next lesson.]

7 Levels of Leadership

Imbedded in the leadership diamond are concentric circles representing the Seven Levels of Leadership, which guide the individual from personal leadership to societal leadership. Depth is provided in seminars and additional writings on *The 7 Levels of Leadership,* though here we summarize to provide greater context for the model and to help you plan for leadership development:

1. **Personal**—focus on self...
2. Life—expands to consider the seven areas of life...
3. Interpersonal—interacting with and serving others...
4. **Team**—first-line supervision of individuals/groups...
5. Managerial—lead leaders of teams and programs...
6. **Organizational**—lead divisions and organizations...
7. Societal—influence from and beyond our organizations...

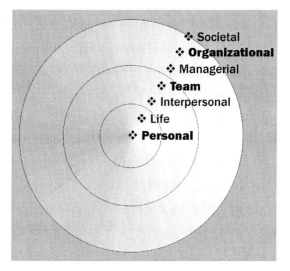

❖ Societal
❖ **Organizational**
❖ Managerial
❖ **Team**
❖ Interpersonal
❖ Life
❖ **Personal**

Leadership and Management

Some people refer to directing people and projects as management. We suggest leadership as the preferred term when referring to influencing plans and people, while management focuses on organizing and controlling resources.

Developing as a Diamond

Diamonds develop from raw material of coal after enduring years of heat and pressure until becoming one of the world's most valuable, useful, and beautiful resources—ultimately called a gem. When you are under stress, remember that without pressure the coal does not become a diamond. Choose to persevere at your callings, at what is most important. Everyone makes mistakes, experiences disappointment, and causes disappointment for others even with the best of intentions. The life leader persists, even under stress of what feels like intense heat and pressure, renewing commitment to callings and improvement while reconciling what we can and cannot change, as we develop into *diamonds* that are useful, strong, and valuable.

[The model and applications receive more explanation in additional lessons on professionalism and stress and in our seminars. We sought to provide a simplified summary here.]

Symbolism of the Diamond

The Dyson Leadership and United States Army models share the diamond as a metaphor for personal leadership development. Former Army Chief of Staff General Edward C. Meyer described the Army Leadership Framework:

> *Just as the diamond requires…carbon, heat, and pressure, successful leaders require the interaction of…character, knowledge, and application. Like carbon to the diamond, character is the basic quality of the leader…. But as carbon alone does not create a diamond, neither can character alone create a leader. The diamond needs heat. Man needs knowledge, study, and preparation…. The third property, pressure—acting in conjunction with carbon and heat— forms the diamond. Similarly, one's character, attended by knowledge, blooms through application to produce a leader.*

The Dyson Leadership Diamond symbolizes and seeks to remind us about internalizing wisdom, beliefs, and best practices to prepare and take action, persisting through stress over time.

When you finish this book, you should have at least a basic understanding for developing a plan for life that helps you define and live closer to your best-self. The Be a Pro model reinforces development of an ethical foundation from the start that matures as one grows in leadership responsibilities. Imbedded in these models is learning how to self-regulate and enforce desired ethical standards within an organization. Then, you can prepare further by reviewing the twenty-three dimensions of the Army Model to identify where to place priority in your development to earn higher levels of empowerment and effectively influence others.

> *That which we persist in doing becomes easier—*
> *not that the nature of the task has changed,*
> *but our ability to do has increased.*
> -Ralph Waldo Emerson-

Professionalism Lesson 2

Earn empowerment rather than wait for it. Admit that you are more responsible for your performance and career growth than is your supervisor. Identify your desired results and actions in your professional plan. Anticipate what your supervisory leader needs to trust you have earned empowerment. Help your manager serve as a mentor by stating your intent through your plan and seeking coaching. Proactively seek to develop higher levels of trust in your competence and character for the seven levels of empowerment: (1) Tell, (2) Teach, (3) Direct, (4) Coach, (5) Support, (6) Delegate, (7) Empower.

Earn: to deserve or acquire as a result of action.

Empower: to give power or authority; to give ability; to enable.

Earned Empowerment Mindset

The Army's Field Manual (FM) 22-100 teaches that empowerment is expected:

> *…When you train them to do a job, give them the necessary resources and authority and get out of the way…inculcate the principle of…training for bottom-up action…. This is a tremendous statement of trust in subordinates and one of the best ways to develop leaders.*

Understanding that leaders are taught to think and act toward empowerment of troops and team members, the true professional will do more than his part to prepare to earn empowerment. He will state intent for what he wants to be, know, and do—with respect for instruction of the leader—so together the soldier, the leader, and the unit will succeed better and faster than if the soldier waited for instruction and relied only on verbal communications.

Some of the best professionals and leaders are *ordinary people who do extraordinary things* because of callings and choices that foster desire and commitment to earn empowerment to be, know, and do at the highest possible levels. Adopt the mindset that gaining responsibility, even preparing for promotion, should mainly be a function of earning empowerment instead of waiting for a leader to direct you. The Dyson Empowerment Model illustrates this principle and how to act on it.

The trust assessed as correct for the level of character and competence can be simplified to three: **Tell, Coach,** and **Delegate**. Once mastered, the nuances of all seven levels should be developed.

Dyson Empowerment Model

The lower half of the Dyson Leadership Diamond addresses empowerment. You can use this to support stating intent with your supervisor. You as a leader can use this lesson in interviews, staff meetings, and coaching to state intent and agree on shared vision with people, teams, and divisions.

The model shows how one earns trust in self and from others through attitude/character combined with ability/competence. Trust is determined for each key activity. In one role you may need to be told how to start; in another, you may deserve delegation. As trust in your attitude and ability increase, your need for supervision decreases.

As trust increases,
empowerment increases and supervision decreases.

Core Concepts

Trust: Belief in Attitude (character) + Ability (competence)
Activity: Each important role, project, task, or position.
Empowerment Level: As trust increases, supervision decreases.

Personal Characteristics

Attitude: Callings/Choice + Commitment + Character +
Courage + Confidence + Connection + Charisma
Ability: Knowledge (knowing what to do) + Skills (able to do
something well)

Leadership Characteristics

Inspiring: Leaders attract others with charisma created by
commitment, character, courage, and confidence.
Caring: Value purpose, people, and projects.
Learning: Set an example and encourage improvement.
Servant Leadership: Serve people and the greater good.

7 Levels of Empowerment from Leaders

Leaders use these few pages to state intent and expectations.
Professionals also can use this chart to clarify expectations.

Level	What I'll do (leadership)	What I expect of you (personal empowerment)
Tell	Tell what to do, when, where, how…	Wait until told to act
Teach	Tell, plus explain why, follow up	Learn, ask, act on what I say for important actions
Direct	Teach & coordinate	Recommend actions, follow directions
Coach	Direct and advise	Plan goals and actions, seek coaching, act
Support	Coach and reinforce decisions/actions, assist/serve	Plan, seek support for goals and actions, act, report results
Delegate	Support and give you responsibilty, monitor results	Plan, gain support for goals/strategy, act, report; accept responsibility
Empower	Delegate and give you authority	Plan; communicate goals, strategy, results; cooperate; accept accountability.

7 Components of Attitude/Character

Use these components of attitude (character to do the right things) and questions to assess trust in your preparation and perceived trust from a leader. A leader also considers these:

1. **Choice**—Have I decided to seek my *callings*, plan and lead my life, and develop qualities to succeed in this role?
2. **Commitment**—Do I have a strong desire to succeed? Am I dependable in behavior? Will I persist to see the job through even amidst difficulties?
3. **Character**—Do I have good intent? Good impact? Do I keep promises? Am I trustworthy to do the right thing for the organization and people involved, serving above self? Will my integrity help me persevere after the emotion in which I make promises has passed?
4. **Courage**—Am I committed enough, tough enough, to act facing fear? Is my motivation/my reason for succeeding big enough to sustain me if times get tough or disappointing?
5. **Confidence**—Do I believe in myself, my attitude and ability, and my chances for success? Can I earn trust in myself and from others in my potential?
6. **Connection**—Do I feel connected to our purpose, people, and projects? Am I inspired about the organization and its impact? Do I see the cause and group as bigger than my needs?
7. **Charisma**—Am I the kind of person sought as a teammate? Am I a worthy example and encourager? Do I have the *right kind* of charisma, which comes from character-based values and actions, not just personality? Can I attract people by communicating a vision, doing my part, persuading others to serve, and helping them?

Assess yourself and what you need to be prepared instead of wait for the leader to assess you. State your assessment and intent for developing, sharing how the leader can help.

7 Components of Ability/Competence

Understand that a mature, savvy decision-maker will instinctively assess what level of trust he has for the attitude and ability you have to fulfill a task, role, project, or mission. Key components of ability include skills (competence to do something well) and knowledge (knowing what to do). These components help you develop *knowledge* and *skills* leading to honed instincts:

Key ways to develop your *knowledge*:
1. **Education**—academic preparation in general studies and areas of major focus or professional preparation.
2. **Training**—instruction and/or coaching in principles and practices for doing your job well technically and in *strategic skills* like planning, time and energy management, motivation, ethical decision-making...
3. **Self-study**—continuous improvement of knowledge.
4. **Observation**—watching others to emulate.

Key ways to develop your *skills*:
5. **Experience**—doing something, performing...
6. **Practice**—preparing in advance for doing, performing...
7. **Rituals and Habits**–combining traditions and time priorities to invest in practice and experience to develop ability to do the right things well, instinctively.

The leader can use this model to state intent—how he decides on level of empowerment—and expectations of you (what is needed and when). The true professional includes in his plan ways to develop in priority areas to earn trust in self and from a supervising leader. You and your leader must each develop trust in your competence and commitment to maximize delegation, minimizing over-supervising and conflict. State your intent for development and achievement to help your leader understand your motives and find ways to help you succeed in reaching your goals for giving as well as gaining.

Earning Empowerment

Earning empowerment is a concept critical to fulfilling higher values like self esteem, success, and significance in service. The mindset of earning empowerment breaks with past thinking on waiting for direction from the "boss." True professionals respectfully anticipate and ask for feedback on their plans to increasingly add value.

A belief underlying the Dyson Empowerment Model is that the professional is primarily responsible for his plan, performance, rewards, and career path—along with the leader. True professionals respectfully adopt the mindset that gaining responsibility, even preparing for promotion, is a function of seeking and earning rather than waiting.

The supervisory leader takes responsibility for setting the right example and encouraging the professional toward his expressed goals—developing a strong and effective partnership. The leader typically is best prepared to state intent of the organization plan and the requirements of the team member's position. However, when the true professional sees a need, he acts or suggests how he can serve rather than wait for a request. Take the lead to offer what you can contribute and seek win-win shared vision with the leader.

Learn with intent to be and do your best. Write your professional plan and share it with others, which will help you improve your focus on priorities and discover how best to serve others. Your written plan, taken as far as you can take it, will help your leader and colleagues understand where you need coaching, just as it improves synergy and cooperation. Your statement of intent expressed through your written plan, specifically showing what you want to give and gain—as well as how you want to grow—will help your manager function more as a mentor. This helps the leader see gaps in his own coaching with you and suggests to him how he can improve his leadership and support of you. And, your plan may inspire him to develop one—or to use it more effectively.

It is an act of wisdom for the organizational leader to make sure systems are in place to require and reward development, communication, and focus on professional plans. The basic knowledge supporting this practice has been in place for centuries though relatively few organizational leaders have a system for stating intent through plans and assessment in place at a high level. *Performance rewarded is repeated.*

Also, it is an act of personal leadership for the professional to state intent through a professional plan to facilitate improved communications, coaching, and cooperation. Your doing so will help the leader serve more effectively and enjoy working with you more. It is much more gratifying to support motivated people wanting to succeed aiming at targets of shared vision than it is to try to "motivate" people and follow up to make sure they are working toward fuzzy roles and goals, which can lead to micromanaging, conflict, and deflated commitment to the job, team, and organization.

To earn empowerment, assess your attitude and ability for current and prospective roles. Consider what it takes to earn empowerment from your leader's perspective as well as your own. Determine where and how you can develop to earn trust. In our call to action we provide a professional assessment as a tool to help you assess and seek coaching. Present to the leader what you believe he needs in order to trust your attitude and ability to do the job, and invite him to coach you. Both of you can start any project with better anticipation for success, greater trust in each person's intent, and sharper focus on the desired results and action. You both can benefit from reduced negative stress and conflict, which can result from misunderstanding, inadequate direction, or unspoken disagreement. Preparation and action on this lesson can boost performance, retention of good employees, and results.

Professionalism
Lesson 3

Practice "no excuses" accountability. Own it! Focus on solutions and results, taking responsibility for the mission and your part. Mitigating circumstances often affect an outcome, but only one person, partnership, or alliance is ultimately accountable.

Excuse: attempted justification for not keeping a promise; a pretended reason.

Accountability: called to account; answerable.

Accountability means no excuses! Mitigating circumstances often affect an outcome but one person, partnership, or alliance of leaders is ultimately accountable. When military officers take their oath they make a choice to give up their right to blame others. You may delegate responsibility, but never accountability. This is a useful lesson in any profession.

In the book, *Ranger School: No Excuses Leadership,* Brace Barber has several themes, one of which is to emphasize that in every team situation, regardless of the conditions or challenges, one person is ultimately accountable for the outcome of the mission. Many reject this concept, going to great ends to explain why a negative outcome is someone else's fault, why they had little or no control of the situation—any excuse to shift accountability away from them. Many otherwise good people shift blame because they do not embrace this concept or their instincts have not been developed to overcome the urge to protect their personal security and esteem. Only through mature attitudes, habits, and instincts can we accept accountability and move on to fix the system flaw or effort that caused the failure.

Denial of accountability creates counterproductive habits and limits one's ability to be a true professional and exemplary leader of others. Complaining usually results in nothing more than lost time and energy, which creates added stress. Further, focusing on excuses instead of solutions ingrains patterns of negative thought.

Prepare for threats to your ego. When you make a mistake or results fall short, focus on solutions to accomplish the mission, learn from the experience, and improve systems, training, and habits to do better next time. What else can you do that helps?

The warrior ethos ingrains the notion of accountability. On the first day as a cadet at West Point, upper classmen instruct four acceptable responses to almost any question:

"Yes Sir."   "No Sir."

"Sir, I do not understand."   "No excuse Sir."

When you are in charge, "the buck stops at your door." This is true of any endeavor, whether it be a team completing a task in a company, a volunteer effort, or an individual functioning within a family.

When an organization has a weak performance record, we often find that accountability is blurred and systems of follow up are underdeveloped. Success is most likely when one person, or a group of dedicated people, takes ownership of key goals, makes resolutions, and keeps them. Until this happens, people in underperforming organizations can fall prey to an attitude of "wait and see," creating unspoken beliefs that keeping promises is optional. This erodes commitment, confidence, and results.

Some ideas to combat "wait and see" and boost action:

♦ Add the value *accountability* to the written values of your organization.

♦ Set up systems to make "no excuses" ownership of accountability automatic. For example, include in your system of performance evaluation and rewards a means of assessing (with feedback and suggestions) the results each team member is accountable for attaining.

♦ Tell stakeholders often how accountability is implemented as a value in projects and processes.

♦ Share this as a core value with prospective employees and other potential stakeholders—choose only prospects that align with the value.

- Provide staff members and others you mentor with a Professional Plan template. Require them to complete them in writing to help both of you understand and focus on desired actions and results. We offer a template as part of the Call to Action tools, and we have more.

- Ask professionals to share their professional plans for action and accountability with their supervisors in order to receive coaching that will speed the process of learning what it takes to earn empowerment, especially in new roles.

- Implement a process for identifying priorities and establishing accountability and follow up. Give added emphasis to this tactic until the organization gains or regains a high trust culture where most feel a high level of confidence in the organization and its ability to succeed.

- Make sure training focuses on preparing people to act on and achieve stated results. Focus on desired results as well as topics. Keep criteria for assessment in mind as you design and deliver training and coaching.

- Add an "accountability" statement of value to your personal life plan, whether you call that part a mission and vision statement, constitution, or simply your list of values. State what keeping promises means to you and how it influences others.

- Share this value with those close to you to boost internalization of your intent and invite mentors to positively hold you accountable.

- Implement the action ideas selected, then introduce them to others at the beginning of the relationship. This makes expectations clear from the start instead of following the frequent practice in organizations of introducing evaluation criteria at the end of the performance period.

Applying these suggestions will encourage people to step-up to *champion* roles—the subject of a later professionalism lesson.

When we help an organization assess how to get better results, a few simple steps toward accountability often are needed and help increase trust and motivation. Organizations commonly go on strategic planning retreats and create great goals. Yet, without clear accountability and an action plan, these worthy goals often go unfulfilled until the next planning retreat when they repeat the cycle. Without accountability, the internal culture can foster skepticism and paralysis where initiative dies and personal and organizational results suffer.

The good news is that a single person can begin a positive turnaround in such a culture by seeking accountability and empowerment and insisting the team give noble effort to achieve desired results. One person can set an example and encourage others until a critical mass of people adopt standards that help the organization operate at a higher level. My own corporate experience reflects that constructive change and results that "stick to the wall" start with one or two champions that hold themselves accountable. A dedicated core of champions can change a culture.

We encourage individuals to write a vision for their best-selves, which includes a statement about accountability. Read your vision statement regularly to remind yourself of your desired behavior, improve focus, and internalize patterns of thinking that will help you do the right things automatically more often. While perfection may seldom come, we can increase the probability of thinking and living as our best-selves.

Sample Excerpt from David's Plan for Life that Addresses Accountability and Disappointment

I lead from wherever I am, doing my best with my important roles and goals. I make and keep promises for my areas of responsibility plus those where others need me.

*When results fall short of desired expectations, I **admit** what happened, **accept** the impact on others and me, and **act** to make the best of this situation while learning how to do better next time.*

Professionalism
Lesson 4

Develop ethical fitness and decision-making from the start. Loss of trust in character is more damaging and harder to restore than well-intentioned mistakes or under-developed competencies. People are more willing to forgive failure through valiant effort than intentional violations of trust. Have personal and organizational training reinforce how to make tough ethical decisions and choose *the harder right*. Know that good intent does not always equal good impact and that perception and truth do not always match. Have a strategy to earn and re-earn trust with vital relationships.

Ethical Fitness: ability to make the right ethical choices even under extreme stress; doing the *harder right.*

Harder Right: decision that most positively affects the widest circle of people for the greater good, even if requiring sacrifice.

In our course, *Harder Right Ethical Decisions and Actions, a* key reference is the *Be a Pro* Leadership Model, which emphasizes developing a foundation for harder right decisions and action:

Dunn-Donnithorne Be a Pro Leadership Model

Societal/ Influencing Leadership *Be a Statesman*	Set example of how to live balanced, healthy lifestyle in global, competitive environment for good of organization and society Be a coalition builder Lead organizational and societal change/improvement Live and leave a legacy
Organizational/ Team Leadership *Lead Leaders*	Lead and develop leaders Be a mentor and succession planner Clearly state intent, expectations, parameters Balance mission, resources, and people for *"triple-win"* Manage systems, processes, and best practices
Direct/ Interpersonal Leadership *Apply Ethical Reasoning with Others*	Practice *face-to-face* leadership of employees/troops Gain mastery of more complex aspects of profession Coach and care for people (praise progress, redirect, or reprimand) Build successful teams using different leadership styles Improve communication and conflict resolution skills
Personal/Life Leadership *Absorb Values and Learn Behaviors*	Learn how to be a *follower* Learn how to be a *true professional* Know "how to's" of profession (Skills and Knowledge) Develop strong self-concept **"The Harder Right"** Win within the rules (ethical fitness) ➡ *Decision that most positively affects the widest circle of people for the greater good*

The concept was developed by Col. Larry Donnithorne (U.S. Army Retired) while serving at the United States Military Academy and adapted by Stretch into the *Be a Pro Model*. Col. Donnithorne wrote about the U.S. Military Academy's approach to leader development in The *West Point Way of Leadership*. West Point provides the nation with "leaders of character." The model has value in every sector of society—not just West Point or the military. A foundation of inspiring trust and keeping it lies at the base of the development model to provide *lifetime leaders* of character as one practices winning within the rules and recognizing and doing "the harder right." They build this idea into everyday life, maturing the ability to exercise leadership in increasingly complex settings with a solid ethical foundation.

Many of these young people have never taken the time to reflect on and anchor their beliefs. As a result, like many others, they struggle with ethical decisions until they are firm in their values.

The Be a Pro Leadership Model illustrates how important this ethical building block is in the development of personal leadership first (leading oneself) before leading others. The person develops from knowing about ethical behavior, to adhering to it, to securing it as a belief. A desire to "do the harder right" applies equally well in the private or public sector. When motivation to live this way is combined with a strong sense of personal worth, plus knowledge and skills, then the ability to become *ethically fit* in real life can be realized.

Your personal integrity and earned trust from others are more valuable than money and tangible perks. Fulfillment in life comes from finding your callings and gaining respect from the people with whom you share life. That respect is earned every day based on behavior. Make decisions mindful of the greater good for the widest circle of people, and you will trust yourself and win the trust of those who matter.

With earned trust and a mission that has been internalized with a high level of commitment, a combat unit will "go to the gates of hell" for a worthy cause and commander. Loss of trust in a leader will swiftly erode unit cohesion and performance. An ethical foundation built in peacetime enables winning with honor in war. To do their best, people must believe in what they are doing and the people with whom they are serving. The same is true of "corporate combat."

Right versus Wrong

Many people believe they understand *right versus wrong*. Most people, however, need preparation and practice to consistently choose right over wrong. For many well-intentioned people, *right versus wrong* is not as clear as they think, and there is ample evidence of ethical scandals in our public culture and private lives, which proves the point.

People and organizations often overlook the importance of identifying and internalizing desired beliefs in building a strong ethical foundation. People under intense stress revert to those behaviors that are most ingrained. Even if well-intentioned, a person with underdeveloped or inappropriate beliefs may take undesirable action, lacking the will to do the right thing even when they know it is wrong.

Beliefs Leading to Bad Behavior

Consider these statements common in the psyche and language of our culture that lead to unethical behavior by people who mean to do right.

+ "If the boss does it, it must be okay."
+ "What they don't know can't hurt them."

- "It's okay to cover up this mistake because I can make up for it on the next project."

- "Nice guys finish last."

- "I've paid my dues and have it coming to me."

- "When I get a job I like, then I will work hard."

- "If I am caught up and nobody tells me to do anything, I should be able to do what I want."

- "Life is chaos, so my behavior doesn't matter."

- "It is genetic, it runs in the family."

- "Let the buyer beware."

- "I just 'borrowed' the money; I will put it back after this deal pays off."

- "You have to adapt your ethics to the situation."

- "To be competitive, we can't be honest all the time."

These *bad beliefs* often lead to justification of unethical behavior under normal stress and are exacerbated under intense stress. Sometimes people *don't know that they don't know.* They do not realize they are acting on flawed principles because they have internalized undesired beliefs, maybe because they never learned better or because they work in a culture that accepts or reinforces bad behavior. These people may operate with good intentions without understanding that their behavior can lead to inferior, even unethical, outcomes.

A simple example of how beliefs can unknowingly hurt the motivation of employees with good intent follows. A client organization struggled with mediocre performance. Of the top two reasons discovered through simple assessment, one was an underlying belief by many of the employees that, "if the phone isn't ringing and I've completed my current task, I should be able to do what I want." During such times, many "surfed" the Internet, read magazines, and made personal calls—wasting time. They could have been using that time to be productive—

seeking to help other employees, work on important long-term but not urgent priorities…in general being a good steward of their time—for themselves and their employer. Management's initial perception was the people were lazy. Digging deeper, we found most of the people liked their jobs and believed in "a day's work for a day's pay." With good intent, they were, at best, wasting time and violating the value of stewardship or, at worst, stealing by getting paid for not working. Most of these employees had entered a culture that accepted such behavior and had not embraced stewardship of time and talents. Their belief systems were not prepared well, so they lulled themselves into the accepted thoughts of the group they joined.

To change a culture like this, leaders need to assess the situation. They also need to identify and articulate the beliefs, values, and results they desire, then implement rewards to educate and motivate those with good intentions. People can improve thinking, decision-making, and behavior by identifying and internalizing desired beliefs and values using beliefs inventories such as the one used in our *Ethical Decisions and Actions: Choosing the Harder Right* seminar.

Beliefs Leading to Ethical Behavior

A person who internalizes the following type beliefs will tend to choose to act ethically, even when it is difficult to do so.

- *I demonstrate a strong work ethic even if no one is watching.*
- *What I sow, I shall reap.*
- *I do my best even if that means exceeding the requirements of my job.*
- *If I finish my work early, I look for additional ways to serve and make the most of my time.*
- *Even if I am not in my ideal job, I deliver my best and develop myself until I earn a job I desire.*

- *Even if I pay a price for my honesty in this decision, my integrity is worth it.*

- *I make decisions as though my parent or child is watching.*

To internalize desired beliefs, write these or those you choose in your plan for life to read regularly. Organizations can adapt and use them as well.

Good people sometimes do less than their best, even questionable or bad things, because they have internalized incorrect beliefs and values. We strongly recommend that people commit to preparation before stressful situations arise. We also view ethics as much more than merely avoiding illegal acts. Ethics also includes stewardship, how we work, and "The Golden Rule," how we treat others.

Right versus Right

In addition to "right versus wrong," there are "right versus right" dilemmas. The toughest ethical dilemmas may not require deciding between right and wrong, one good and one bad, but rather between two seemingly right choices.

If one has truly prepared and knows right and wrong, *right versus wrong* is not a true ethical dilemma—it is a choice. When we do what we know to be wrong, we have given in and made a choice to do what is wrong.

The most challenging ethical dilemma comes when two ethical values or beliefs conflict. This situation is one that can create intense frustration and many opportunities for attempted justification. Most of us believe in values like integrity, honesty, compassion, stewardship, reliability, caring, courage, loyalty, and truthfulness. They are all worthy qualities.

What happens though when two of these ethical values conflict?

- When justice conflicts with mercy?

- When stewardship collides with compassion?
- When truth opposes loyalty?

My West Point education taught that it is right to violate one ethical value/belief only when another ethical value/belief produces the greater good. Our Seven Step LEAD Decision Guide (to follow) is designed to help one sort through these tough dilemmas and make the ethically right decision.

Ethically Fit Support Systems

Some are fortunate to learn as children beliefs and habits that support ethical behavior. Those who start life without good role models usually have beliefs, habits, and actions that need correction. It is possible to change beliefs if one chooses to become ethically fit and identify and replace undesirable habits. Embrace the assistance of positive and trusted mentors such as family, friends, colleagues, and clergy.

Trying to help an intentionally unethical person behave ethically is almost impossible until he chooses to change. A person who decides he wants to become a character-based person can succeed, though it will require preparation, action, and perseverance.

Retaining ethical fitness is made much easier if one's organization has an imbedded culture that supports ethical behavior. The U.S. military and many civilian organizations have strong congruence between their institutional values and those it demands of their soldiers or employees. Ethical meltdowns do occur such as the Army's at My Lei in Vietnam or a slew of corporate scandals such as Enron, MCI WorldCom, and HealthSouth, but in general employees or soldiers are more likely to behave ethically in an organization that legitimately embraces an ethical climate.

A legitimate ethical culture has business advantages, including increased loyalty. Dr. John Schinnerer, author of "The ROI of an Effective Ethics Program," cites a Hudson Institute survey that quantifies loyalty to a company:

> "Employees [who perceive their organization is ethical] are six times more likely to be loyal than workers who believe their organization is unethical. Only nine percent of the workforce who believed their management to be unethical was willing to remain with the company."

Dr. Schinnerer also reports other benefits from an imbedded ethical culture:

♦ Reduced ethical meltdowns

♦ Greater customer loyalty

♦ Fewer fines and criminal charges

♦ Less pressure and boycotts from social activists

♦ Decrease in employee theft

♦ Stronger financial performance

Finally, Dr. Schinnerer cites a DePaul University study of 300 large public companies, which found that an effective ethics program provided more than twice the value to shareholders than companies whose ethics programs were judged to be superficial and a study by the University of Southwestern Louisiana, which reveals that publicity about unethical company behavior lowered stock prices for at least six months. Clearly, ethical behavior impacts the bottom line.

To assist well intended people to analyze and make *harder right* decisions, we developed the Seven Step LEAD Guide to Ethical Decision-making.

7 Step Guide to Ethical Decision-making

Our decision-making model developed for the *Ethical Decisions and Actions* seminar helps people:

♦ Understand and use a sound decision-making process that is helpful, especially when you face tough decisions;

♦ Boost awareness and strengthen commitment to ethics;

♦ Prepare for making *harder right* decisions based on identifying and internalizing desired beliefs and values.

The 7 Steps

1. **Prepare**
2. Clarify
3. Consider
4. Plan
5. Test
6. Decide
7. **Act**

Many decision-making models focus on the steps 2-6; we add and emphasize preparation and action, steps 1 and 7.

1. Prepare—Identify what you need in order to think, decide, and act.

♦ Quiet Your Mind

♦ Assess Your Beliefs

♦ Assess Your Motivating and Ethical Values

Quiet your mind to synthesize and process information. Assess your beliefs, values, fears, and priorities that drive your instincts and internalize the ones you want to guide you. Identify and write desired beliefs, values, and priorities in advance, which will boost your capacity for ethical fitness and better performance. When an ethical dilemma arises, you will be prepared to analyze a situation or act on instinct.

Assess Your Priorities in the 7 Areas of Life

Everything we do falls within the seven areas of life, shown here in this portion of the *Dyson Life Leadership Model*. This model correlates with the Dyson Hierarchy of Seven Motivating Values (next page).

When an ethical dilemma faces you, be aware of what area of life and motivating value is impacted so you will be aware of the motivation driving your instincts.

- Physical—Is the dilemma a survival or health pressure?

- Financial—Is there pressure from loss of income?

- Professional—Does this pressure threaten loss of job or important career goal?

- Personal—Will I feel embarrassment or lost esteem?

- Social—Is my relationship with someone threatened or will a loved one think less of me?

- Philanthropical—What impact will this dilemma have on my ability to contribute to and serve the community?

- Spiritual—How will my actions match with teachings, rituals, practices, beliefs, and values I have internalized?

The more you have internalized desired motivating values, the more they will serve as a source of strength when facing ethical dilemmas. By having a prepared mind and knowing what you value most, you will be more likely to rely on those values when they are challenged by the dilemma you face.

Assess Your 7 Motivating Values

SIGNIFICANCE

SUCCESS

SELF ESTEEM

SOCIAL CONNECTION

SECURITY

SAFETY

SURVIVAL

The *Dyson Hierarchy of Seven Motivating Values* expands knowledge learned from Abraham Maslow, who identified five basic needs of people—physiological, security, belongingness, esteem, and self-actualization. The Dyson model uses seven motivating values to help people make advanced distinctions and places greater emphasis on significant living while serving interdependently with others to serve society beyond self-actualization.

Maslow determined that people tend to be motivated by higher-level values only after lower level values have been at least partially satisfied. After the needs of *survival* and *safety/security* are met, people increasingly seek to connect with people, groups, and purposes greater than our basic needs. The type readers we have targeted want to be their "best-selves" by fulfilling higher values.

Our seminars explain more about the meaning of the hierarchy of values and how you can use them in greater depth to aim at being your "best-self." Each of the motivating values has a list of sub-values that help a person identify what is most important in life to include in your Plan for Life to improve focus, decision-making, and instincts.

2. Clarify—State what must be decided, what happened, should have happened, what the ethical dilemma is, and who might be affected.

3. Consider—Gather information. Assess the important facts and assumptions, internal issues, and external factors. Separate truth from perception and critical decision factors from extraneous information. Involve others if needed. Ask:

- Is this an actual dilemma or a misunderstanding?

- What are the relevant facts?

- What assumptions are in place? Are they reliable?

- What internal issues (policy, procedures, and existing cultural norms...) should be considered?

- What external considerations (client needs, economic, legal, political, social, competition...) should be evaluated?

- What are the potentially positive outcomes and the probability of achieving them?

- What are the possible negative outcomes and their probability of happening?

4. Plan—Generate options with the corresponding probable results of doing the *harder right*. These filters will help you consider the course of action to take:

- Golden Rule

- Greatest good for greatest number

- Consistent with highest ethical value

- Legal

- Financial

- Precedence/consistency with prior decisions

- Instincts (gut test, inner voice, calling…)

- Rewards values you seek

Make a preliminary course of action or best-option decision. Consider if others should be involved in deciding and, if so, who should participate.

5. Test—Present your tentative decision or best option to selected stakeholders for feedback If acting alone, test your trial decision against your calling, your feelings, and applied logic.

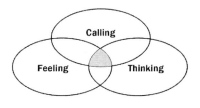

♦ Listen to your spiritual *calling*, your "gut," what you feel led to do.

♦ Consider your emotional *feelings*, what you want to do.

♦ Test your decision by logical *thinking*—what you deduce is correct based on rational assessment and trusted advice.

Write what you determine from this process in an effort to find the center—*the sweet spot*—of the three sources of discernment. Consider trusted advice from mentors, peers, parents, friends, or spiritual leaders. Consult references for knowledge and insights of people who may have faced this decision. Adjust your decision if needed.

People can feel called to do something and not want to do it. Pastors and other professionals have said they "ran for years before accepting their call." Others resist a calling or a feeling because they fear or deduce low probability of success.

People who have prepared with a plan for life that identifies callings, beliefs, values, and priorities will make better decisions more often. Reconciling the three sources of a sound decision—calling, feeling, thinking—can help you, whether through in-depth assessment over a major decision or a quick mental check of what you are about to do. After you internalize this decision-making model, you can make better decisions instinctively.

6. Decide—Choose your desired option; involve key persons if needed for approval.

7 Levels of Decision-making Options

Randy Sain, upon becoming president of Sain Associates, found himself in need of tools and skills to deal with decision-making at more advanced levels because his decisions now influenced more stakeholders and required input from more people. He asked me for a set of best practices for decision-making that could serve as a guide for him, the vice presidents, and managers.

This tool provides a list of options for making a decision from deciding alone to gaining unanimous agreement.

1. Decide without consultation or communication of decision—just do it.
2. Decide, then communicate the decision.
3. Decide tentatively and communicate the decision, then implement unless feedback influences you to change.
4. Decide after consulting with key stakeholders for suggestions.
5. Decide after presenting your tentative decisions to one or more stakeholders and inviting feedback and suggestions.
6. Decide after your group reaches consensus and informs you of their recommendation.
7. Decide based on a vote (majority, unanimous…).

Having a strategy for decision-making will help you reach a good decision in a timely manner. Identifying a process for decision-making proves particularly valuable when team members are under pressure, which can cloud the relevant issues. One of the gunfighting lessons is to *be aggressive, clear, and decisive* so subordinates need to know there are times when the more authoritative styles of leadership and decision-making are necessary. Learning a decision-making model helps you make better ethical decisions and along the way develop your instincts to help you do the harder right automatically.

7. Act—Communicate your decision to stakeholders, then implement. Design and install systems and best practices to guide and reward desired behavior and results automatically.

Action normally should be planned and implemented at three levels for maximum effectiveness:

- Personal—your decisions and follow through

- Team—applications for team members and stakeholders

- Organizational—development or improvement of systems, best practices, and training automatically leading to desired results in the future.

Place special emphasis on steps one and seven—preparation and action. Honestly assess your beliefs and values because an ethically immature person often operates from under-developed instincts. Take action to plan, learn, and do things that lead to good habits and instincts. Of the seven decision-making model steps, these two crucial steps are most often given less attention than deserved.

Should you wish to develop ethical fitness at a deeper level or develop an ethics program for your organization, our *Ethical Decisions and Actions* course:

- Takes a more detailed look at beliefs, motivating and ethical values, and decision-making as a foundation for making difficult ethical choices.

- Elaborates further on the decision-making guide, provides cases, and suggested actions.

- Emphasizes the action step, since moving forward is often more difficult than making the decision.

- Provides additional information on the LEAD Decision-making Model.

Professionalism
Lesson 5

Decide to think with positive expectancy and make the best of situations. People face many disappointments in war, business, and other areas of life. Learn to make peace with them, persist, and "bounce high" when you fall.

Positive expectancy: focusing on desired positive outcomes and solutions rather than on worrisome negative possibilities.

Positive Expectancy

My son, Steve, played professional baseball for nine years. A major reason he consistently earned over a .300 batting average (excellent in professional baseball) was his belief that he could hit the best pitch a pitcher could offer. Even though Steve and many players "failed" 70 percent of the time, the belief he could hit every time reinforced his ability to bounce back. The best-prepared athletes rehearse swings and catches thousands of times to internalize muscle actions and responses. They mentally rehearse and visualize actions and responses in order to turn their desired actions into reflexes and instincts. A sense of positive expectancy gives them staying power to work through inevitable slumps and treat each at-bat as a new opportunity.

Positive Patterns of Thinking and Communicating

A baseball manager walked to the mound to warn his pitcher about the next batter, "Whatever you do, don't throw to him high and outside!" Where did the pitcher's mind focus? On high and outside, the thought provided by the manager. Home run! The manager should have stated what he wanted, "throw low and inside" instead of what to avoid.

A dad teaching his little girl to ride her bike pushed her off and encouraged, "Watch out for that pothole, honey!" And she did, running the front wheel into the hole and falling. She focused where her dad told her to look. His intent, of course, was to protect her. He could have said, "Stay on the smooth surface" or "drive around that hole."

In these examples, the manager and the parent had good intent. However, their pattern of thinking and communication focused on actions and results to avoid instead of on what to seek and do. The recipients of instructions were forced to engage in a mental process rather than taking simple action, to have two thoughts instead of one. The ball player and child had to think about what to avoid and then try to figure out what the manager and parent wanted.

The adult can process two thoughts—what to avoid and then what to seek—better than a child. Parents whose communication patterns with children have been monitored send negative messages more often than positive ones. Many use "don't do" messages more than often than they use instructive "what to do" messages. This pattern of one-dimensional thinking often carries over into professional life when people give "constructive criticism" on what they do not like and complaints more often than they give specific feedback and suggestions for desired results and actions.

Pay attention to your thoughts and speech. If you feel the need to tell someone what not to do, consider what you hope they will do. Then, you can more likely state a request or suggestion positively. You also simplify communications. Practice thinking of solutions and suggestions before you speak. You can reduce confusion, shorten learning curves, get better results, and save time.

Breaking Through to Improvement

Dr. Norman Vincent Peale, author of *The Power of Positive Thinking,* influenced millions of people through his writings and sermons. One of his habits was to plan for worry—yes, plan for it. He understood that worry did not help him much, though he could never quite abstain from it. So, he set aside two hours weekly for worry, keeping the rest of the time focused on positive expectancy. Therefore, if he felt worry restricting his optimism and ability to take action, he could mentally postpone the worry until the time set aside for it. This habit helped him minimize the negative impact of worry and maximize thinking about solutions.

Some religious leaders affirm and use Dr. Peale's teachings, though I have heard a few warn against them. Some have internalized and passed on an incorrect belief that a person choosing a positive attitude and developing a plan for life means she is relying less on God. The opposite is true. Spiritual faith calls for positive expectancy as well as action when facing negative influences and possibilities. We are called to live at the highest possible level, and it is our choice to try.

To achieve a "break through" typically requires a "break from" past patterns. The message from *Proverbs* provides truth, "As a man thinketh, so is he." As someone thinks, his actions and habits follow. Pray for direction and strength. Plan for how your best-self should act. Take action. Persevere.

If Not Bliss, Then Bounce

Attaining a constant state of bliss is humanly unattainable, though earning a sense that one generally has his/her act together with the capacity to absorb the "hits" life brings and bounce back is attainable. We believe learning to "bounce" is a direct result of being fit in each area of life and keeping them in balance, in alignment with your values and circumstances.

A major ingredient for stardom
is how high you bounce when you hit bottom.
-General George Patton-

Professionalism
Lesson 6

Fulfill your callings and live a legacy to find meaning. Money is like oxygen; you need it, but it does not give meaning to life. Design your life to be a masterpiece that fulfills your mission.

Calling: what we discern as our highest purpose; divine summons; mission; vocation; profession; trade; occupation.

Legacy: something handed down; a gift, a tradition.

Mission: the special task or purpose for which a person is destined in life; calling.

Mission (Military): the combat operation assigned an individual or unit.

Mission Statement (Personal): a written summary of a person's purpose in life; or of personal and professional purposes; the essence or summary of a vision statement. It usually starts with "To" followed by the purpose.

Vision Statement: visualizing and describing desired outcomes; the result of your plans developing as you desire. If the mission statement is the title, the vision describes the painting.

Make your life a masterpiece.
-John Wooden-
Former basketball coach, UCLA

Callings and Missions

In the Dyson Hierarchy of Motivational Values, the highest level is *Significance.* Here, you can focus beyond success to seek spirituality, stewardship, service, and other higher-level values.

To reach that level of meaning in life one begins with a calling. To make one's calling *come alive,* we suggest writing a plan for life with mission and vision statements. We offer excerpts from our statements for life and professional life as examples to help you get started or continue to develop yours.

Life Mission/Vision Statement Example

David's mission statement, inspired by someone asking him to define the purpose of life, has been constant for more than a decade and is considered by some as a universal life mission statement:

To live a spiritual journey—faithfully;
love and serve others—meaningfully;
and do my best—joyously.

The *seven core values* within this mission and their meaning:

1. **Live**—*Love life, respect and enjoy living things*
2. **Spiritual**—*Connect to our Creator and my callings*
3. **Faithfully**—*Make courageous choices to fulfill my callings on my journey*
4. **Love**—*Care for and serve others*
5. **Meaningfully**—*Do unto others as they need and want*
6. **Best**—*Be my best-self as a good steward of my callings, gifts, and talents as a "ten-talent" person*
7. **Joyously**—*Make the best of circumstances happily with appreciation for blessings.*

Life Vision

While a mission states purpose, a vision describes what you desire as you lead your life. It focuses on the core results you seek to fulfill. Again, a sample from David's description of his best-self. While I have not achieved this vision, admitting the truth about my callings helps inspire me to take action at a higher level:

1. *I seek understanding of my highest spiritual callings and seek enlightened truth, sharing what I find with those who also seek truth.*
2. *I love and serve others according to their needs and wants, matched with my gifts and talents, helping them to fulfill their callings, gifts, and talents.*

3. *I do my best joyously—to serve God, care for others, and grow in enlightenment. I fulfill my callings and leave a legacy by doing my best—improving my mind, body, spirit, service, and stewardship—preparing my soul for greater life and my capacities for greater service.*

Vision statements for the seven areas of life affirm desired results and also provide inspiration, direction, and reminders for accountability. Summaries from his plan:

1. **Spiritual**—*My highest priority is to live a close, connected relationship with God and his natural law—understanding my callings with heightened discernment, from which all areas of life flow.*
2. **Personal**—*I do my best joyously—discovering and developing my callings, gifts, and talents.*
3. **Social**—*I love and serve others meaningfully—adding value with encouragement, example, and enlightenment.*
4. **Professional**—*I am a man on a mission—to help others in my state, then country and world, to prayerfully develop and fulfill their plans for life so they can discover and devote themselves to fulfill their highest callings.*
5. **Physical**—*I develop health and energy through nutrition, work, fitness, inspiration, renewal, and positive, harmonious relationships.*
6. **Financial**—*I live beneath my means and earn beyond my needs, contributing first fruits and excesses as investments in expanding capacities of others in need according to my callings.*
7. **Philanthropical**—*I serve my community and country through my profession, public service, and daily acts of kindness.*

The next sample vision statement focuses on professional life. I use this to state intent, boost inspiration, and match with those who share like values. We advocate *match versus sell* so it is a good thing, especially long-term, when this statement also helps someone assess they do not match because "we cannot be all things to all people."

Professional Mission

On my Professional Constitution and Capabilities Summary, the first thing listed after my name is my professional mission, the purpose of my professional service:

> *To help people and organizations*
> *PLAN and LEAD in LIFE*
> *to fulfill their callings.*

Professional Vision

Next, my vision summary describes the core of what I seek to give and gain:

1. ***Individuals*** *understand their callings, gifts, and talents—and make great choices to fulfill them—designing and using a PLAN for LIFE that inspires and guides them to learn and LEAD their lives, leaving a legacy.*
2. ***Organizations and teams*** *succeed and distinguish themselves with improved design of purpose, values, desired results, strategies, systems, structures and best practices that support and reward to live their priorities. They implement through leadership, training and coaching to help people develop their attitudes and abilities to become their best-selves and serve others at the highest possible levels.*

My professional vision summarized on a second page includes seven statements focused on callings, results, service, preparation, matching, commitment, and rewards; an excerpt:

> ***Callings:*** *I discern that my highest callings include helping people PLAN and LEAD in LIFE. Each of us should focus on callings and choices, plus the principles and practices of personal, interpersonal, and organizational leadership. If we can help someone develop a plan for life that inspires and guides, then we help that person fulfill the principles of "as a man thinketh" and*

"design before construction." We increase probability of greater inspired service instead of aimlessness and escapism, develop fitness and success in the seven areas of life, and over time increase focus on higher-level values like spirituality and stewardship beyond esteem and success.

The purpose of a vision statement is to affirm our highest possible expectations so we can aim at them. While I often fall short of my vision, I do better aiming at noble targets than if merely "going with the flow" reacting to random thoughts.

A third page given to prospective sponsors, clients, and students provides a checklist of results and seminars with which I can help. Stating intent increases my clarity and focus, plus helps both of us determine better and faster if we match.

Stretch's journey to a written statement of life mission and vision took a different path. In 1990, he went on a sabbatical to assess how he needed to make changes and to renew his focus on what was most meaningful. He started with the mission, "To take charge of my life," then went on to summarize vision statements about how he wanted to live his life, such as:

- *Make money my servant, seeking financial independence and simple elegance; make it an enabling resource.*
- *Keep possessions secondary to people.*
- *Make living an adventure in opportunity.*
- *Seek the counsel of mentors while respecting their privacy.*

These and other vision statements gave him the sense of direction he needed to make changes productively.

Stretch's plan divided life into eras. For the first fifty years, he went "all out" to "be all he could be" in his chosen military profession. Next, he envisioned spending ten or fifteen years serving in a private sector organization, then the remainder of his life giving back by doing what he is passionate about with those with similar values. This book is part of that legacy.

Legacy

A legacy is prepared to be passed on after we die. A legacy can also be lived, passing on gifts of love, service, and lessons while alive. Statements of legacy tend to focus on obituaries, eulogies, and wills. Obituaries typically include biographical information while eulogies include more about relationships and influence. Wills typically describe final requests written for executors and legal entities.

We recommend writing a will as an extension of your plan for life. Go beyond that to write a draft of your obituary to have ready for your executor. Further, write your desired obituary and eulogy—not for traditional purposes of "what you want people to say about you," but for a higher one: to identify the experiences and influences you want to have occurred during your life. These writings can provide great insight, especially when you review them regularly to internalize the values you discover and use them to guide your priorities. As importantly, they serve as keepsakes and sources of wisdom for loved ones. This approach is suggested again in Gunfighting Lesson Seven as a way to show loved ones a "mirror to your soul."

David affirms his written constitution is a great source of inspiration and accountability, as well as an important motivator and aid in time management. Once you write your legacy, ask "If I keep living with the same priorities, will I fulfill my callings and legacy?" The answer may prompt you to start making more time for important people and projects in your life to help you *live your priorities.*

Stretch cites his father as one of his motivations for writing. His dad wrote numerous books, documenting his hard-earned wisdom as a written legacy, with his wife serving as editor. Stretch wants to do the same for his children and their generation. He calls it a *living tradition,* coming from the Latin word "traditio" meaning to hand down.

Stretch's mission and vision statement gives him a sense of direction and focus. Having sought to live his legacy, he wants to earn, "Let it be said well done, be thou at peace." That phrase is part of the West Point Hymn that he wants engraved on his tombstone at Arlington National Cemetery when his watch has ended. Internalizing valuable lessons and our callings inspire us to serve with greater commitment and courage, and then pass on our story.

What is the use of living
if not to strive for noble causes for those who live on.
-Winston Churchill-
Former Prime Minister, Great Britain

Your mission and vision will help you write goals and plan your time priorities. Share them with colleagues and clients who have similar callings so you can boost cooperation.

We are always a work in progress.
The process of getting there is more fun
and personally rewarding than being there.
-Claudia Kennedy-
Lieutenant General, United States Army

Chris Crouch, co-author of *The Contented Achiever* and an adjunct member of the Dyson Institute faculty, advocates reaching contentment and achievement, which he defines as "both fulfilled and materially successful." This state is more easily achieved when you find your calling and choose to leave a legacy with those who matter most.

Finding and pursuing your calling
gives you the gravitational pull toward your best future.
-David Lipski-
Author, *Absolutely American*

Callings in Common

Many professions and civic organizations set standards inviting members to accept a common calling or creed as a basis for inclusion and inspiration to do the right things. Some examples to inspire you and your organization:

The Commissioning Oath to be an Officer in The United States Army

I, [soldier's name],...having been appointed an officer in the Army of the United States...do solemnly swear...I will support and defend the Constitution of the United States against all enemies, foreign and domestic, that I will bear true faith and allegiance to the same; that I take this obligation freely, without any mental reservation or purpose of evasion; and that I will well and faithfully discharge the duties of the office upon which I am about to enter, SO HELP ME GOD.

Stewards of the Code—Keepers of the Flame

The United States Military Academy Cadet Honor Code states, "A cadet will not lie, cheat, or steal or tolerate those who do." Having such a code provides cadets opportunity to practice what is expected of them as future officers. The purpose is to exhort them to a lifetime commitment to honorable living. Every profession must have a non-toleration requirement that it self-regulates if it is going to prosper and retain credibility. When cadets from the academies graduate, they act as keepers of the flame for the military profession. Learning and practicing how to "do the harder right," especially when it comes to non-toleration of those who choose not to comply, is a difficult challenge. To help meet that challenge, West Point includes in its curriculum opportunities for graduates to return to have substantive dialogue with cadets about the importance of continuing to "do the harder right" after graduation—both while in the service and when they retire into civilian life. The responsibility to be trusted for a lifetime as stewards of the code is retained by every graduate.

The Sentinels' Creed

The Sentinels' Creed describes the commitment of soldiers who serve, *even when no one is watching*. Those who guard the Tomb of the Unknowns serve as examples of those who do their jobs without concern for who gets credit.

My dedication to this sacred duty is total and wholehearted. In the responsibility bestowed on me never will I falter. And with dignity and perseverance my standard will remain perfection. Through the years of diligence and praise and the discomfort of the elements, I will walk my tour in humble reverence to the best of my ability. It is he who commands the respect I protect. His bravery that made us so proud. Surrounded by well meaning crowds by day, alone in the thoughtful peace of night, this soldier will in honored glory rest under my eternal vigilance.

Civic Club Creeds

The U.S. hosts numerous civic clubs that attract citizens united by areas of volunteer service and/or professional advancement. They typically communicate their purposes and creeds prior to membership and include in their rituals reading or reciting the purpose and core values of the organization, which helps members internalize desired thoughts and actions.

Civitan Creed

I AM CIVITAN: as old as life, as young as the rainbow, as endless as time.

MY HANDS do the work of the world and reach out in service to others.

MY EARS hear the cry of children and the call throughout the world for peace, guidance, progress and unity.

MY EYES search for others to join in fellowship and service of Civitan.

MY MOUTH utters the call to daily duty and speaks prayers in every tongue.

MY MIND teaches me respect for law and the flag of my country.

MY HEART beats for every friend, bleeds for every injury to humanity and throbs with joy at every triumph of truth.

MY SOUL knows no fear but its own unworthiness.

MY HOPE is for a better world through Civitan.

MY MOTTO: builders of good citizenship.

MY BELIEF: do unto others as you would have them do unto you.

MY PLEDGE: to practice the golden rule and to build upon it a better and nobler citizenship.

Four-way Test of Rotary

1. Is it the truth?
2. Is it fair to all concerned?
3. Will it build goodwill and better friendships?
4. Will it be beneficial to all concerned?

Rotarian Declaration in Businesses and Professions

As a Rotarian engaged in a business or profession, I am expected to:

♦ *Consider my vocation to be another opportunity to serve;*

♦ *Be faithful to the letter and to the spirit of the ethical codes of my vocation, to the laws of my country, and to the moral standards of my community;*

♦ *Do all in my power to dignify my vocation and to promote the highest ethical standards in my chosen vocation;*

♦ *Be fair to my employer, employees, associates, competitors, customers, the public, and all those with whom I have a business or professional relationship;*

♦ *Recognize the honor and respect due to all occupations which are useful to society;*

♦ *Offer my vocational talents: to provide opportunities for young people, to work for the relief of the special needs of others, and to improve the quality of life in my community;*

♦ *Adhere to honesty in my advertising and in all representations to the public concerning my business or profession;*

♦ *Neither seek from nor grant to a fellow Rotarian a privilege or advantage not normally accorded others in a business or professional relationship.*

Kiwanis Six Permanent Objects

- *To give primacy to the human and spiritual rather than to the material values of life.*

- *To encourage the daily living of the Golden Rule in all human relationships.*

- *To promote the adoption and the application of higher social, business, and professional standards.*

- *To develop, by precept and example, a more intelligent, aggressive, and serviceable citizenship.*

- *To provide, through Kiwanis clubs, a practical means to form enduring friendships, to render altruistic service, and to build better communities.*

- *To cooperate in creating and maintaining that sound public opinion and high idealism which make possible the increase of righteousness, justice, patriotism, and goodwill.*

Exchange Club Covenant of Service

Accepting the divine privilege of single and collective responsibility as life's noblest gift, I covenant with my fellow Exchangites:

- *To consecrate my best energies to the uplifting of Social, Religious, Political and Business ideals;*

- *To discharge the debt I owe to those of high and low estate who have served and sacrificed that the heritage of American citizenship might be mine;*

- *To honor and respect law, to serve my fellowmen, and to uphold the ideals and institutions of my Country;*

- *To implant the life-giving, society-building spirit of Service and Comradeship in my social and business relationships;*

- *To serve in Unity with those seeking better conditions, better understandings, and greater opportunities for all.*

The Optimist Creed

Promise Yourself

♦ *To be so strong that nothing can disturb your peace of mind.*

♦ *To talk health, happiness and prosperity to every person you meet.*

♦ *To make all your friends feel that there is something in them.*

♦ *To look at the sunny side of everything and make your optimism come true.*

♦ *To think only of the best, to work only for the best, and to expect only the best.*

♦ *To be just as enthusiastic about the success of others as you are about your own.*

♦ *To forget the mistakes of the past and press on to the greater achievements of the future.*

♦ *To wear a cheerful countenance at all times and give every living creature you meet a smile.*

♦ *To give so much time to the improvement of yourself that you have no time to criticize others.*

♦ *To be too large for worry, too noble for anger, too strong for fear, and too happy to permit the presence of trouble.*

Youth Development Organizations

The Boys and Girls Scouts are but two of the many organizations dedicated to help young people develop character and competence. Professionals and volunteers devote time to help children and teens gain experience beyond school and sports to practice service and achievement with others.

Boy Scout Oath

On my honor I will do my best
To do my duty to God and Country and obey the Scout Law;
To help other people at all times;
To keep myself physically strong, mentally awake, and morally
straight.

Boy Scout Law (12 Values)

A Scout is:

Trustworthy	*Loyal*	*Helpful*
Friendly	*Courteous*	*Kind*
Obedient	*Cheerful*	*Thrifty*
Brave	*Clean*	*Reverent*

Girl Scout Promise

On my honor, I will try:
    To serve God and my country,
    To help people at all times,
    And to live by the Girl Scout Law.

Girl Scout Law

I will do my best to be
    honest and fair,
    friendly and helpful,
    considerate and caring,
    courageous and strong, and
    responsible for what I say and do,
and to
    respect myself and others,
    respect authority,
    use resources wisely,
    make the world a better place, and
    be a sister to every Girl Scout.

Most professions have a statement to inspire and guide members, such as engineers and family physicians.

Engineers' Creed

As a Professional Engineer, I dedicate my professional knowledge and skill to the advancement and betterment of human welfare. I pledge:

- *To give the utmost of performance;*

- *To participate in none but honest enterprise;*

- *To live and work according to the laws of man and the highest standards of professional conduct;*

- *To place service before profit, the honor and standing of the profession before personal advantage, and the public welfare above all other considerations.*

- *In humility and with need for Divine Guidance, I make this pledge.*

The Family Physician's Creed

I am a Family Physician…. This is what I believe:

You, the patient, are my first professional responsibility whether man or woman or child, ill or well, seeking care, healing or knowledge.

You and your family deserve high quality, affordable health care including treatment, prevention and health promotion. I support access to health care for all.

The specialty of family practice trains me to care for the whole person physically and emotionally, throughout life, working with your medical history and family dynamics, coordinating your care with other physicians when necessary.

This is my promise to you.

Professionalism
Lesson 7

Be a champion for your calling, your profession, people you serve, and your organization. Choose to develop a world-class "A" level attitude with commitment and courage toward seeking mastery in your competence. Work on your plan for life until you give yourself an "A" for discerning and writing your callings and choices. Identify and describe your desired legacy, then persist with commitment to fulfill it. Demonstrate character to keep promises and do the right things, even under stress. Develop confidence as you take action, rather than waiting for confidence before you take action. Grow in your sense of connection to projects and the people working on them, matching on mission and values more than on personality. Develop from the inside-out genuine charisma based on character and competence that attracts people who want to work with you on common goals. Serve as a champion for people and organizations of good intent, helping them identify and fulfill their callings, gifts, and talents through stewardship with distinction.

Champion: An ardent defender or supporter of a cause or another person; a warrior; has attributes of a winner....

Those who seek to be true professionals and serve as such, who "champion" people and professions, develop attitude and character first to increase commitment and capacity to serve. Callings and choices fuel desire and decisions to prepare and act. Those who focus only on technical competence in their development—and in the development of others—fall short of stewardship and the best long-term results.

Barriers to Higher Levels of Attitude and Character

Barriers typically stay in place unless we break through them, which often requires a break with past thoughts and habits. The source of many of our problems and the barriers to our progress usually has more to do with components of attitude like commitment, character, courage, and confidence than with competency. Often the primary barrier to increasing competence is found in the levels of commitment and confidence a professional feels toward the task as well his preparation for it. Improvement often starts through identifying callings and choices.

Comments from CEOs, program managers, and other professionals, as well as personal observations for decades of what does and does not work, helped me discover a simple, though powerful breakthrough, an "aha" insight that has affected the way we teach and coach. Consider if you have stated or heard any of these statements:

- "Years ago we told our people they were empowered; what if your people don't want to be empowered anymore?"
- "What if you have given the best training and coaching available, but some employees don't even try to improve?"
- "What if you've done everything you know to improve the work environment and your staff still evaluates job satisfaction as a "C?"

Paul Earle, Executive Vice President of Colonial Properties Trust Multi-Family Division, shared their goal to be a market leader and how they were instilling key performance indicators to guide benchmarking. He then posed, "What if some of our people don't want to be world class—or don't believe they can?" The "aha" and "tipping point" followed. We need to look deeper than training topics and satisfaction surveys.

Taking the components of attitude and ability in the Dyson Empowerment Model, which guide professionals to earn empowerment and leaders to delegate it, I designed a survey to ask professionals and students to assess where they were and wanted to be on commitment and confidence—in self, job/profession, and team/organization. The results proved so valuable that the survey was expanded and offered to additional groups. The summary results of research reported in the next table reveals a key barrier to maximum motivation—levels of beliefs about trust in attitude and ability. For some individuals and teams, this survey and supporting tools and plans have provided a breakthrough in understanding how to prepare for earning higher levels of empowerment as well as shifts in strategy for leaders who train and coach people. Some have adapted plans, performance evaluations, and other tools.

In a leadership class at Sain Associates enrolled by people seemingly with initiative, the average level of commitment and confidence was "C." I was so surprised that these people who were motivated enough to enroll in a course that required four hours of effort monthly for a year would assess themselves below "A" or "B." One woman assessed herself as a "D" on character (based on keeping promises to self and others). I met with her privately. After some reflection on past patterns, she concluded she rarely kept promises to herself. Although she was more than fifty years old, she realized for the first time she had a pattern of thinking that kept her from believing she could succeed; she had a barrier to confident action. This belief barrier kept her from doing her best—sometimes from even trying—which meant not keeping promises to herself, others, or the organization at a high level.

With this mindset, the president would encourage the company through presentations and written plans—or the team leader would encourage big goals for the people and projects—though her belief barrier instinctively blocked hope and action. She would feel energized for awhile, though inwardly she thought success might come for others but not her. She did little differently.

Summary of Survey Results

Assessing Current and Desired Levels
of Trust in Attitude/Character

Scale=A-F, just like school, the system familiar to most people. Groups include corporate professionals and executives, professional society members, and college students who attended conferences or enrolled for seminars/short courses.

Your Beliefs/Assessment about Yourself 7 Components of Attitude (Character)	Now Range Average	Desired Range Average
Callings—I have identified my callings, gifts, and talents.	A-F C-	A-B A-
Choices—I have decided to fulfill my callings and have written plans for my life/legacy.	A-D C+	A-B A-
Commitment—I am dedicated to my callings, legacy, and priorities; pursue…passionately.	B–D C+	A-B A-
Character—I do what I say I will, with good intent, keeping promises to myself/others.	A-F C-	A A
Courage—I act on what is important even before feeling totally confident.	B-F C-	A-B A-
Confidence—I believe in my attitude and ability (attitude, skills and knowledge).	A-F C+	A A
Connection—I feel connected to the people I serve/work with and to my projects.	A-F C	A-B A-
Charisma—I attract, inspire and encourage people who match values to work with me.	B-D B-	A A

Now, look at results from a narrowed study of commitment and confidence in one's profession and organization.

Your Beliefs/Assessment about Your Commitment and Confidence In Your <u>Profession / Position</u> (career, job…)	Now Range Average	Desired Range Average
Commitment to my profession / position, roles, goals, and responsibilities…	A-C B-	A A
Confidence in my professional ability (skills, knowledge) to serve and succeed…	A-C C+	A A

Your Beliefs/Assessment about Your Commitment and Confidence In the <u>Team / Organization</u>	Now Range Average	Desired Range Average
Commitment to the team and organization, my accountability to my part in our success…	A-C C+	A A-B
Confidence in the organization, plan, leadership, and our ability to succeed…	A-C C+	A-C A-

These assessments proved essentially the same, with the current assessment of "C" and a desire for "A." The self-assessments tended to yield the highest scores for owners, senior leaders and managers, followed by professional staff and students. We presumed some of the more motivated personnel in the organizations would participate in training and coaching. A range of "C-" to "B-" seems like low assessments for commitment and confidence. If the assessments had been from a broader sampling of the company, they probably would have been even lower.

Goals such as market leadership and world-class service are not likely to be internalized deeply for those who have a level of commitment of "C" or worse. The highest correlation with low confidence is low commitment.

Similarly, low confidence tends to produce low commitment. The highest correlation for low commitment is low-level design of callings and choices.

A correlation appears to exist between feelings of commitment and confidence with employee satisfaction. During a two-year period when levels of employee commitment and confidence increased amongst leadership class members at Sain Associates, employee satisfaction increased as well.

As a result of these assessments, we are better teachers because of what we have learned about people. We coach participants to:

- Identify what they need to do to reach the desired level of callings and choices, commitment and confidence, and other components of attitude in their plans.

- Share their professional plans for performance and improvement with their supervisory leader during the course, the performance evaluation, and the planning process.

- State what they need from a leader, team, and organization to achieve maximum results and fulfillment.

- We give them a professional plan template that includes self-assessments and goals for improving attitude and ability as well as earning empowerment. We include an excerpt of the professional plan template as one of the tools in the Call to Action section. Using the survey results, we adapt the course curriculum to help them achieve specific desired results rather than just teach topics. In virtually every case, people grow faster and get better support from those they identify as important to them.

Earning a Higher Level of Attitude and Ability Leading to Empowerment and Service as a Champion

We often find the barriers sound relatively simple and are significant only because they have not been identified with action taken. Sample strategies for professionals to boost commitment and confidence in *self:*

- Identify callings and choices in a written plan that inspires and guides. One of the most common admissions of low commitment is the person who has little clarity on callings or purpose in life. Writing and reading a plan for life to improve and internalize priorities and focus can be accomplished in 10 to 15 minutes daily (1% of your time).

Sample actions that boost commitment and confidence in *job/profession:*

- Your professional plan states what you want to give and gain. Review it with your decision-makers to make sure your goals align with the goals they and the organization have for you. Some hold back from giving full commitment to an organization because they are not sure if they will be able to earn the level of rewards they desire. This diminished feeling often lingers because neither the professional nor the leader initiates action to identify the desired results. If desired roles and rewards are not available to you, it is better to know rather than work for extended periods with the anxiety of not knowing and ultimately leaving disappointed—or worse, remaining with a low commitment. Either way, seek a service to which you can give an "A" level of commitment and action.

- Confidence often is boosted—and stress reduced—by preparing a learning, training, and development plan that will prepare you for current and desired roles. Outline what you need to earn empowerment, then get coaching for suggestions and assistance. This process helps people prepare for promotion, earn trust faster, and increase commitment to the process.

Sample actions that boost commitment and confidence in the *team/organization:*

- CEOs and other leaders typically need to present the mission, vision, and desired results repeatedly to help people see where the organization is going and how they fit into the plan. Some staff report their level of commitment remains low because they are not clear about the direction of the organization and their opportunities within it, even though the leader believes he has communicated adequately.

- Use the organizational chart as a positive tool that communicates how the organization fits together, its channels of communication and cooperation, and potential career paths. Employees often tell us they are "riding the fence" of commitment and "keeping their ears open" for other opportunities because they are not aware of career paths. Even if the organization has done all it can, if the professional has not reconciled that opportunity exists, commitment can be undermined until clarity improves. Organizational charts are often viewed negatively as sets of boxes that limit people. They can be positive tools. Along with plans, position profiles, and performance evaluations, organizational designs can provide a framework for stating desired results, behavior, and rewards.

- Identify what you need to earn and maintain an "A" or "B" level of attitude. Admit that your character is reflected, in part, by your attitude toward your work and other people. Employees are most open and positive with leaders when they take perceived complaints like "this is why I have a low commitment to my job and this organization" to a higher level that focuses on "my goal is to get from 'C' to 'A' levels of commitment and confidence. My professional plan includes what I seek to do and how you could help me."

Sain Associates, an engineering and survey consulting firm founded by Hack Sain and now led by Randy Sain, sponsored classes that met monthly at lunch in a year-long course on leadership and professional preparation. For several years, we compared the current and desired levels of attitude and ability at the end of the given year with the ones they had stated the previous January. On average, participants improved at least one grade in their assessment of attitude and ability. Most of these professionals had ten or more years of experience and technical training that did not address assessment and development of components like commitment and confidence. The first assessment revealed a "C/C+" average in commitment. Commitment improved to "B" or better in one year with an investment of one hour weekly. Further, in the annual company survey that assessed employee satisfaction, Sain Associates improved from "C" to "A" in two years.

Commitment to values like professionalism, service, ethics, and leadership affects success in any field of service. Ask any caring and credible CEO or team leader about what they want more of in their team members, and you will likely find agreement that commitment is a core part of taking their people and their organization to the next level.

Attitude and character development are within our control. In addition to competency training, forward-thinking organizations also focus on development that boosts character, commitment, confidence, and other components of attitude as well as skills, knowledge, and other areas of ability. We can help people break through to higher levels of development and performance through a combination of training and coaching, plus tools and systems that improve focus on planning, action, and results.

In the Call to Action section near the end of the book, you will find Assessment and Action Plan templates for Professionalism, Gunfighting, and a Fitness Package designed to help you decide what you need to do to improve your quality of life and build a comprehensive stress strategy. You have the option of reading the rest of the book, then completing the assessments and action plans. Or, while the lessons from this chapter are fresh in your mind, you could go to the Professionalism Assessment and Action Plan and respond to what you just learned, plus decide what you need to do.

Preparation for Stress Lessons

Stress: strain; pressure; tension; strained exertion that affects the body and mind; change to which you must adapt.

Ambushed: an instantaneous surprise; being or feeling attacked.

Pragmatic optimist: one who "looks at the bright side" in a practical way.

Trauma: a very disturbing, stressful experience; emotional shock from a real threat or one's interpretation of circumstances.

Triage: A process in which things are ranked based on likely benefit when limited resources must be allocated.

Preparation for *Under Stress*

We offer this book about doing our best as professionals and leaders with the backdrop *under stress* because stress can bring out the best and the worst in people. Under intense stress, our preparation for it–or not—can mean the difference between life and death, or at least affect the quality of life we enjoy as well as our influence on others around us.

A soldier, especially a combat leader, must be mentally, physically, and emotionally prepared for the stressors of combat. The military spends extraordinary amounts of time in training and simulations to prepare people for the anticipated stressors of combat and other hardships. We believe more attention should be given to stress preparation in civilian professions. The ability to respond to stress correlates with the quality of ethical fitness and decision-making. Corporate scandals often stem from ethics violations because good people do bad things because they are unprepared for stressful pressures and temptations.

Also of great importance is the impact of stress on personal life and social relationships that is both documented and observable with great impact on relationships between family members and interactions within the fabric of society. Some simple things can be done in our families and schools as well as spiritual and professional organizations to help people prepare to be their best-selves. We believe, if more people embrace the spirit of true professionalism and commit at a higher level to prayer, planning, practice, and performance to do what is most important well, we as individuals and as society can serve better under normal as well as intense stressors.

Gunfighting and Other Intense Stressors

Unfortunately, gunfighting has been a part of our lives though military conflicts that seem to occur every decade or so and a part of the lives of law enforcement and other professionals who "serve and protect" our homeland daily. We use the *gunfighting* label in both a literal sense and as a metaphor for extreme stress or trauma for those pragmatic optimists in any military or civilian profession.

Virtually everyone faces stressful situations, some life threatening. Some military professionals get ambushed in combat. Some corporate professionals feel ambushed at work. Other civilians can feel ambushed by unexpected physical, financial, and personal threats. Many people feel stress from time demands, financial responsibilities, conflicts, and other pressures.

Productivity usually drops when stress gets out of control to the point thoughts and actions lose focus. If unprepared, low morale and inappropriate behavior can follow.

Pragmatic Optimist

Stress is a fact of life. We wrote this book for the pragmatic optimist, who faces normal stress each day and likely will suffer trauma at times. According to Clayton Tucker-Ladd, "over half of us by the time we are 20 have suffered at least some trauma." Researchers estimate that at least 60% of men and 50% of women experience serious trauma; yet only 5-10% have been diagnosed with serious traumas such as post-traumatic stress disorders (PTSD) or dissociative identity disorders (DID). This latter group needs professional assistance beyond the scope of this book. We use the term *trauma* to represent an assortment of the type *ambushes* faced by many people, even pragmatic optimists—death of loved ones, stressful divorces, natural or man-induced disasters, loss of jobs, debilitating diseases, and the like. Given the complexity of the subject of stress, we focus on how to help people prepare to live as their "best-selves" against a backdrop of stress.

Pragmatic optimists prepare to control stress and not allow it to control them or hinder them from living as their best-selves. *Admit* it is there. *Accept* the consequences of dealing positively or negatively with stressors. *Act* to prepare for and respond to stressors as your best-self.

Triage

Our approach to such a complicated topic is to address it according to priority and circumstance. The normal daily life stressors are dealt with separately from the less frequent but more intense stressors. Either normal or intense stress can be instantaneous, requiring immediate action, or prolonged, requiring the ability to cope for an extended period of time. We place priority on skills and actions that help make one resilient in handling prolonged normal stress and develop reflexes and instincts for immediate stressors.

Approach

The seven lessons are organized to help you uncover your sources of stress, differentiate between good and bad stress, then use good stress to help achieve peak performance while mitigating the impact of bad stress. We provide several "nuts and bolts" tools to enable serious students to move forward.

Lessons for Stress

7 Lessons for Stress

1. Develop your *Fitness Package* for the seven areas of life. Get good at the basics.

2. Identify sources of stress.

3. Distinguish between *good and bad stress*.

4. Develop a strategy for *normal and intense stress*.

5. Use *stress* to help you achieve peak performance.

6. Practice *safe stress* in advance before the stakes get too high.

7. Create structures, rituals, and habits to proactively leverage positive stress and mitigate negative stress.

Stress Lesson 1

Develop your *Fitness Package* **for the 7 areas of life.** Be good at the basics. *Physical*: the basics of sleep, breathing, nutrition, and exercise provide a platform for health and fitness. *Financial*: living within your means helps your attitude, health, and relationships. *Professional*: a plan with priorities leading you to desired results centered on your callings boosts inspiration, performance and rewards. *Personal*: a plan for life with life leadership habits create stewardship, meaning, and peace of mind. *Social*: handling stress positively helps build positive relationships and minimizes self-inflicted conflicts from reacting to painful stress and broken trust. *Philanthropical*: making time to contribute beyond ourselves gives an extra sense of meaning and joy. *Spiritual*: identifying, developing, and fulfilling callings, gifts, and talents is at the heart of significant living.

Balance: the act of mentally comparing or estimating two things; mental or emotional equilibrium; to compare by estimating the relative, importance, or value of different things.

Fitness Package: developing fitness and balance in the 7 areas of life—a major negative stress reducer and source of preparation for living as our best-selves.

Balance

Dyson Life Leadership Model

The *quality versus quantity* topic inevitably comes up when discussing fitness and balance. Of course, quality of results is a key goal that almost always requires a balanced investment in quantity of time, energy, and resources. An obvious example is to state physical fitness as a value will require you to work out and/or do physical work to get and stay fit for other areas of life while balancing the need to invest time and energy in those other areas. We recommend developing fitness balanced in the seven areas of life with a continuum of best practices that build habits of life leadership with purpose and priorities.

It rarely makes sense to focus on only one area of life long term. Some Olympic athletes sacrifice all else for physical and mental fitness. For some professionals, their "blind ambition" makes only their work matter. We seek to help those who want a *sense of flow* in living that comes from a meaningful slice of time for each area and from the resulting synergies of fitness in all the areas as a whole.

Core values and temporary circumstances dictate what balance means for different people. In a seminar series for Project Corporate Leadership, approximately 40 professionals in the Birmingham area seeking to prepare for senior leadership, they varied in current and desired weekly time priorities.

♦ Time for professional life invested per week ranged from 40 to over 70 hours

♦ Spiritual time ranged from 0 to 20 hours

♦ Social time ranged from less than 10 hours to almost 30 hours.

Even for these people with so much in common, their values and time priorities varied significantly and, thus, so did their view of balance. We assert that there are few circumstances, unless survival is at stake, where "0 hours" in an area leads to long-term fitness.

A key action is to identify priorities in and between the seven areas of life and decide how much time, inspiration, money, and energy should be invested in them. Many people have periods when circumstances or goals require them to re-define balance, at least temporarily, such as is the case for Olympic athletes, professionals completing graduate school at night, and military professionals on tours of duty in combat zones.

In *Absolutely American*, David Lipski relates the major benefit of balance in the well-rounded program cadets receive at the United States Military Academy. He stayed at West Point for four years and followed a class from entry through graduation. He writes, "Cadets complain all the time…plebes (freshman) about upperclassmen, cows (juniors) about not having their own cars…but I came to see West Point as *the happiest complaining place on earth.*" The post feels like a small town under jolly martial law. And yet, t*he secret result of mental, spiritual, physical, ethical, and emotional fitness is a sense that one is in the flow of living, not being dragged along by the current."* A person who senses he is in charge of his life combines purpose and passion with a healthy level of structure and discipline, grounded with nonnegotiable standards.

Balance matters! Captain J. Charles Plumb, a Navy pilot in Vietnam, ejected when his plane was hit by a surface-to-air missile. He was a prisoner of war (POW) for six years. In his lectures on his experiences, he points out that he needed his physical, mental, emotional, and spiritual parachutes to make it through each day. By having all these areas *fit*, he was able to endure under extreme stress. So with fitness and balance in the seven areas of life as our goal, we review each.

Physical Fitness

Combat drains one's physical and mental state. To minimize the impact of combat fatigue, military leaders exceed minimums on the Army Physical Fitness Test. Leaders make steady progress from the minimum standard of 180 (out of 300)—they expect more of themselves. A unit standard often is at least 250, and a leader standard at 270. We include maintaining good health here as well. Avoidance of substances that degrade one's health or capacity for mental fitness is a must. Maintaining physical fitness serves as an *energy platform* to stay fit and perform in other areas.

Making changes in the physical area of life is the number one New Year's Resolution, followed by financial resolutions. A body builder worked out 4 hours per day. He got great results.

Yet, that means he is not investing 3 or more hours in other important projects and people. Many people can maintain physical fitness with an average of 30 minutes of exercise per day. If you feel the need to do more in exercise and sports, make sure the price you pay is balanced with other priorities and desired legacy. Reconcile your standards and find fulfillment in them. Using school as a metaphor, sometimes it is better to earn "B+" or better in most areas than "A+" in one and "C" or worse in others.

Nobel laureate Herbert Simon advocates, "satisficing." Near-perfection is not always a good goal. Deciding the importance and the degree of excellence merited in key areas makes more sense to achieve meaningful balance than seeking maximum excellence in all areas—some areas are likely not as important as others.

The reality is that most people need to do more, not less, in the physical area of life. Most blame lack of time. Actually, for most, the barriers are inspiration (motivated want to), energy (juice to act on inspiration), and personal leadership to act.

Energy gives us courage. On days when you get squeezed on time, do something! Even if you only have 1% of your time (10-15 minutes), even 5 minutes, you can do a lot of sit ups and push ups—or the equivalent. *Are you saying to yourself, "I don't' have time?"* You probably agree that doing your maximum push ups and sit ups daily will help you instead of doing nothing because you feel rushed. Time yourself as you do as many push ups and sit ups as you can; you may be surprised— or humbled—that this may only take a minute or two. The point we offer is that when pressed for time, even 1-5 minutes will do you good physically and mentally because this keeps you in the habit of taking action under less than ideal circumstances instead of accepting a habit of doing nothing, which will lead to degrading your physical fitness.

For those with a sedentary lifestyle, you may need extra effort and support to get started toward positive habits. A few ideas for your consideration:

♦ For 30 days, invite someone to exercise with you and help you hold yourself accountable.

♦ Hire a reputable personal trainer.

♦ Associate more often with people who live healthy lifestyles you would like to emulate.

♦ Read books or periodicals that educate and encourage you to think about health and fitness.

♦ Go to a Physical Fitness Boot Camp. There are a growing number of civilian programs in the United States, many run by ex-service members.

Financial Fitness

Money is like oxygen—you need it, but it does not give meaning to life. However, when there are insufficient financial resources to meet the basic needs of one's family, then the soldier or civilian must take steps to rectify the situation.

Assess your general level of financial fitness by answering three questions:

♦ Do you live within your means?

♦ Do you invest to satisfy future financial security needs?

♦ Do you have a working knowledge of budgeting and financial planning?

Physical and financial fitness provide the foundation for fitness in the other areas. Basic financial fitness takes care of survival, safety, and security needs with some for the fulfillment of higher values such as connection with others, church or charitable contributions, philanthropic causes, personal development, as well as help for family members in need.

Although there are many pluses to the military, many not-for-profit service jobs, and some other worthy professions, financial abundance is usually not one that helps with living or leaving a financial endowment to loved ones. Following the simple, but sometimes difficult path, of spending no more than you earn, with some set aside for when you cannot earn or emergencies, will give added meaning to your life.

Professional Fitness

Mastery comes through developing and earning trust in character and competence. Develop increased competence through knowledge and skills.

U.S. soldier in Iraq, 2003.

Some of those competencies needed by professional soldiers:

Technical/Tactical subject like…

- Rappelling
- Squad Tactics
- Land Navigation/Reading Terrain

- Military Law
- Military History
- Organizing for Combat

Conceptual subjects like…

- Stress Management
- Assertiveness Skills
- Counseling/Motivation
- Team Cohesion
- Tuning in to Troops
- Intuition/Perception/Instincts
- Inquisitiveness

Professionals—military and civilian—typically need knowledge and strategic skill in areas like these:

Personal/Life Leadership

- 7 Best Practices for the 7 Areas of Life
- Planning
- Motivation
- Time and Energy Management
- Earning Empowerment
- Ethical Fitness and Decision-making
- Professionalism
- Organization
- Stress, Adaptive Coping, and Resilience

Interpersonal/Team/Managerial Leadership

- Delegating Empowerment
- Performance Assessment and Coaching/Mentoring

- Staff Development/Team Building
- Project Management
- Shared Vision and Win-Win Agreements

Organizational/Societal Leadership

- Strategic Planning and Management
- 7 Diamonds of Organizational Excellence
- Evaluation and Rewards Systems
- Best Practices for Key Processes
- Financial Management
- Organizational Structure
- Multiple Stakeholders
- Communications, Public Speaking, and Media

More people hold themselves back, sometimes losing opportunities or even jobs because of under development in *below the surface* (recall the iceberg model) character and attitude than in their skills and knowledge. The motivation to develop abilities leading to competence originates with developing character and other components of attitude.

Recall from the data presented in Professionalism Lesson 7 that the average self-assessment for professionals and students has been "C" (using the school grading system). When confidence is at the "C" level, that person will prove less likely to try new ideas that fall outside her comfort zone. Part of the motivation for developing the instrument came from CEOs and team leaders asking, "What do you do when you state in goals that you want to be world class and, years later, you find out the team does not want to or think they can?" Identify what it would take for you, other people, and from the organization to get you to the next level. Key components like commitment and confidence can help you develop your professional plan to include actions to expand your capacities.

Sharing your professional plan with your leader and mentor helps him/them know better how to support you. This is a key concept for leaders as well, because many are trying to inspire world-class performance before the people want to, believe they can, or make a commitment to try.

Personal Fitness

Mental, intellectual, emotional, and ethical fitness are included here, as are attitudinal outlook and other personal traits. The Army's desired mental fitness qualities are: will, self-discipline, initiative, judgment, intelligence, cultural awareness, and inquisitiveness.

Cultural awareness, simply stated, is sensitivity to different backgrounds, cultures, and traditions. Our aim is to build a cohesive team with the same underlying set of values—not to make everyone the same. Building these qualities should be continuous from K-12 and on through age 100+. Preparation must provide you with commitment and focus, self-control, and capacity to stay emotionally strong to get the job done even if that means enduring hardship circumstances under extreme pressure over long periods of time.

Social Fitness

Having a social life adds fun, allows one to decompress, reunites one with friends and family in a wholesome and invigorating way. One of life's great mysteries is why we are in such a hurry to grow up, then when we are older we long to be children again. One of the expressions from a cartoon character created by Bill Cosby, Fat Albert, is "Just because you are grown up [doesn't] mean you have to be an adult." You can have fun and still be a class act.

We are always a work in progress. The process of "getting there" is more fun and personally rewarding than "being there."
-Lieutenant General Claudia Kennedy-

People as Blessings or Burdens

Beliefs and values affect fitness in the social area of life heavily. John Croyle, founder of the Big Oak Ranch, reminds parents that children sense whether you view them as a "blessing" or a "burden." How much you value people will influence the quantity of time you invest with them and the quality of attention to listening, sharing, connecting, and giving. One way to develop greater social fitness is by writing a vision for the relationships you seek to have with the people who matter most. It adds inspiration and guides your thoughts to improve behavior.

An example of a sentence in my vision statement for the social area of life:

I love and care for my family.
What is important to them is as important to me as they are to me.

We practice habits of listening to understand instead of being too quick to respond with our thoughts. We can be direct, though kind, to share honest feelings about behavior while honoring the feelings of another.

Fitness in the other areas affects social fitness. Stressors in your physical or financial life affect your social interactions. If you are regularly *on edge* due to bad habits leading to insufficient sleep or nutrition, you can change those habits and build your energy for others. Sometimes, something simple like turning a late-night TV show off to get 30 extra minutes of sleep can change the way you feel as well as greet and help people the next day.

Philanthropical Fitness

Many of the great colleges and universities, libraries, and centers of arts and science have been established because a person or group succeeded significantly beyond their financial needs to have resources to donate to society and valued generosity with others through a lasting legacy. Developing financial fitness so your capacity meets your needs with excess to share can help you donate to people and causes. To do so will improve financial strength, social relationships, and volunteerism to the not-for-profit organizations or causes that can do greater work with greater resources of time and funding. As you write a description of your desired legacy, consider the schools, agencies, and other organizations that have or can serve your loved ones and can help fulfill the contributions you feel called to make.

Many philanthropists give because someone asked them to help. The practice of personal leadership to plan for life and identify desired legacies through philanthropy would lead more people to volunteer before they are asked and make better decisions about how and where to serve. This book is one way we chose to contribute as part of our legacies. We donated our intellectual property rights to the Institute so proceeds from its sale will be invested in programs to serve others beyond our time.

Create greater value through synergy when you volunteer or accept invitations to serve. If a person gets asked and accepts to volunteer for a role, that may prove good though not necessarily best. Consider your spiritual gifts, talents, and callings when you volunteer to serve or donate. Communicate your goals for service and growth to people in your family as well as current or prospective organizations you may serve such as community groups and churches. This planning and communication will increase the probability that you will get invited to serve where you can make the greatest impact. Loyal volunteers support our programs—among them the Personal Leadership Association, Leadership Education and Development, Professional Development Education, Life Leadership Academy, and the Plan for Life Ministry—because they find their callings match ours. We encourage each member and friend to write a plan for life, and from that to prayerfully discern their callings. When people find that working with us helps them and us fulfill callings, then we create more synergy than if we merely asked for help. In the future, more charities and churches will help their members discover their callings, gifts, and talents to serve the people and to help them serve in the most meaningful ways.

You can decrease disappointment by not serving in areas for which you are not suited. By volunteering and getting asked to serve in areas suited for you, you will accept more often and decline other requests for which you are not suited gracefully and rationally.

Spiritual Fitness

This book is not about advocating a specific religion, but does embrace a belief in God. We affirm the solace and comfort of those who believe in a higher power acquired from faith. One needs to keep spiritual focus from which to draw strength. By maintaining spiritual habits leading to spiritual fitness, one can fulfill his callings and retain a personal calmness of heart as well as courage to persevere.

> *Focus on worshipping and serving God*
> *more than on the different methods*
> *practiced among the divisions of the House of God.*
> -Suggestions for Successful Living-

We believe many people would gain a higher level of spiritual centeredness and peace by focusing more on our own purposes in life instead of focusing so much on differences in beliefs amongst our neighbors—a major source of stress for many that has caused conflicts, even wars.

Gaining a sense of joy and peace is a divinely offered stress strategy.

Respect others who believe differently—
almost everyone does.
-Suggestions for Successful Living-

Most people believe in a higher power from which they draw strength and comfort. When you identify, develop, write, and internalize your highest purposes, beliefs, and values, you can live closer to your best-self. PLAN (Pray, Listen, Act, Now) on your callings and choices. It will add to your sense of spiritual centeredness. Invest time and energy in prayer, study, and service, seeking higher levels of spiritual understanding and development.

A movement is taking place that is long overdue and will escalate in emphasis. Spiritual organizations have started helping people identify spiritual gifts and talents. Many people, especially in churches, are reading *The Purpose-Driven Life*. This is great news. Those spiritual organizations we have seen help with gifts and talents inventories to identify areas in which the person can best serve the organization. This is a great start.

We recommend a more powerful approach. Identify callings, gifts, and talents. Continue to consider how to use them in spiritual service to the ministry. Emphasis should get expanded to include how to develop and use spiritual gifts and talents for use in the seven areas of life—not just the organization. Our callings, gifts, and talents should drive our development and service in professional and philanthropical lives as well. Through our Plan for Life Ministry, we seek to help spiritual leaders help people develop plans for life that inspire and guide them to identify, develop, and use their callings, gifts, and talents synergistically.

Stress Lesson 2

Identify sources of stress. Ask and answer what causes stress for you—and why—so you can prioritize ways to leverage good stress and mitigate bad stress.

You have power over your mind—not outside events.
Realize this, and you will find strength.
-Marcus Aurelius-

Stress comes from many internal and external sources. Your brain interprets changes and creates thoughts. These interpretations tell your body how to respond—whether to feel anxious, irritable, fearful, tense, or relaxed.

Interactions with others can create interpersonal stressors from sources such as disagreements, demands on your time, loss of loved ones through death, divorce, or displacement, and financial pressures. The setting we are in can affect us—beach or traffic, pollution or mountain air, rain or sunshine. These and other changes happen frequently, so we constantly have to adapt.

Deciding what it means to live as your best-self—and why—is a foundational step to prepare for living significantly as well as for handling stress. For most people, identifying sources of stress and solutions for handling those stressors is a prerequisite for developing our best-selves. Awareness of how you react to stressors is a starting point for knowing the appropriate response and how to prepare in advance for the next time you face that stressor.

Problem or Pattern in Thinking

Assess honestly if the feeling of stress is caused by a real problem or if it comes because of a pattern of thinking that you have internalized even though it does not serve you well. Many people form habits of worry and stress, even when the problems are minor, beyond their control, or even self-induced.

Remember the woman who assessed herself with a "D" level of character and confidence? She discovered that her assessment came from a pattern of thought that started 40+ years earlier. Her pattern of thinking increased stress in her life because every time a new idea came along, she suffered a quiet frustration based on the belief she would not follow through. Every day, she faced life with a weak level of hope and confidence. The resulting weakened commitment and action added to the disappointment and stress. The solution to improvement included admitting, accepting, and acting to define and internalize who she wanted to be. That gave her a stronger foundation on which to start building the patterns of thought and instincts her best-self longed to have.

Circles of Influence and Concern

Is the source of your stress something you can influence or is it just an area of concern? Many people add to their stressors by worrying about things beyond their control and by taking time away from things they can influence by wasting time talking about mere concerns with others who cannot influence the situation either.

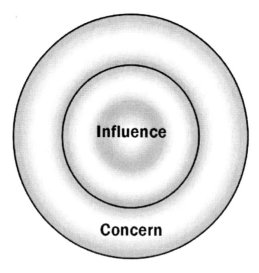

Circle of Influence and Concern

Acknowledge your concerns, though aim at priorities in life you can influence. Focus on solutions to minimize stress.

Time, Inspiration, Money, and Energy (T.I.M.E.)

Beliefs about time and strategies for time management often hold people back from their best possible results. Many people focus on time management as a one-dimensional effort to make time and motion more efficient. An interconnected view of T.I.M.E. (Time, Inspiration, Money, Energy) serves you better.

Time includes the quality and quantity of time for the most important roles and activities in life. Include the right amount of time. Improve the quality through attitude and development of competencies to do better with the time spent.

Inspiration provides emotional energy and commitment to create good stress pursuing worthy aims. A person *on fire with enthusiasm* for the right things can accomplish much more than someone "going through the motions" or "watching the clock."

Money is part of what we get from investing time, inspiration, and energy. Understand what it takes to earn rewards. In a profession, ask early what gets rewarded there based on values, actions, and results. In many organizations, new employees do not learn the criteria for their evaluations and compensation until the end of the first year. A major source of stress comes from working on things you assume are important only to find out later that there is little connection to mission, goals, or rewards. We recommend improving that system by using the assessment tools we offer in the Call to Action section to hire, train, and coach people to aim at the behavior and results that will produce what is good for the person and the organization.

Energy provides the platform for work and other parts of life. Jim Loehr and Jack Groppel, authors on performance, define energy as "capacity to do…." We suggest building more sustained capacity "to do" through supercompensation techniques and leveraging natural body rhythms. Create a transition ritual between work and home to decompress.

T.I.M.E. Checkup

Excerpts from the Dyson Institute T.I.M.E. Checkup can help you look beyond just time management efficiencies to help you get to the source of your time and stress solutions. You can answer some of these and others when you get to the abbreviated T.I.M.E. Assessment tool we provide for you. Consider how well you match these:

Time

- I spend enough *quantity* time on *what* matters most—*personal*.

- I spend enough *quantity* time on *who* matters most—*social*.

- I spend enough *quantity* time on what gets rewarded—*professional*.

- The *quality* of the time I invest is high in energy and enjoyment.

- I learn from teachers and writings about how to use time well.

- I assess my time use in relation to my priorities regularly.

Inspiration

- I have identified and written my callings, gifts, and talents.

- My personal plan includes my mission, vision, legacy, and priorities.

- My plan includes my written desired values and beliefs.

- I feel a sense of mission in life and for callings, gifts, and talents.

- I feel inspired by my desired legacy.

- I feel wanted and valued in my relationships.

- I have the commitment to do what is important.

- I have the ability/competence to do most of what is important.

Money

- I understand what results and actions get rewarded in my profession/financial life.
- I invest enough time and effort in what gets rewarded financially.
- I am living within my means.
- I am investing to satisfy needs for future fiscal security.
- I have knowledge of budgeting and financial planning.

Energy

- My physical energy keeps me going at work and home.
- My intellectual energy keeps me interested and focused.
- My emotional resilience to setbacks is high; I bounce back.
- I can work with focus for as long as needed.
- I have energy for important people and things after my professional work is done.
- I sleep well and feel rested when I wake.
- I eat nutritious foods most of the time and fun foods in moderation.
- I do the basics well, like drink 6-10 glasses of water daily.
- I breathe deeply multiple times per day.
- I do vigorous exercises at least 30 minutes a day three or more times a week.
- I know my natural body rhythms and take advantage of them.
- I supercompensate to add to my physical and emotional capacity.

Wheel of Balance

This *wheel of balance* helps you quickly assess in which areas your life might be out of balance and need attention.

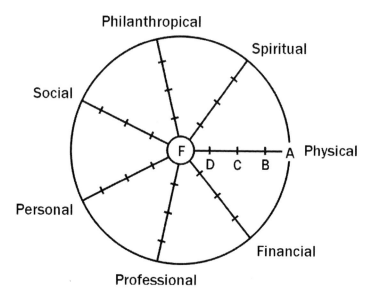

When you complete the Professionalism, Fitness, and T.I.M.E. exercises, you can mark your grade on each spoke from "F" (failing/frustrated) at the hub out to "A" (excellent/fulfilled) on the edge of the wheel life. The wheel on the right is a sample for someone who assessed each area of life, then connected the dots to see the level of balance of his *wheel*.

The goal should be relatively equal balance based on your values and circumstances—not an equal amount of time, inspiration, money, and energy invested in each. Fulfilling good results and balance in one area might take fifty hours and only five in another. When you identify your values and priorities to achieve balance, you will live with greater peace, less negative stress.

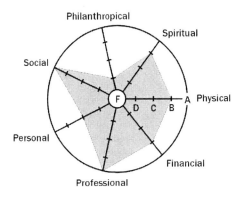

Your view of balance may vary with each stage in life. A parent and professional who adds *graduate student* to her mix of roles might redefine balance to shift 20 or more hours most weeks to school for a few years and adjust after graduation. If your assessment reveals this would cause too much imbalance in other areas for an extended time, then you may choose to redefine success in terms of grades or speed of completion, choosing to feel good about earning a "B" instead of "A" or taking longer to graduate so that success takes less time per week. An Olympic athlete may consider life balanced with training eight or more hours daily the year before world competition and training an hour or less to stay in shape following the Games.

Significant imbalance in any area will add stress to the journey. Assess where you need more balance to "roll on" with manageable stress on your well-maintained "shocks" to prevent damaging "the engine and chassis" —you.

Sources of Imbalance

If you feel distress, keep asking why until you get to the source. You may be reacting poorly to a situation because you are tired with too little mental energy to do the task well. Honest assessment might reveal that you are tired because you did not get enough sleep the night before and you did not get enough sleep because of poor choices such as staying out too late or watching television too long. Or, you might have low energy today because of poor choices such as the type or quantity of food to eat.

You might feel stressed because you are running behind and worried that you cannot accomplish the task or arrive for an appointment on time. Honest assessment might reveal that you procrastinated on starting this important task by spending too much time on the unimportant or even escaping excessively into diversions like television or hobbies. The word *excessive* is key because time for relaxation, entertainment, and creative outlets is important when balanced with other priorities—after the mission is accomplished.

Those who habitually purchase unnecessary things before they can afford to pay for them often add significant levels of stress —not just for them but also for the small-business owners and their families who get affected through slow or non-payment. Unfortunately, a surprising percentage of people file for bankruptcy.

Many people shop to relieve stress, which might have been caused by excessive shopping. *The Millionaire Next Door* even recommends minimizing time for shopping by seeking a satisfactory value in a reasonable amount of time instead of shopping excessively seeking the best deal. For example, instead of spending hours or days checking all over the country to find the very best deal for a car, check a few key sources and find a good value—using the time saved on your important priorities instead of a secondary priority such as shopping.

The mindset regarding debt of the entrepreneur is different from the person earning a salary or in debt from poor budgeting. The new business owner often must seek debt and plan for losses for months or years before creating critical mass in a self-sustaining organization. The entrepreneur has high expectations. His debt may serve as a positive stressor. The person in debt from poor money management has low expectations and the debt is a negative stressor. Both had bad debts—one used it responsibly to motivate, the other negatively. The assessment tools we offer in the Call to Action chapter are designed to help you identify areas where the greatest difference exists between where you are and where you want to be. These are frequently sources of significant positive or negative stress. Using stress in positive or negative ways is the subject of the next lesson.

Stress Lesson 3

Distinguish between good and bad stress.
Good stress can provide a positive edge that
leads to motivation, focus, and energy to act
on priorities. *Bad stress* often comes from
feeling unprepared, unsatisfied with actions
and/or results, and unsure if competencies or
resources will meet demands. Think through
your stressors to put them in the good or bad
category before you address your response to
negative stressors.

Good stress: eustress; positive pressure to perform and improve aimed at important priorities, which boosts energy, results, and fulfillment—as in working on an important project with limited time or resources.

Bad stress: distress; negative feelings often caused by poor preparation or effort and/or aiming at incorrect priorities, which weakens energy, results, and fulfillment—as in falling short on something important because of bad choices or investing time in something you should not be doing.

Edge: keenness, as of desire or enjoyment; zest.

Dynamic Tension

Stress creates dynamic tension. When you feel stress, ask yourself *why*. This can help you understand if you are feeling stress because you are driven to do a good job in an area of importance or if you feel stressed because you spent limited time, energy, and resources on low priority activities. The more you identify and internalize your callings, the more stress you will feel when you are not acting toward them or otherwise not using your time and energy in alignment with your priorities. The dynamic tension of stress generated from acting on what is most important is good for you.

Assessing Importance

If you feel stress because you are working on something that is relatively unimportant or the task should be delegated to someone better suited for it, this is a source of bad stress (distress). The solutions typically include adjusting roles and time priorities. This might motivate you to become more successful financially so that you can hire an assistant or a consultant specialized in that area. An entrepreneur can feel stress because of investing more time than desired on administrative matters when an administrative assistant would be better prepared, do a better job, and enjoy those duties more. A small-business owner might feel stress over spending extended hours on bookkeeping and tax forms. That can lead to either frustration or increased motivation to earn the right to hire a bookkeeper or accountant to handle these roles for which he is better suited educationally and mentally.

You may feel stress because you are not confident in your preparation. That can be a good form of stress because it can show that you care about the people and project to feel driven to prepare for it. Like the professional athlete going into an important game, this anxiety can create positive motivation to prepare through education, training, and effort to do a great job. If you do not seek solutions and prepare, the stress will likely linger and restrict you from your best performance.

Stress related to important matters often produces adrenaline so you can prepare and perform. Stress related to unimportant matters often produces frustration because you are investing precious time and resources, which means you are taking time away from important matters.

The source of your stress might be for a good purpose, but you still feel frustration or fatigue because you are attempting to do too much in too little time. This insight might give you motivation to realize that you need to simplify or do some secondary things less often—at least for a period of time.

First things first is a key principle. Stephen Covey listed it as habit 3 in *The Seven Habits of Highly Effective People*. People who have internalized the idea that it is okay to play first and work later usually end up creating stress for themselves and others. Those who work and then play can minimize distress and enjoy the reward of recreation after promises are kept.

Self-induced Stress

The true professional assumes that most stressors are self-induced, and therefore we can do something to improve the situation. We take that view because this is a stronger approach than looking at sources of stress as something done *to us*. *No excuses accountability* may appear to add stress by adding responsibility or even guilt when results fall short of expectations or promises. Actually, the reverse is true. By taking ownership of what is happening to us, we increasingly can look at what we did, or did not do, that at least contributed to the situation and then move on to solutions. If we feel stressed about time pressures or financial responsibilities, we typically contributed to those through our decisions to seek or accept commitments. We should admit when our stress is self-induced and act on solutions.

Attitude and Expectations

Attitude has a lot to do with whether a stressor is beneficial or not. In her book *The View from Gabbratha*, Judge Colleen McMahan tells an amazing story about attitude. A young man she called Larry wrote her after serving a year in a prison boot camp. Most prisoners have a poor attitude and low expectations. Larry thanked her for his having to learn to live life honestly with self-discipline. He turned the stress associated with confinement into a source of motivation and high expectations. We can learn from Larry. We can choose how many stressors affect us. Having a strategy to deal with normal and extreme negative stressors in the best way possible is the subject of the next lesson.

Stress Lesson 4

Develop a strategy for normal and intense stress. Anticipate stress; feeling pressure is inevitable, especially if you seek to serve in significant ways. Decide in advance how you will handle negative pressure to behave as your best-self. Discern if the solution is a greater immediate investment of time and energy working on priorities or improving your *fitness package* to prepare for and respond to stressful pressures.

Normal stress: everyday changes, strains, and pressures such as from time demands, financial needs, relationship conflicts, and disappointments.

Intense stress: excessive changes, strains, or pressures, such as getting ambushed or suffering from trauma.

Simple Wisdom

When faced with a problem, Hack Sain has a simple, positive approach. He writes on a piece of paper a description of the problem along with his ideas for possible solutions. Then, he says, "I go to bed." He expects an answer or progress toward a solution when he wakes. This simple wisdom helps you move from negative stress about the problem toward positive feelings that you have done all you can do at this time. Plus, it puts your mind to work processing options.

Planned Stress

Induced *planned stress* like deadlines to finish ahead of schedule allows for the unexpected—Murphy's Law seems to always strike when we least want it. A deadline to complete the task in advance, allowing for time to review and make improvements and the possibility of unexpected challenges adds stress but does so before the stakes get high and helps assure a positive outcome by allowing extra time if plans do not go perfectly.

My grandfather was a farmer during the day and had a job at a food processing plant at night. Even though his job in Dothan, Alabama was less than 20 miles from the farm, he would leave over an hour early just to make sure that he could get there on time in case his truck "broke down." And, when his truck did break down he had time to fix it or get a ride to work. This helped earn him a reputation as someone you could trust to keep promises without excuses.

Stress Junkies

"I wait until the night before to do a paper because I do better under pressure." I have heard students say that. What that usually means is that they had to perform under pressure before and adrenaline of the stress helped them perform at a peak level. They were able to complete the tasks, though likely with minutes to spare, and earned a decent grade. Therefore, they remember that they did okay and liked the increased energy and focus, so they internalized that incorrect belief that they do better under that kind of pressure.

Some of the students are now professionals working with the same mindset that purposely procrastinating is good because they believe they work better under stress. Some do this because they believe they are correct. Others have become *stress junkies* preferring to work under stress rather than manage the project well and make progress until the job is done—with time to spare. They are mildly addicted to the stress adrenaline. A solution is to create safe stress demands on yourself to prepare early so you can adapt if needed.

Stress and Ethical Behavior

Corporate CEOs have been arrested and ridiculed for ethics violations. People who do not know them cast blame without suggesting solutions for what caused the problem. Look closer.

Many of these people were "regular, church-going, choir-singing people," liked by many. While some displayed excessive greed or arrogance, in their intent, we believe many were unprepared for the stress from situations in which they put or found themselves. Some slid into bad behavior that continued and escalated. Then, in critical moments of choice, they reacted motivated by instincts to maintain values like survival, security, and esteem.

Recall the Dyson Hierarchy of Values, which identifies seven values that drive people: survival, safety, security, social connection, self esteem, success, and significance. Most people seek higher level values after they have satisfied lower level values. When someone focused on success is unprepared for a stressful ethical dilemma, he may revert to lower level values like security and survival. He may instinctively justify the "animal-like" behavior of a "dog-eat-dog" mentally driving lying and cheating others for self-preservation. Fulfillment of the higher values of significance under stress requires development and internalization over time of clarified beliefs, values, and habits. Learning and acting on lessons of professionalism and leadership under stress can improve professional performance, ethical fitness, and decision-making leading to better behavior and leadership of others.

Professional and spiritual organizations should and can do more through education, training, and coaching as well as systems to communicate and reward desired results and behaviors. This will help people do the right thing more often under normal stressors and can help prepare them for more intense stressors as well. Key decision-makers—especially people like presidents, pastors, and parents—often need more thorough preparation in ethical decision-making for those times when intense stress could produce ethics violations or other decisions that affect a large circle of influence. They can use their education and developed instincts to teach and guide others to do the right thing more often.

We applaud efforts to put ethics programs in place in a growing number of organizations in reaction to ethical violations with significant social and financial consequences. The federal government has responded with more laws and promises of closer scrutiny to monitor the system. This should help keep people focused on doing the right things even though the key motivation seems to come from increased awareness and fear of punishment. We understand that focusing on ethics programs to react to past problems, whether to do the right thing or put on a good face for regulators, provide steps in the right direction to the ultimate goal of doing the right thing merely because it is the right thing.

Dealing with Disappointment

Many people waste lots of time worrying about what happened—or might happen—instead of making the best of a situation. When worry outweighs solutions and positive actions, lack of focus follows. Patterns of thinking can lead to habitually "wallowing in pity" or "feeling like a victim" and attempting to justify why we are not at fault. Excessive complaining wastes time, inspiration, money, and energy.

Everyone with a conscience experiences disappointment and worry. Allowing negative feelings to create excessive stress often creates more problems than does the problem causing the stress. When disappointment hits, some seek excessive alcohol, food, drugs and/or cigarettes to escape. Some immediately pick up the phone and call someone to talk about their most recent setback. Without seeking solutions or understanding sources of the problem, they then call someone else; and the cycle continues with most of their energy going toward expressing frustration and seeking support instead of developing and acting on solutions.

It is a choice and instinct for the mature person who excels at personal leadership to move quickly into positive thinking and action. A simple strategy to internalize is, *admit what happened, accept the consequences, and act to do the best I can.*

Beliefs as Barriers and Irrational Thinking

Some people have internalized beliefs that increase stress and decrease productivity. In the *Ethical Fitness* lesson we touched on some of the beliefs that lead to ethical behavior, such as "I demonstrate a strong work ethic even if no one is watching."

Beliefs also can lead to irrational self-talk that needlessly adds negative stress, such as:

"I can't change…"
"I can't overcome my problems… "
"It is important that everyone approve of me…"

David Goodman's *Emotional Well-Being through Rational Behavior Training,* asserts that at the heart of irrational thinking is a belief that things are done *to you.* Accept that "stuff happens" and decide how you will respond. Adopt the strategy of *Admit, Accept, and Act.*

We anticipate that the mindset of most readers of this book is to believe you can change or improve in most cases, if you resolve to do so and take action. You may have people in your circle of concern who have internalized another belief, which we think is largely incorrect and potentially harmful. Many believe that the formative years are so powerful that people cannot change beyond a certain age.

The formative stages of infancy through the teenage years are very powerful influences, and we should do all we can as adults to teach and guide young people. We should also state our intent with young people, and encourage them to practice developing habits and instincts as well as increasingly making independent choices. Further, we should internalize that we are always *works in progress* and that we can change when needed. Many people attempt to justify bad behavior and unwillingness to change on external influences, such as genetics, circumstances, and cultural environment.

A man I knew well at one time had a habit of staying out late drinking alcohol—and worse—with people other than his wife. He told me: "It's genetic; my dad was that way, and my son probably will have the same problem." His belief supported his irrational justifications for bad behavior. Rather than tackle the stress of getting control of his drinking, which would help him deal with other temptations, he kept building momentum with his irrational thinking until lack of honesty and accountability for his actions resulted in the extreme stress of intense hurt and divorce from his deceit. The division of his family affected him, his wife and children, as well as friends and business associates. The lack of solutions oriented action required by one man hurt many. If he accepted no excuse accountability and a belief that he could change, he may have still divorced though could have done so with a much higher level of integrity and much less damage done to the innocent. Deeply imbedded beliefs are a source of great good—or great harm.

Defining Standards

Nobel laureate Herbert Simon recommends, "satisficing," which challenges us to decide the importance and degree of excellence merited. Some people enjoy more peace and spend more time on what is most important by adopting a strategy that "the house looks good when it needs to" instead seeking a standard of near perfection all the time. This advice has helped many working parents. Some I know, especially first generation working moms, have tried to emulate the perfect home like their full-time homemaker moms while emulating the professional efforts of their full-time working dads. They create stress by seeking equal excellence in both. This expectation is not likely to match reality, resulting in bad stress from frustration and fatigue. There are times to seek *excellence* and times to seek *satisfactory*, especially in matters of appearance. A few extra minutes with a child, a project of calling, or for yourself may prove more valuable than maintaining perfection at times it is not needed. Stephen Covey reminds us to be careful of getting "in the thick of thin things."

Performance Anxiety

Performance anxiety affects most anyone who tries to do anything challenging. Dr. Dale Feldman, a professor attending one of my lectures to students at UAB, came to me to discuss how he could coach his daughter with performance anxiety when she played music in competition. He had given her good advice: *define success*. His daughter sometimes would focus on perfection, and when she made a mistake, her disappointment affected the rest of her performance. He encouraged her to set an expectation of excellence, preparing for those times when she did not achieve perfection, to help her keep going after making a mistake. Another strategy is to identify things that could go wrong so she could admit they exist though decide how her best-self could prepare for them. And, if they happen anyway, what she could do in the moment to make the best of the situation.

Some misinterpret the principle of positive thinking as not worrying about what might go wrong. Better advice is to admit problems can occur though prepare for the good and bad so you can focus on the good, respecting though not succumbing to the pressures of possible problems.

Many of us feel added stress when the stakes get high. A summary of a few basics to help:

1. Define success—the results you seek. Get clear about your mission, vision, and motivation for the goal.
2. Define the success strategy for preparation—what you can, should, and will do to be prepared—as well as feel prepared and deserving of success and joy from the effort.
3. Define your success strategy for the performance—what you will do prior to and during the performance. This can include visualization and rituals you identify that put you in your peak performance mindset. Professional athletes and performers often visualize themselves performing well and, if disappoint happens, responding in a positive way.

Entrepreneurs

One of the most common sources of stress and frustration for people who start their own businesses or private practices is that they get to spend less time on the main reasons that they went out on their own in the first place. Most people end up spending more time on administrative and financial requirements of running an organization than the amount estimated or wanted, which means they have less time and energy for the primary services or calling that drives them positively to serve. Identifying desired and actual time priorities can help you move in the right direction about how to spend your own time and how to balance that with others such as volunteers, consultants and contract service providers, and employees.

Most new businesses fail within a few years. Michael Gerber, author of *The E-Myth*, warns against acting on the impulse to over-organize. Many with entrepreneurial enterprises, especially those birthed inside a home office, face temptations to clean and organize before the main thing gets attention. Many entrepreneurs who go into business or practice to do one main thing actually spend less than half their time on the main purpose of the enterprise. Some fail and do not understand why. Focus first on what matters most, and learn to feel good about seeking the right priorities instead of feeling stress over not fulfilling standards designed incorrectly from the start.

Time and TV

A *USA Today* study showed that the average American watches over 20 hours of television per week. A single decision to watch programming that you find educational or entertaining has helped people plan to watch 7 to 14 hours of television per week instead of twice that much then choose more meaningful ways to use the time previously spent watching programming that was merely filling a void.

Home Remedies for Stress

As research for our strategies menu for proactive ways to handle stress, we asked family members and friends what works for them when they feel stress. Here are a few of their tips along with a couple of our own. Perhaps some are reminders of those you have used.

Pray/Read Scripture—ask for strength and guidance as you decide and act. Sometimes, you should slow down and refocus on and reconnect with your Creator to help you feel renewed peace and energy. Rick Warren in *The Purpose Driven Life* recommends these scriptural stress busters to have peace of mind even with stress: make a habit of prayer (Mark 1:35); know who you are (John 8:12); know who you want to please (John 5:30); set clear goals (John 8:14); focus on one thing at a time (Luke 4:42-44); do not do everything yourself (Mark 3:14); take time to enjoy life (Mark 6: 30-31).

Quiet your mind (my mom's advice)—you will recall that is step one of our ethical decision-making guide.

Visualize—see yourself succeeding and practice doing what is needed mentally.

Cry—crying can release positive chemicals in the brain and body that can make you feel better.

Stay in the now—Counteract excessive regret about the past or worry about the future by focusing on what you seek—short and long-term—and what you can do—today.

Listen to peaceful music—some researchers claim that Baroque style classical music is a good choice because the instrumental sounds include approximately seventy beats per minute, similar to the human heart.

Leverage recreation—reduce overall stress by using your recreation or hobby to accomplish several worthy ends.

Whether fishing, golfing, playing bridge, skiing, jogging, many professionals participate with clients, family, friends or support charity of church events through their sport.

Grow a garden—it takes tending and soothes the spirit.

Pets—for many, pets in the home provide a source of joy and calmness. Care and feeding of young animals may cause more stress until they mature and learn from your training.

Breathe deeply—take deep abdominal breaths several times per day to help relax and oxygenate your blood and fuel the body and mind. I was first made aware of the benefits of deep breathing when sent to Westminster Choir College as a youth. I was taught to shift from breathing from the chest to breathing from the abdomen. To know if you are deep breathing properly, lie flat and see that your abdomen rises as you inhale. Later, when I began serious training for running marathons and training in martial arts, I discovered the same benefits were realized.

Meditative fitness—exercise removes tension from the body. Thomas Jefferson lived to be 83 at a time when the average life expectancy was over 10 years less. He walked 4 miles a day and believed the purpose was to "relax the mind." I embrace walking meditation taking deep, quick breaths as one-foot touches the ground and breathe out with the other step. Once in a rhythm, my body becomes relaxed and my mind "does its own thing" often generating ideas that I capture on a small notepad I take with me. Of course, such a routine of *mentally getting in the zone* should be done along a safe route away from traffic or other hazardous situations.

Stretch your muscles while relaxing your mind—long, slow stretches help prepare your muscles for vigorous exercise like running or sports. You can also use that time to relax or focus your mind. "Stretch's" nickname came from giving stretching exercise instructions to soldiers in the 2nd Infantry Division in Korea.

The blessing of slow motion — My mother lived her own lessons. One she called the blessing of slow motion. When I slowed down enough to listen, she told me how some of the timesaving devices aimed at making our lives less hectic could have the opposite effect if taken to extreme. She passed away never having used a computer or cell phone—and yet she kept marvelous records of everyone's birthdays, anniversaries, addresses...and every letter my father had written to her from the time they dated through three wars over 62 years of marriage. She clearly preferred the tools of slow motion. I was unaware of the extent of the legacy she lived until she passed and literally hundreds of people from teens to her contemporaries wrote to me about the difference she had made in their lives. She had a way of shedding stress and getting everything important done. Her "secret" was the power of the pause—she learned to slow down, pause, then keep going without stressing over "easy choices." When she went to the grocery store she didn't get caught up in the potentially stressful mundane task of choosing between 100 types of cereal—she grabbed her shredded wheat and went on. We can choose not to make every choice a mountain, not to have to have every latest gadget, and to pace ourselves. The net effect is less daily stress and more joy.

Take five—when trying to break a habit or addiction (like chocolate), make yourself wait five minutes from the time of the urge. Often this will be enough for the temptation to be conquered. Nic Niedermann of the European guitar duo *Tonic Strings* told us he used this approach to stop smoking.

Use software and services to remind yourself—keep track of tasks, appointments, and events with software or use an Internet reminder service to provide added peace of mind.

Power naps—I try to start each day at 5 a.m. After lunch, when I start "the second shift," I sometimes need renewal. A nap of 10-30 minutes does wonders. When time does not allow, I recline with my feet above my head for five minutes on my Total Gym or with my head off the edge of the bed. My mind relaxes, blood flows to my head, my spine relaxes, and tension seems to escape. Over the years, I have gotten better at relaxing this way and can sometimes fall asleep within a minute and wake up in 10-20 minutes feeling refreshed. Thomas Edison often took short naps on his work bench every few hours to help him work over long periods when he needed to stay close to the flow of important projects. Power naps are a helpful way to the use your natural body rhythms to your advantage.

Strategies for Intense Stress

Conditioned responses are the key to the ability to function effectively under acute stress. Experienced practitioners are able to relax on demand and respond effectively. Rapid relaxation and coping skills training can enable you to relax on cue or command. Rapid relaxation training involves knowing how you respond, then matching your responses to refined techniques for responding in a way beneficial to you. Researchers in the treatment of phobias, especially fear of heights, advise writing a stressful-events hierarchy—listing likely stressful situations from least anxiety producing to most, practicing feeling the tension from each situation and countering with coping thoughts that become so rehearsed that they kick in when actually encountered. For more on this skill, refer to *The Relaxation and Stress Reduction Workbook* by Davis, Eshelman, and McKay.

There are several safe and useful ways to practice responding to intense stress. One of the best is to become knowledgeable about simple, yet effective techniques to deal with emergencies. As an example, know the three statements to ask someone who might be having a stroke:

- Ask the individual to smile—check to see if both sides of the face are the same;

- Ask him or her to raise both arms—this is difficult for a stroke victim;

- Ask the person to speak a simple sentence—this will reveal if there is noticeable speech difficulty.

When a person knows these type immediate response drills and a situation arises where their use is necessary, their confidence in responding to stressful situations is enhanced appropriately. Though such medical emergencies may be low probability events, knowing about several such techniques (CPR, having a person cough repeatedly if suffering a heart attack, or the stoke response just noted) increases the probability while making you more confident.

Consider potential threats that would require your immediate action, visualize the response, and then practice it until it is a conditioned reflex. For example, learn basic personal defense moves—use of pepper spray, hand-to-hand combat techniques, flight, etc. To be effective, these must be aggressively practiced to activate without hesitation. Many require a qualified coach or trainer to be sure the techniques are learned properly and the student becomes proficient.

A coach is someone who tells you
what you don't want to hear,
who has you see what you don't want to see,
so you can be who you have always known you could be.
-Tom Landry-
Former Coach, Dallas Cowboys

The desired result from conditioning and coaching is self-confidence in reflexes and instincts for the serious threats you may encounter. Legitimate confidence in your instincts will help conquer fear and improve performance, both as an individual and as a member of a team.

Stress Lesson 5

Use stress to help you achieve peak performance. Stress from challenging goals and pressure to perform can boost success if you master actions through mental and physical rehearsal and are both prepared and focused on priorities. Use these experiences to improve your capabilities to live and work in a sense of *flow*.

Peak Performance: the psychology and practices of performing as your best-self.

Flow: the essence of the most enjoyable, satisfying moments in our lives; condition in which you so involved in something that you forget yourself. "Performing at your best and loving it" (Csikszentmihalyi, 1991).

As we have said, stress is not necessarily bad—and can be very good for you. Psychologists and professionals in mind sciences usually suggest we need stress in our lives to achieve at peak levels. We need good stress and committed drive to solve sources of bad stress.

Sports Applications

Sports psychologists affirm that a healthy level of stress provides that needed *edge* to motivate you to prepare and get into the game mentally. Athletes generally perform better when stakes are high and work harder if there is some stress from the risk of losing their job as a player or of losing the game than if the challenge or competition is easy. In sports, like other areas of life, there is a balance between stress that is needed to hone our senses and stress that can exceed our capacity, which can result in tightening of muscles and "choking," which relates to worrying or trying too hard and restricting performance.

Motivation based on Probability

The Project on Human Potential at Harvard University determined that across a large spectrum of people, a 50-50 chance of success was the best level of probability to produce motivation. For individuals within that group, some were most motivated when the chances of success were almost assured, and if probability was low they hesitated to even try. For others, they were more motivated when someone told them "it couldn't be done." With low probability of success, some respond positively to use this stress to do that which others cannot or will not while others spend more time worrying, which dilutes their focus and energy. Therefore, the stress of uncertainty can work positively or negatively for people— determine what scenarios and strategies work best for you.

If you respond best to "big audacious goals," set them and go for it. However, if your goal-setting maturity is still developing and you need to go for goals that are definitely achievable, admit that is best for you and achieve smaller goals and build momentum. You can demonstrate more courage and build resilience to anxiety, thus managing stress better.

Peak Performance Research

Dr. Charles Garfield began researching "peak performance" after observing significant contrasts between NASA teams prior to and following the Apollo Eleven project, our first lunar landing. In an abridged article, he lists 10 distinctions between average and above-average performers, good and great executives, among them:

- Driven by a sense of mission
- Write goals and plans
- Review and update them regularly

These are primarily actions to take. An additional distinction among peak performers, which we assess as a by-product of the actions:

- Make better, faster decisions

Your Plan as a Tool for Motivation

If you are driven by a sense of mission, you will prove more likely to write a plan for life with goals and actions to inspire and guide you. If you write and review your plan for life, you will prove more likely to feel driven by a sense of mission. If you do, by-products will include making better, faster decisions because you have internalized at a deeper instinctive level your purpose and priorities. You can use your plans to internalize your callings to boost inspiration and performance.

Plans can cause higher forms of good stress. Setting a goal that pushes you to grow outside your comfort zone can cause stress, though it can be good stress that builds inspiration and healthy adrenaline and ultimately capacity to do more to fill the gap between what you seek and current reality.

Admitting reality sometimes is needed to "jolt" one out of a pattern of thinking and action that is leading to somewhere different than the vision. Internalize how you feel over the inspiration of the vision and the disappointment of the reality. Your Professional and Personal Plans are roadmaps to close the gap and propel you toward your best-self.

Stress Lesson 6

Practice *safe stress* **in advance.** Seek opportunities to practice and test yourself to expand your *comfort zones* before the stakes get high. Practicing under realistic conditions can help you be and feel prepared, with greater confidence and less stress, plus improve performance with fewer mistakes by staying sharp and focused.

Ambushed: an instantaneous surprise; being or feeling attacked.

Battle Drill: used to denote repetitive, rigorous training in how to attack, defend or respond to serious likely threats or situations.

Simulation: an artificial representation of reality used to practice decision-making.

When enemy soldiers ambushed my unit in Vietnam, the training from Ranger School saved my life. I was better prepared to handle this intense stress because I had already practiced what to do. My instincts took over and helped me take action when, with less preparation, I might have been less capable of dealing with the threat of death.

In the military, law enforcement, and first responder professions "battle drills" are continuously updated for current threats. People in other professions can follow the same model. In the military, repetitive training in how to attack or defend from serious threats is a primary means of preparing soldiers for combat. Proactive in nature, the drills are continuously updated for current threats. For example, in Iraq, the drills include tasks such as how to respond to an ambush or how to properly inspect a vehicle. Today in Afghanistan and Iraq, the Army and Marines respond almost instantaneously to the changing situations. When terrorists suspend a string of bombs from an overpass to hit a convoy or booby trap a dog lying in the road, soldiers are training in battle drill responses to these threats the next day. Training realism is enhanced by adding civilian volunteers to represent enemy non-combatants. Drills are designed and practiced on the assumption that the "game" has no rules and your foe will cheat. Soldiers are drilled to the point the procedures become reflexes and instincts. In civilian law enforcement, SWAT teams have similar drills for hostage rescue, vehicle take down, active shooter response, drug busts and other tasks they may be called to perform. People in any profession can follow the same pattern with preparation for emergencies. Learning the Heimlich maneuver or CPR is a good response example of a valuable skill, which must be practiced to the point of instinct.

Gunfighting Lesson 2 addresses facing fear by preparing your instincts through simulations. Simulations are a mental form of Battle Drill—a way to address fear or anxiety while gaining competence. Even though they are not absolute representations of actual events, the events they generate build confidence and give the mind the decision-making practice it needs to learn from mistakes. There are expensive simulations like those used to train pilots and inexpensive ones like the Dunn-Kempf manual board game explained in Gunfighting Lesson 2.

There are many companies that offer highly interactive business simulations where participants make decisions that affect staffing, marketing, outsourcing, and other operational concerns. Zodiac Financial and Business Strategies provided such a simulation to my former company. The Center for Creative Leadership has another. Look around, ask; do an Internet search to determine what is available in your field. It will pay dividends.

The importance of practice under stressful conditions grows in importance as the stakes get higher. The military spends more time in simulations than do most professions because the consequences of getting it right — and not — involve human lives as well as the protection of great values like our freedom.

Seeking to practice and expand your comfort zones in safe stress scenarios also applies in civilian life. One of the great benefits of students getting involved in athletic and academic competitions is that they not only receive motivation to learn more, they develop habits of working under pressure of deadlines as well as performing under pressure in front of spectators. Even though the audiences and scenarios change over time, the experience of facing and performing under pressure develops life skills that can help you regardless of what you do.

Commentators prior to the Super Bowl talk about the advantage of experience from veterans who have played at the professional level for the most years or those who have the advantage of having played in a Super Bowl. The next best thing to being there is practice.

A person who will perform or speak to audiences of a thousand or more might start with small audiences and work up to larger ones. If time or opportunity for this type transition is not an option, you can create scenarios as close to realistic as you can. This practice helps you identify areas of improvement, possible problems, and helps your mind get ready for the possibility of anxiety from performance anxiety or *stage fright*. Some of the strategies for stress presented earlier also serve as strategies for safe stress—to prepare and experience stress in advance of the actual threat.

Pastor Doug Giles, who sees the church as a source of strength for avoiding the secure, suggests that a truly spiritual person will be able to expand his comfort zone for stress. He cites Leon Podles' charge "Go find your Holy Grail; go meet the strange, meet the unfamiliar." We embrace this charge as a way to prepare for the inevitable, unexpected ambushes in life.

Stress Lesson 7

Create structures, habits, and rituals to proactively leverage positive stress and mitigate negative stress. Identify priorities and create appointments with self and others to invest in doing the right things to make time for them and to form constructive habits. Spending T.I.M.E. (Time, Inspiration, Money, Energy) in alignment with your priorities leads to greater peace even under pressure.

Structure: to give form or arrangement; to structure a curriculum; structure one's day.

Habit: an automatic behavior done often and hence, usually, done easily; an act that is acquired; a practice or custom.

Ritual: a higher level habit with added meaning performed regularly so as to reinforce a desired end, as in a family tradition or desired habits to fulfill a resolution; a set form or system as in ceremonies.

Structured Flow

The Path of Least Resistance reminds us that energy flows along the path of least resistance, not against the grain or natural flow. Many people misunderstand the term when they complain to someone, "You always take the path of least resistance" when they refer to laziness. When understood, taking the path of least resistance is an act of wisdom—after you have designed the path. Some advise to "go with the flow" when the flow might take them to a bad destination. The better advice for most settings is to design the structures for least resistance, then go with the flow. We use the T.I.M.E. Checkup regularly as a ritual to keep ourselves calibrated on the important.

3X for the Important

Our experience has led us to allow at least three times as much time, money, and energy to do a significant activity as we initially estimate. To write a book, succeed in business, prepare for an important event, solve a problem with a loved one, allow for extra time. We set deadlines to finish ahead, allowing for "Murphy's Law." We incorporate this concept in our prime time management and budget estimates, so if we fall short of expectations we can adjust. Many who *play first and work later* create stress and disappointment—for themselves and others.

Prime Time Management

Like television producers, prime time management is the art of matching your best programming with your most important audiences as well as appointments for your priorities. Most important for you might include family, clients (those you serve), fellow workers or partners, close personal contacts, and yourself. Like most people, we use our schedule and calendar to guide us through each day and schedule future activities.

We schedule and do our most important work early in the day. This coincides with our natural body rhythms. We get into a flow early to stay on task for final preparations for a seminar or client service—or whatever is the most important service of the day. We use the "3X" rule to block out sufficient time. Dr. Peter Drucker, author of *The Effective Executive*, advises that setting aside blocks of time for important work boosts productivity more than trying to multitask and invest short spurts of time on projects that require concentration. Usually, a block of 60 minutes proves more powerful than 10 spurts of 6 minutes.

People who seek to do routine tasks first under the belief "I will get this out-of-the-way and then move on to what is most important" typically add stress to their lives and diffuse their effectiveness by spending too much time on secondary things at the expense of not enough time on the most important things. We look for synergy between important projects and people, saving multitasking for the routine.

We seek to focus and stay in the flow of the most important until prepared. We try to discipline ourselves to select only that e-mail which relates to the highest priorities of the day until the afternoon when we seek to respond to all of it that deserves attention. With phones calls, we also focus on the priority promises in the morning and return other calls in the afternoon—after the main things are done. Family and friends know they can call any time they need us, though they know our intent to make and be available for calls late afternoon or evening after we have served our clients and professional purposes for which we earn our living.

We schedule times with ourselves to live our priorities. We treat time for writing, study, and focused work as sacred just as we do to keep appointments with others. This helps us do what is needed to develop as *true professionals* and *live as our best-selves*, as we suggest for others.

Our core prime time for serving clients or others we serve is Tuesday through Thursday. When a vendor of a product or service we want to purchase asks for an appointment, we arrange, when possible, to transact that business on Fridays. We seek to schedule time for planning, purchasing, staff development, and business on Monday or Friday to protect Tuesday through Thursday that the people we seek to serve want most often. Prime time management includes matching time with others.

Our exercise regimens vary but typically come mid-morning or mid-day to rejuvenate us after four or more hours of work. These allows us to use our early morning energy for high impact mental work. After a few hours we typically want and need a break. We can seek natural changes of pace like meetings, phone calls, and workouts. We use our calendar to create structures in advance to help us aim at the right targets and help hold ourselves accountable for our life balance and resolutions.

In the next section, we offer lessons for gunfighting professionals and leaders with knowledge and instruction to help those who serve in the military prepare for the intense stress of combat. This section also can help loved ones of our military and patriotic public understand the preparation and service required in the profession of arms charged to defend us. Finally, gunfighting is an example of intense stress with lessons that apply to civilians.

Preparation for Gunfighting Lessons

Gunfight: a duel or battle with firearms. We also use gunfighting as a metaphor for acutely stressful situations. Although the corporate world is not literally a war, the great Prussian military thinker Clausewitz, in pondering whether war was an art or a science, concluded, "We could more accurately compare war to commerce, which is a conflict of human interests and activities." Such "conflicts of human interest" occur in almost every profession and may result in acute stress. Some economists even refer to gunfighting as "capitalism with the gloves off."

Gunfighting: a fight between persons using pistols or revolvers; "the brotherhood of the close fight" (Gen. Keane).

Leadership: "…the art of accomplishing more than the science of management says is possible" (General Colin Powell).

Stretch in Vietnam
1968

These gunfighting lessons have their roots in 1968 when I was a 24-year-old soldier on my way to Vietnam. Even though I had come from a family of soldiers who served with honor, had been educated at West Point, and had troop unit experience in Germany, I was still in many ways blissfully ignorant of the harsh realities of combat.

Just before I left for Vietnam, a classmate—a close friend who had been in my wedding—was killed in action. I was of course apprehensive about my impending tour of duty, yet determined to serve with honor and, if it were God's will, return alive with my men.

I offer a few narratives from my time in Vietnam that were fundamental to the formulation of the gunfighting lessons.

These short personal stories provide a sense of what it was like, the immediate impact of each experience, and how the remaining years of my career led to a solidification of my views, which I now share in these lessons. Having served more than a decade in the private sector after my time in service, I also believe there are corporate and civilian applications of these lessons.

I made a conscious effort to follow, in my own way, the example of General George Patton. Dr. I. B. Holly related in his *Reflections on Leadership for Would-Be Commanders* that after Patton graduated from the Command and General Staff College, he wrote the school to send to him their current maps and tactical problems, which he then solved himself in order to hone his tactical skills. Such dedication to self-direction and independent motivation are critical to mastering one's craft. For years Patton was accused of making snap decisions. In truth, his dedication to being a profound military student through years of thought and study prepared him to make confident decisions that more often than not yielded results in his favor. A Patton-type intensity of research and study leads to a confidence that seeks control over circumstances. It breeds a belief that with intense desire one's ends can be reached despite intervening circumstances. I make no claims these lessons will enable the practitioner to have control over circumstances. Nevertheless, the stories and thoughts I now share are those of a small unit combat commander—as recalled from my letters, notes, and memories—who believes they have passed the test of time and offer value to those who serve.

Vietnam—1968/1969—Early Lessons Learned

In January of 1968, North Vietnamese General Nguyen Giap launched the Tet Offensive, an assault into South Vietnam that became one of the most well-known campaigns of the conflict. In other years, Tet was the festive and peaceful celebration of the Lunar New Year and the beginning of spring, but not that year. In 1968, the hills of the central highlands of South Vietnam, which are remarkably like North Georgia, were war-torn rather than festive. At the time, I commanded Delta Company of the 4th Combat Engineer Battalion, 4th Infantry Division (a unit of about 200 soldiers) in the highlands of central Vietnam.

As I relate these stories, I must point out that battle should not be romanticized. I find nothing exotic or fanciful about battle. It is hateful and dirty, but at times a necessary last resort. The suffering resulting from war is brutal, not only for the soldiers involved, but also for their families, whether friend or foe. The battles fought in corporate settings also can be frightful even if no actual blood is spilled. From such battles, no matter how distasteful they are, lessons are learned. My experiences and later thoughts that led to these lessons were especially influenced by the writings of Lt. General Harold Moore and Lt. General Carroll Dunn (my father). For a study of Lt. General Moore's experiences, read *We Were Soldiers Once and Young* and Lt. General Dunn's experiences, *Engineer Memoirs*. As a point of interest, Lt. General Moore's fighting in 1965 took place in the same part of Vietnam where I saw combat three years later, the central highlands in the vicinity of the Plei Me Special Forces Camp and Ia Drang Valley.

Loss of a Leader

I knew before I left for Vietnam that I must prepare myself for seeing death and disfigurement. My father's advice had been succinct and pragmatic: "Win the battle first, then allow yourself to mourn."

There was a policy in the 4th Division that soldiers in leadership positions found to be less than proficient in the skills and mindset needed to lead others would be relieved of their duties. Complying with this policy increased the likelihood of mission success and minimal friendly casualties. But this also meant the best small-unit leaders were the ones most exposed to risk and harm. My first experience with the loss of a soldier made the harshness of this policy starkly real. My first casualty was my best squad leader. The Viet Cong in a bunker complex killed him. My immediate thought was the cruel irony that troublesome soldiers were relieved from leadership positions and sent to the relative safety of the base camp in Pleiku, while the best leaders were thrust into harm's way. After the loss, I wrote the first of several letters to the next of kin of fallen soldiers. As I chose my words, I had the initial realizations that would eventually lead to my philosophy on gunfighting.

1. Tough circumstances require equally tough policies that can bring increased risk to the best and brightest. While this cannot be described as fair for each individual, it is necessary for the greater good of the larger group and the mission.

2. Death notification is one of the most solemn duties of the company commander.

Although these lessons may seem foreign to civilians, there is a connection to many civilian professions. First responders and law enforcement personnel also face such harsh realities. All too often most businesses experience the unexpected loss of an employee, and the leaders' sensitivity and professionalism in response will go a long way to either provide comfort or compound grief.

3. In combat, in business, or in many professions, unexpected circumstances will require someone to step into leadership positions with little warning. Prepare in anticipation.

The Ambush

Fourteen miles from the Ia Drang Valley is a Special Forces Camp called Plei Me. In December 1968, I was leading a convoy of bulldozers and earthmovers from the camp under the protection of three M-48 main battle tanks. The route had stretches where the tree line came within 25 meters of the road. We knew the enemy was in the area and expected an attack. While enroute, the enemy opened fire from the tree line. My backpack radio was hit by rounds from automatic weapons, which temporarily limited my communications. However, the enemy was no match for the combined fire from my soldiers' weapons, the tanks, and Air Force F-100 jets, which quickly arrived to give close air support. The enemy broke contact. Those who survived the day were grateful for their good fortune. That night I wrote my thoughts.

1. Preparation through prior planning for artillery and close air support had paid dividends.

2. Our survival that day was more dependent on "pucker factor" (functioning under stress) than the accuracy of our individual weapons—we were prepared to trust our instincts.

3. Deciding to be aggressive enough, quickly enough, is crucial. One cannot hold back. Indecision is fatal.

4. When first fired upon, I don't recall thinking. Instead I recall reacting as I was trained in the ambush battle drill. The ability to react by instinct to this situation came from training received at the Army's Ranger School. The signs that suggested an imminent attack were not concrete, but because we were alert, we were ready. The drills in which we were trained matched the likely threat actions. Preparation of instincts under acute stress was the key. Although there are no "Ranger Schools" for civilian professionals, there are training opportunities that feature teamwork under stressful situations.

Years later I discovered that you can be "ambushed" in a corporate setting as well. The beneficial wisdom of that December day would once again prove useful. In contrast to my experience in Vietnam, I recognize that the more recent Iraq close-combat experiences frequently involve an enemy in an irrigation ditch or behind a courtyard wall where small arms direct-fire weapons are less effective than the "spray 'n pray" bursts of rounds tactics we had used. The military continuously revises its tactics so pre-battle training drills will be matched to the likely threat scenarios and instincts can be trusted.

The Rescue

The central highlands of Vietnam contain magnificent forests with many beautiful mahogany trees 100 feet tall or more. In October 1968, a U.S. CH-47 helicopter crashed into a mountainside. My company had the mission of removing twenty-seven bodies from the wreckage, which required rappelling through the tree canopy from a hovering helicopter. As difficult as this was, an even more trying mission was in store for us a month later when a Huey UH-1C "Snoopy" helicopter crashed while flying along the Cambodian border. My unit's rappelling capability was again called on. When the small unit I used to conduct the mission arrived on the scene, we inserted the platoon leader, Lt. Charlie Friend, and his radioman to check for survivors and retrieve the classified intelligence gear. As my Huey made a wide turn to pass back over the site, I saw red smoke, which meant a "hot" landing zone—our men were under enemy fire. The high tree canopy made it difficult to reinsert the ropes so we could extract the men. While two Cobra gunships and the door gunners on board our Huey laid down suppressive fire, we finally got the ropes to the ground and the platoon leader and radioman "tied off" to the end of the rappelling ropes. The time spent hovering, preparing to pull them up from the landing zone, seemed eternal. With the men suspended on the ropes, the pilot took the Huey up to 3,000 feet to get out of small-arms range. Several minutes later we landed in a riverbed and brought the men inside the aircraft. They had grasped the ropes so tightly they had difficulty releasing them. Our reunion was emotional, but silent, with powerful hugs saying all that was necessary. What impact did this experience have?

1. Real personal risks come with the territory, and while fear under such circumstances is natural, fear tests the true courage and decision-making of leaders and soldiers under extreme stress. The best preparation for decisive action when fearful is a passion for competence and trust, reinforced under the most realistic conditions possible. Soldiers have to respond in any number of unexpected and chaotic environments.

2. However prepared you may be personally, you may be called on to have complete faith in your teammates in order to survive.

3. The true professional seeks to earn greater responsibility, and through this pursuit hones skills and gains confidence. Lt. Friend was chosen for the mission because he was best prepared. He continually sought greater responsibility—from his passion to excel, not for personal glory—and his instincts were prepared to meet the challenges of the situation.

4. Decisions under acute stress have consequences. In this case, Lt. Friend's rapid assessment of the situation on the ground and ability to rapidly "hook up" saved himself and his radioman. In a more recent example, the soldier who uncovered Saddam's hiding pit had to make a quick decision on whether to throw a grenade into the pit or hold back. He obviously had trained his instincts to serve him well, as his preparation under realistic conditions led to the taking of Saddam as a captive rather than killing him. The capturing soldier was at risk, yet made the right call in that situation because of his training and preparation.

The Booby Trap

A booby trap is a concealed device triggered by the actions of an unsuspecting victim. There were two general types of booby traps used against us in Vietnam, explosive and non-explosive. This story involves a personal meeting with a non-explosive type known as a pungi stake. Such a booby trap works as follows. Bamboo, which has strong elastic qualities, is bent and tied off. Moving a trip wire sprang it. At one end are sharp prongs tied so that when the trap is sprung, they impale the victim. The ends of the stakes are treated with feces to infect the victim's wounds. During a search and clear operation to root out Viet Cong, I tripped such a trap, and the prongs wounded me in the back. By combat standards, the wounds were not serious, but two of my soldiers died from similar wounds. I was grateful for being spared. Fortunately, the trap was old and there was less spring in the bamboo. My injuries healed quickly, thanks to the skills of our medic, but the incident left several impressions.

1. While the human body is fragile, it is capable of remarkable recovery.

2. No one should assume "It won't happen to me." Expect that something unexpected will happen.

3. Do not go it alone in potentially dangerous situations. There are sound reasons for units or teams to undertake dangerous missions. This should be obvious, but if one is careless or unlucky, the consequences can be severe.

4. As obvious as the old cliché, it is equally accurate: "that which doesn't kill us can make us stronger."

5. Sometimes a person receives a second chance. I recall a paradox of emotions after the close encounter with the pungi stakes: gratitude for not being seriously wounded, a sense of failure at having tripped the device, and a sense of wonder at why I was spared more serious harm. I finally decided that what mattered was the second chance God had given me, and I resolved not to blow it. I vowed someday to try to pass on what I was learning for the benefit of future soldiers.

My experiences, including these aforementioned stories, became the basis for a group of affirmations for how I wished to live. They eventually took specific form and became a personal creed, from which portions of this book grew.

For most people, the business world and sports are as close as they will come to combat. In many ways, "corporate combat" is a reality that has applications for these gunfighting lessons. Where possible, I have sought to make connections between the gunfighting lessons that follow and their use in other venues where acute stress resides.

I aim to instill these lessons with an increasing rich understanding of the business of combat, professionalism, and leadership that will help you embrace a viable philosophy for being a true professional and earning the respect of others.

Military Terms Used in this Book

NCO	Non-Commissioned Officer (Sergeant)
SGM	Sergeant Major (senior NCO)
LT	Lieutenant (junior grade officer)
CPT	Captain
LTC	Lieutenant Colonel
BG	Brigadier General, one star
MG	Major General, two-star
LTG	Lieutenant General, three-star
GEN	General, four-star
	General of the Army, five-star
Platoon	Unit of 25-50 personnel led by a Lieutenant
Company	150-250 personnel led by a Captain
Battalion	500-1000 personnel led by a Lieutenant Colonel
Division	10,000-20,000 personnel led by a Major General
Huey	Helicopter for transport on combat missions
A10/F100	Aircraft for close air support to ground troops
M48	U.S. battle tank deployed in Vietnam war
Cadre	Military faculty
ROTC	Reserve Officer Training Corps in colleges
NVA	North Vietnamese Army

Lessons for
Gunfighting Professionals

7 Lessons for Gunfighting Professionals

1. Develop a soldier's heart through spiritual centeredness.

2. Anticipate feeling absolute fear under stress and prepare your instincts so you can trust them!

3. Find seasoned Noncommissioned Officers (NCOs) to serve as mentors and teachers.

4. Be tough. Experience extreme physical and mental stressors like prolonged intensity of focus and sleep deprivation to develop habits, instincts, and endurance to function effectively for long periods under tough conditions.

5. Prepare for paradoxes and having to choose the *least-worst option*.

6. Be decisive, aggressive—even audacious—in clear and simple terms; indecisiveness is a fatal flaw.

7. Put your personal affairs in order.

Gunfighting Lesson 1

Develop a "soldier's heart" through spiritual centeredness. Prayerfully internalize your purpose through sincere introspection to know the reasons you fight. Reconcile suffering and killing before going into combat. Internalize the warrior ethos. Believe in yourself and the cause you serve. The noble warrior is an instrument of his people with a honed sense of civilized equilibrium in a harsh profession.

Warrior ethos: professional attributes and beliefs that characterize a noble soldier; refusal to accept failure, tight fabric of loyalty to other soldiers, leader accountability, and will to win battles while living up to military values.

The soldier, above all other members of humanity,
is required to perform the highest act of religious
offering—and that is the sacrifice of life.
-General of the Army Douglas MacArthur-

Soldiers do not claim to be perfect, but good soldiers aspire to be heroic and place others before themselves. Winston Churchill observed, "at any moment in history the world is in the hands of two percent of the people, the excited and the committed." The good soldier is part of that two percent.

There is considerable literature that argues that war is morally neutral. My thoughts are not an effort to rationalize the consequences of killing in combat. Rather they are centered on pragmatism and reality. The warrior ethos consists of professional attributes and beliefs that characterize a noble soldier. The noble warrior's specialty is the improvised yet disciplined application of violence. The noble soldier is an instrument of his people and a tool of his government's policies, sworn to obedience in accordance with their decisions. Such soldiers deserve acknowledgement for the difficulty of their trade and its many paradoxes. In combat, the soldier aims to destroy the enemy, yet when vanquished, the noble soldier treats them with dignity. To do less makes us little better than the thug, criminal, or terrorist. I find it helpful in preparation for combat to differentiate between the noble warrior and thug or barbarian. Recall the shoe bomber on the plane? Judge William Young had some interesting remarks when sentencing Richard Reid. Reid had admitted his allegiance to Osama bin Laden and Islam. Said the Judge, "You are not an enemy combatant, you are a terrorist. You are not a soldier in any war; you are a terrorist. To call you a soldier gives you far too much stature…. You are no warrior. I know warriors. You are a terrorist…a species of criminal guilty of multiple attempted murders…."

A fragile line of discipline and integrity separate honorable warriors that embrace the warrior's ethos and such barbarians. Noble warriors improvise violence but within civilized boundaries (for example, seek to minimize harm to civilians). Our nation's warriors have both men and women of extraordinary mental, emotional, and physical character and a few liars, tyrants, bullies, and cowards. The warrior ethos seeks to attract and keep many of the former and as few as possible of the latter. The situation at Abu Ghraib prison in Iraq illustrates the dichotomy between a few soldiers' conduct and that of Pat Tillman (the National football League player who was killed in the line of duty in Iraq). Thorough training, ingrained discipline, and solid leadership take a generation raised on Hip Hop and Jerry Springer and bind most of them with the glue of a noble soldiers' warrior ethos. I believe that spiritual centeredness is an essential tool in the binding process. Its role in combat preparedness is to help come to terms with likely harsh realities before the fight so your instincts can serve you and costly hesitation can be avoided.

Some combat paradoxes a soldier has to come to peace with:

- Having to take someone's life to save the lives of others, especially when your spiritual foundation values life;

- The possibility of harming innocent people or fellow soldiers through "friendly fire;"

- Witnessing death, disfigurement, and destruction;

- The possibility of making a mistake of dire consequences when an instantaneous decision is required;

- Harming women or young enemy combatants when one's own culture has an ingrained desire to protect women and youth;

- Facing fight-or-flight situations where instantaneous decisions are necessary;

- Having to sacrifice for all, even those whose actions seem undeserving or unappreciative.

A spiritually-centered heart goes a long way toward living afterward with the consequences of seeing comrades die and the killing of enemy soldiers, noble or otherwise. Such a heart is not an irrational dedication. Soldiers seeking to prepare in advance for combat find solace in a spiritually-centered heart. Our country was founded on a transcendent belief in a higher entity.

The enormous psychological and physical pressure of combat derives from the ever-present knowledge that someone is trying to kill you. Combat is a confusing, amorphous, and bloody struggle. Invariably there will be situations where events do not take place as planned and units are isolated, communication breaks down, soldiers are captured, and unrestrained, self-destructive fear can creep in. Every military member must develop the individual wherewithal to keep panic at bay. Firmly grounded confidence in one's preparation, trust in the cause and in those leading them, and considerable soul-searching creates service members who fight with a warrior's ethos, complying with the codes that govern their behavior regardless of the codes of the enemy.

The following strategies can prepare a soldier's mind and instincts at a higher level of spiritual centeredness and fitness before facing combat:

- Decide what kind of soldier and person you will be. Professionalism Lesson 6 suggests deciding what you seek as your "best-self."

- Write, review often, and internalize your beliefs, values, and strategies for developing competence, gaining trust, demonstrating courage, and earning empowerment.

- List the paradoxes, apparent contradictions, and other challenges you can imagine, and describe how you will act if faced with them. Answer how your best-self will handle fear, loss of life, paradoxes, and the inevitable "fog of war."

- If you are a person of faith, pray regularly, seeking strength, guidance, and serenity.

- Seek quality time with spiritual mentors, such as chaplains or combat veterans, to help you be grounded and decisive in a firefight.

- Read the works of authors like Colonel Roger Nye where the role of the warrior as a moral arbiter is addressed.

- Contact the Simon Center for the Professional Military Ethic at West Point for material on the warrior ethos.

- Accept in advance the unfairness of a few having to sacrifice for all, even those you may think are undeserving of the sacrifice. During any conflict there will be dissent. That is a greatness of this country. Address with veterans whom you respect ways they came to terms with those Americans who "aid and abet the enemy" through inappropriate dissent that hurts our country's cause.

The importance of the spiritual dimension of a soldier is aptly described by one of our nation's greatest generals:

I look upon the spiritual life of the soldier as even more important than his physical equipment. The soldier's heart, the soldier's spirit, the soldier's soul is everything. Unless the soldier's soul sustains him, he cannot be relied upon and will fail himself and his country in the end. It is morale... and I mean spiritual morale...that wins the victory in the ultimate. And that type of morale can only come out of the soldier who knows God and who has the Spirit of religious fervor in his soul. I count heavily on that type of soldier and that kind of Army.

-General of the Army George C. Marshall-

Pastor Doug Giles of Miami speaks eloquently about re-establishing the definition of a strong warrior in his book, *Ruling in Babylon*. He sees the church not as an extended womb to keep members in therapy for life, but as a source of fuel for avoiding the secure, for accepting the tasks of the warrior—as a base of strength.

These thoughts can be applied to your role as a "corporate warrior." In the "heat of battle" in business, you cannot pause to review your values, revisit your goals, or rework your strategies. You should enter high-stress work scenarios with as many paradoxes as you can identify already reconciled and your values solidified. Develop your instincts so you can trust them before the stakes get high. Make your intellect the regulator of your instincts.

U.S. soldiers praying in Iraq, 2003.

Gunfighting Lesson 2

Anticipate feeling absolute fear under stress and prepare your instincts so you can trust them. Fear freezes. The ability to maintain control starts with one's frame of mind. Successful outcomes to stressful engagements are often dependent on "pucker factor" (functioning well under stress). Fear often comes from the unknown. Learn in advance as much as you can about the realities of what you are likely to face. Train your mind in advance under realistic conditions using simulations and drills to hone reasoning and decision-making skills with absolute trust in your instincts as your goal. Once confronted, you only have time to execute!

Battle is personal.
Under the body armor there is still the body—
the flesh, blood, and sinew of soldiers
experiencing the concussion of combat.
-New York Times editorial-

Although modern weapons have tended to make killing more detached, ultimately the soldier has to confront the enemy—be they uniformed soldiers, gangs, street thugs, organized criminals, tribesmen, or terrorists—in a very personal battle.

In many stressful situations, you will not be alone. You will be scared but know that others will be too. Shared fear beats alone fear. Soldiers do not stop fear; they control it and use it as a survival technique to stay alert. Fear can compromise soldiers if their thoughts are not disciplined to buffer them.

Resolve that you will do what your comrades trust you will do. Prepare your instincts by visualizing yourself running toward a goal rather than away from fear. Practice under the most realistic conditions so you will do the right thing well—automatically—rehearse, again and again.

We gain strength, and courage, and confidence
by each experience in which
we really stop to look fear in the face…
we must do that which we think we cannot.
-Eleanor Roosevelt-

Simulations can be of great assistance. Even though they are not absolute representations of actual events, the events they generate build confidence and give the mind the decision-making practice it needs to learn from mistakes.

While a student at the Command and General Staff College, I worked with a classmate, Steve Kempf, to develop a tactical instructional war game called "Dunn-Kempf." The game developed from a need to have a cost-effective way to hone military leaders' conditioning in quick problem recognition, analysis, and decision-making based on reason. Similar board games have been used for centuries. Manual board games are credited with the Prussians' success in the Franco-Prussian war of 1870. The game generated stress by pitting live opponents against each other in an intense, yet physically safe, environment. Unexpected events led to mistakes without the consequences of actual combat. The simulation had limitations. Intangibles such as the state of unit training, esprit de corps, special weather conditions, shock, physical stamina, or the infamous "fog of war" were not well simulated in the model. Nevertheless, brains were actively engaged as players contended with many simultaneous battle parameters. Such "safe stress" mental simulations, combined with physical toughness conditioning, makes a winning combination.

There are good performance simulations for many professions. While heading an organization responsible for supporting the Federal Emergency Management Agency after hurricanes, I trained using a simulation in effectively gathering resources. Pilots and doctors use simulations. Lawyers have mock trials. The Center for Creative Leadership in North Carolina has a simulation for business leaders. Law enforcement agencies have courses that address dealing with fear when faced with a home intruder or assailant. Look around; ask; do an Internet search for help in your field. It will pay dividends.

When seconds count, instincts and decisiveness come into play.
In quick-developing situations, the leader must act fast,
impart confidence to all around him, must not second-guess
a decision—make it happen! In the process, he cannot stand around
slack-jawed when he's hit with the unexpected. He must face up
to the facts and deal with them and move on...
-Lt. General Harold Moore (U.S. Army Retired)-

One caution is called for here. Do not make the mistake of using drugs to help deal with fear under acute stress. Enrique

Lang, a former Kansas City Chiefs professional football player and marine in Vietnam, shared with me stories of men that used marijuana to heighten their mental state before going on patrol. Although their senses were enhanced, there were consequences to taking the drug; in this case, physical coordination was impaired. As a result, the men could acutely sense a danger, yet were less capable of reacting appropriately to it. The consequences were catastrophic in loss of life. The bottom line: develop and depend on your natural best-self.

One of the best ways to prepare instincts is to practice the "what if" technique taught by the National Safety Council in its defensive driving course. Drivers should always be observant for hazards by looking at what is behind them, what is around them, and where they are going; then, mentally think of what they would do if a hazard appears. Learning and practicing this technique while driving becomes useful in many settings and is a good example of a positive habit.

An extreme example of the power of training to prepare one's instincts is the Secret Service Protective Division personnel. They are trained in the unnatural act of taking a bullet for another person as a purely instinctive action.

In a later lesson on having to choose the least-worst option, we relate the story of a State Trooper. Its message also applies here as an illustration of preparing one's instincts. The trooper's finely honed competence and ethical fitness led him to put a severely injured driver out of his misery in an extraordinarily humane manner.

All the ways we offer to internalize our lessons are intended to make you a practitioner of this lesson. A passion for the character and competence that makes a true professional will have you prepared with on-call habits and instincts that will give you the confidence to respond effectively to acute or prolonged stress by being disciplined in actions in spite of fear.

Gunfighting Lesson 3

Find seasoned Noncommissioned Officers (NCOs) to serve as mentors and teachers. Seasoned veterans help you move from "book smarts" to "street smarts" in learning the profession. They provide a bridge to learning the meaning of caring for others.

The military is blessed with a special group of leaders called Noncommissioned Officers (NCOs). The Noncommissioned Officer Guide describes the NCO in this manner:

Noncommissioned officers are the backbone of the Army. First-line supervisors execute day-to-day operations with precision whenever and wherever duty calls. NCOs provide the leadership required to fulfill our nonnegotiable contract with the American people—to fight and win our Nation's wars, decisively. Train hard and to standard to improve readiness—the cost of not being ready is paid in soldiers' lives, and that cost is too high to pay. As a noncommissioned officer, it is your job to train and lead soldiers to accomplish the unit's mission. NCOs make it happen—they inspire soldiers to work toward common goals, lead from the front, and provide an example of what right looks like. They do not walk by deficiencies either in training or in individual departures from Army Values—NCOs are the front line in enforcing and reinforcing our institutional values.

Sergeant Major Victor LeGloahec, a senior instructor at the Army's Sergeant Major Academy, offers this synopsis:

Noncommissioned Officers (NCOs) are leaders, especially in small units where many times officers are not present. They are masters of supervision at all levels. A plethora of "headhunters" for the business world now actively seek senior NCOs for management positions within their organizations. Primarily of course because they are there 24/7/365 days of the year. The NCO possesses skills that are in high demand as a middle manager: ability to handle people of varied economic, cultural, racial, etc., backgrounds in an efficient manner; capability to use limited resources to accomplish a multitude of tasks; discipline to conduct operations/business in a professional manner. They possess the wherewithal to be a multi-echelon task organizer and executor.

Given these credentials, the NCO is expected to know everything about each soldier relevant to his or her ability to function. This often includes considerable knowledge about personal life. In the business world, or in most civilian professions, there is less encroachment on another's personal business. Therefore, there is no NCO equivalent in many civilian professions. A construction crew foreman has some similarities. The respected retiree comes close. Seek the guidance of those noted for knowledge of the business. Strive to be part of organizations with mentoring programs that embrace the intent in this lesson.

For those in military service, it is imperative for young military officers to observe and listen to NCOs. They are the bridge to caring for troops. They teach that caring for troops is not about emotion. It is about making sure the troops are fed, receive mail from home, obtain fair promotions, and have use of a phone to call home. A soldier will have a renewed spirit after he has had a chance to talk to his family. Officers set the course, but NCOs implement it.

U.S. soldier's letter from home, 2003.

While soldiers are legally adults, most are young; officers and NCOs are their surrogate family. They teach officers what they teach the troops, the many "how to's" of the profession: first aid, how to operate in total darkness, how to conduct a vehicle check point, field hygiene—the list is endless—a soldier's confidence will swell as he learns these basic field skills.

For a superb example of the NCO's role and importance as a mentor, read *We Were Soldiers Once and Young* and see the movie "We Were Soldiers." Study the actions of Sgt. Major Basil Plumley (played by actor Sam Elliott in the movie) to see a strong example of training, leading, and caring for troops.

Dr. Byron Chew
Professor of Management
Former Dean of Business
Marine

This is true for civilians as well. Teachers and professors can be a great source of learning about subjects and life—in school and beyond—for civilians and military personnel. Learning about strategic thinking, planning, decision-making, business, leadership and management can equip you for many areas of life. Military training enriches contributions of teachers. Shown at left is Dr. Byron Chew, who trained and served in the U.S. Marines and was David's major professor in graduate management school at Birmingham-Southern College.

Your leader and/or organization officers set the course, but there are many other valuable people who can serve as mentors and offer you guidance and meaningful service. Look beyond professional associates for mentors. For many, grandparents or their contemporaries can impart timeless wisdom. For some, clerics are a valuable resource. It makes no sense to waste the wisdom learned by others. You do not have to learn everything the hard way. Find your "NCO-type" mentors and teachers. Most often, they will appreciate the chance to pass on their experience to your generation.

Gunfighting Lesson 4

Be tough. Experience extreme physical and mental stressors like prolonged intensity of focus and sleep deprivation to develop habits, instincts, and endurance to function effectively for long periods under tough conditions. If in the military, attend Army Ranger School, Navy SEAL Course, Marine Recon, Air Force Special Operations School, or other training that prepares your mind and body for real conditions. If a first-responder, seek SWAT training or the equivalent. The public can attend conditioning, sports, and other training camps. Reputable similar experiences work to help you supercompensate through systematic exposure to greater stress followed by recovery. Develop discipline to self-start, stretch capacities, and maintain your fitness package. Short-term "pain" pushing your comfort zones is a prerequisite to prepare for intense stress, though the experience yields lifetime benefit.

Toughness: resilience; able to withstand great strain without breaking down; rugged.

Supercompensation: challenging a physical, emotional, or spiritual "muscle" past its current limits to build more sustained capacity. Being skilled at replenishment of energy sources by the body in balance with exertion.

> *A working intellect under intense psychological pressure*
> *and physical exhaustion is an entirely different quality*
> *than a working intellect languishing in a library.*
> -Stan Ridgley-
> President, Russian-American Institute

The U.S. Army's Ranger School (and similar type training in the other services) is a mind and body numbing experience. It is a journey that must be taken one day at a time that has a cumulative impact. The purpose of the grueling regimen of work, deprivation, and misery is to develop combat skills to the point they can be executed under the stress of a combat environment. These skills take many forms—hand-to-hand combat, land navigation, adjusting indirect fire, camouflage, negotiating the "worm pit" (a shallow, muddy 25 meter obstacle course negotiated on one's back and belly), priming explosives, preventive medicine, employing mines, using night vision devices….and much more. These tasks must be performed effectively as a unit, a feat that demands the best in application of sound leadership principles. [For those interested in more detail, go to www.armyranger.com.]

While individuals in many professions will not think they need to endure hardship on a par with a Ranger School type experience, toughness is a near-necessity in many fields. Just as we extolled in prior lessons the virtues of spiritual centeredness to train the heart and simulations to train the mind, the ability to be resilient in the face of overwhelming odds is not developed without effort. Occupational risk takers (soldiers, mountain guides, firefighters, law enforcement personnel…) are thought by some to be adrenaline addicts. Perhaps some thrive on extra environmental simulation, but I contend we all need a good dose of experience in physical stress in circumstances that are not only safe but also beyond our comfort zones. Physical toughness can be crucial in situations with a prolonged exposure to stress. The Navy SEALs affirm this in their creed, "the more you sweat in training, the less you bleed in combat."

Football is a useful analogy to explore toughness in the business environment. Football players must execute a sophisticated battle plan swiftly and decisively, becoming progressively exhausted while a similarly equipped and talented group of athletes does its best to stop them. There is no substitute for learning the "street smarts" of blocking and tackling, then engaging one's brain and body in practice. The discipline to practice procedures (plays) enables initiative under pressure. A CEO should have *plays* his company practices, with the understanding that like a football game, one must improvise—the game is not static.

Many games in sports, life, war, or business are won or lost near the end of the fourth quarter. The best-conditioned team will have the most stamina and, therefore, a decided edge.

There are times in most lines of work where one needs a sustained energy platform to function without burnout. In professions like law enforcement, emergency medical technicians, emergency room doctors and nurses, and surgeons, one's ability to remain fully engaged while making life-saving instantaneous decisions can be significantly enhanced by such training. It is shortsighted to consider the corporate world as only a brain challenge. While smarts beats brawn in the short run, sustaining mental sharpness over a prolonged period of stress is immeasurably enhanced when the brain-smart business person has an energy platform built on such a conditioning experience.

A poster on the wall in the boxing room of a gym at West Point reminds us of Coach Lombardi's observation, "Fatigue makes cowards of us all." The body always tests the mind. When one's body is tired and hungry, it taxes the ability to think clearly and act in accordance with higher values. It is difficult to reach the higher motivational values of fulfillment, success, or esteem when safety, survival, and security are at stake.

In his book, *Ranger School: No Excuse Leadership*, Brace Barber refers to "living-in-synch with yourself." Said Barber: "Every time I have a bad experience or what I thought was a tough day, I remember that I had it worse, and I survived and accomplished the mission at hand."

Ranger School (or the equivalent type experiences in other services) acts to define persons to themselves and to others who know what that experience means. These kinds of courses develop endurance, hone gunfighting habits (prepared instincts), and build capacity to extend the limits of fitness—physical, mental, and emotional—that one can handle and have available on demand.

Most people under-appreciate their true limits. The combination of firm discipline, hardship, conquering the ravages of dust, heat or cold, road marches, rappelling—and numerous actions to demonstrate essential military skills—ingrains the military professional with a sense of confidence in self previously unrealized. I credit Ranger School for saving my life in the ambush encounter.

Discovering the full range of your physical abilities will make you better able to respond immediately to difficult circumstances and prolong your competence until the mission is accomplished. Toughness is self-sustaining. Facing fear and physical strain over and over in a controlled conditioning course increases your ability to be strong—not to back down or give up. Law enforcement SWAT teams repeatedly train in hostage rescue, vehicle take downs, drug busts, and active shooter drills—all aimed at conditioning the team to perform by instinct. Whether in the military or law enforcement, such rigorous training strengthens the mind, body, and spirit to perform under intense stress.

Navy veteran Patrick Avon runs The Sergeant's Program in Rockville, Maryland where more than 700 clients huff and puff their way through calisthenics and other grueling events. Avon, and others like him, run civilian boot-camps. The best are experienced enough to add discipline and encouragement in the right doses so an individual can progress from doing nothing without doing too much too soon. Directors of fitness suggest that those civilians seeking a military fitness type program first see a doctor, observe the class, consider the class environment (instructors will probably yell at you), talk to the instructor, and check his certifications before enrolling. According to Julie Bryan, director of fitness and recreation for the United Services Automobile Association, some certifications to look for are American College of Sports Medicine, Aerobic and Fitness Association of America, American Council on Exercise, Coopers Institute for Aerobic Research, and National Strength and Conditioning Association.

Many progressive organizations include aggressive fitness programs for their employees. General Mills, Motorola, and Coors Brewing Company have reported a return on investment of $3 to $6 for every $1 invested in employee fitness.

The International Council on Active Aging with financial support from Fifty-Plus Lifelong Fitness, created a simple tool to estimate the financial ramifications of physical inactivity. Their online calculator uses a formula based on the cost of medical care, workers' compensation, and lost productivity data once decision-makers have provided answers to six general demographic questions.

While the main focus of this lesson is safely and purposely pushing yourself to determine and expand your limits, there is another important aspect of toughness. It involves the science of learning how to take maximum advantage of circadian rhythms and increasing maximum performance by alternating periods of activity and rest. Jim Loehr and Tony Schwartz provide a comprehensive treatment of how to balance energy renewal and expenditure in their book *The Power of Full Engagement.* Combining a "Ranger School" type experience and lifestyle adjustments to take better advantage of the body's ability to sustain long periods of high performance through supercompensation techniques is a powerful formula for success. Complete a "Ranger School" type experience, preferably while young. The short-term pain yields long-term staying power that will last a lifetime.

Gunfighting Lesson 5

Prepare for paradoxes and having to choose the *least–worst option.* Many times in battle and in life there are no desirable options—all have negative consequences. In war, tough decisions have to be made under extraordinary circumstances, such as when the enemy has no regard for non-combatants. Innocent people are sometimes casualties, clearly an undesirable option, but sometimes the "least-worst" choice available. Noble soldiers will go to any length to protect their own and other innocents, yet the "fog of war" sometimes means losses through "friendly fire." Soldiers of honor detest loss of life, yet must anticipate and prepare for the possibility. Most civilian professions have their own harsh paradoxes to face, such as budget cuts affecting good people and projects for the greater good.

To be a good soldier you must love the Army.
But to be a good officer you must be willing
to order the death of the thing you love.
That is…a very hard thing to do.
Few other professions require it.
That is one reason why there are so few
good officers, although there are many good men.
-General Robert E. Lee (at Gettysburg)-

Soldiering is a remarkable profession. On one hand, it prepares its fold for combat, gunfighting, and killing. Then it takes those same people and trains them in the "humanitarian maneuver," which is to retain respect for people and their welfare.

The prolonged struggle in Iraq is an example of making the best of such contradictions. The Iraqi people have an understandable distrust of authority, and our military has been the authority figure in their country. Many Iraqis pre-judge us as "infidels."

No one likes to have foreign occupiers within their borders. Into such hostile conditions we insert troops and civilian contractors who, as a general rule, have a marginal appreciation and education of the society and history of the occupied country. While our soldiers and civilian contractors are, for the most part, excellent representatives of good will, the circumstances can inspire fear almost to the point of paranoia. Still, the military professional has to be at peace with kicking doors down to eliminate a threat, then respectively drinking tea with local leaders later the same day. In our relative ignorance of Arab customs, our progress has sometimes been excruciatingly slow in the Middle East, especially for people not bred on patience. In such challenging situations, progress cannot be rushed artificially.

Several more examples follow that illustrate combat paradoxes. A classmate of mine was killed in Vietnam because he hesitated when a young girl with a weapon aimed at him— then shot. His hesitation, bred in our society 's expectations and protectiveness of women and children, cost him his life.

In training for the D-Day invasion, my father was preparing his combat engineer battalion to land on Omaha beach. Minefields would be a major threat to the landing troops. Their training program required use of live mines to prepare the invasion force for the psychological stress of removing similar mines during the invasion. More than 300 men passed the live mine removal test, but one was killed. Though the loss was tragic, D-Day was only weeks away, and realistic preparation was essential. The live-mine training undoubtedly saved lives on Omaha Beach and in the hedgerows of the Normandy countryside. Nevertheless, it was difficult for my father to write the loved ones of that soldier to explain a training accident. Despite the best efforts, training casualties occur— clearly an undesirable outcome, but also the "least-worst" one available.

Having to choose from a set of undesirable options is not unique to war. While working in Latin America with ambassadors and their staffs, I quickly discovered that most of their decisions were of a *least-worst* type, with the down side of any decision being loudly criticized by their opponents. Similar stories could be told of the corporate, educational, legal, and medical domains, among many others. Only the naïve live in a world where paradoxes do not exist and the making of "least-worst" choices do not occur.

This final story dramatically illustrates both the inevitability of *least-worst* decisions and the need for ethical fitness combined with competence as part of the foundation of true professionalism.

Shoot Me! Shoot Me!

A large flatbed truck had gone off the highway and hit a tree head-on. On impact, its load of steel tore loose, slid forward through the back of the cab, and pinned the driver helplessly inside. The cab caught fire and was in danger of exploding. A state police car arrived and the trooper ran to the open cab window. The driver inside screamed. "Shoot me! Shoot me!"

It was obvious the trooper could not free the driver. He removed his service revolver, then paused, reconsidering, and slid the revolver back into the holster. At this point, he did a remarkable thing. Running back to his cruiser, he grabbed the small carbon tetrachloride fire extinguisher and returned to the cab. He sprayed the driver's face with it. The chemicals from the extinguisher put him to sleep. Soon after, the cab exploded.

-How Good People Make Tough Choices-

Here we had not only the ethical dilemma of the desire to preserve life (not shoot) versus mercy (put him out of his misery), but also a situation of extreme stress and urgency. The trooper had no time to consult anything or anyone, but his finely honed sense of ethical fitness and competence (knowledge that the chemicals in the fire extinguisher would put someone to sleep) led him to the best possible decision under the circumstances even though the outcome was unavoidable. He had faced a *least-worst* case and performed admirably.

All these paradoxes demand that one make the best of each situation, avoid making the same mistake twice, strive for becoming the best "true professional" one can be, and persevere until the mission is accomplished.

Gunfighting Lesson 6

Be decisive, aggressive, even audacious — indecisiveness is a fatal flaw. Visualize and prepare for taking decisive action in anticipated scenarios. Audacious, daring action can help "rally the troops" and turn a battle in your favor. To assure understanding, communicate with simplicity and clarity.

Audacious: bold, daring spirit supported by thorough preparation of instincts.

Be Decisive

A versatile leader must be decisive. The military preaches that indecision is a fatal flaw. Circumstances dictate the time available to make a decision, but generally military leaders are taught that a good (or even mediocre) decision executed with commitment and urgency is superior to a great decision delayed through protracted fact-finding or consensus building.

Business and military share the uncertainty associated with decision-making. In the *decide* step of our ethical fitness decision-making model, we offer options for making a decision—from deciding without consultation to deciding based on a vote of members. Gaining consensus is noble though should not be a crutch for indecisiveness. There are business or political circumstances where consensus is essential, but in many other battle and business circumstances, waiting for consensus can jeopardize a mission, project, or activity—or worse, doom it to failure. Lee Iacocca put it this way: "Even the right decision is wrong if made too late." Or, as Sydney Harris said: "Regret for the things we did [decisions we make] can be tempered by time, it is regret for the things we did not do [decisions we did not make] that is inconsolable."

Indecision is not normally fatal in most civilian occupations. However, it can be costly and potentially harmful to life. There are countless cases to illustrate. One of my most vivid is the 1979 Three Mile Island nuclear power plant near-disaster near Harrisburg, Pennsylvania. One of the reactors lost its coolant causing overheating and partial meltdown of the uranium core. Documentaries of the disaster revealed the value of the decisions made with limited reliable information when the cost of further delay would, most experts agree, have been catastrophic.

Be Aggressive

Unfortunately, some people, such as the 9/11 terrorists, do not respond well to diplomacy. The idea is succinctly expressed by retired Air Force pilot, Brian Schul: "If one must fight, as hard as it is for some to accept, the harder truth is that to win battles against such enemies, you must negotiate with your knee in his chest and knife at his throat." Some people are uncomfortable with this line of thought, but it is naïve to think this attitude is always avoidable.

People sleep peaceably in their beds at night only because rough men stand ready to do violence on their behalf.
-George Orwell-

Gene Veith makes insightful observations about the American culture today, suggesting we have "feminized" our culture to the point that warlike values such as aggression are not appreciated, except in sports. Our peace-loving sensitivities are part of what makes us civilized, but our terrorist enemies do not share such sensitivity. They see our squeamishness about casualties as a weakness that can be exploited. When they read or listen to the rhetoric disparaging our war efforts, they are encouraged to continue attacks on our troops and innocent civilians. Sustained decisiveness and aggressive action against our enemies are essential for victory over terrorism.

Psychologists have long known that two individuals can have the same information and react radically differently. Therefore, some will interpret decisiveness, forcefulness, audacity, and persistence as arrogant, warmongering, or sanctimonious. This is unfortunate, but an acceptable consequence for decisive and aggressive behavior needed in war.

Being aggressive in battle is especially challenging for women in our military. Women raised in Western culture have to both fight without hesitation and be humanitarian (like their male counterparts), while maintaining their stature as a lady. In some societies, women have been part of the fighting force for generations, but women in our country often have to be schooled to respond aggressively. According to Dr. Ray Wood, director of combatives at West Point, "The violence propensity differs greatly between the genders. Men are more socialized to violence." Women are socialized to nurture. In the context of this lesson, both genders have to condition themselves to approach the violence of battle without hesitation.

There is room for the "boardroom gunfighter" especially when it comes to competing against unethical companies. We can compete cooperatively with noble professionals, though we should "fight with abandon" against those who seek to take advantage of the public trust.

Millennia of evolution have hard-wired most ambitious people to compete, to engage, to "conquer." Our society no longer requires us to hunt for our food, instead isolating us in offices, classrooms, conference rooms, and the like. Many assert that much of the violence in our society is because so many individuals lack healthy ways to channel aggression. Approaching business competition incorporating ethics ingrained in the warrior ethos provides an acknowledgment of aggressive desires and a productive structure for their expression for the common good.

Be Audacious

An aggressive, decisive style can lead to audacity, a confidence that one is almost able to control intervening circumstances. To an outsider it may appear that the audacious commander's or CEO's instincts are controlled by divine guidance as they seem to take over at just the right moment, attacking where the enemy is vulnerable, even if the opponent is stronger. Such leaders seem in command of the mind of their enemies. As A.L. Long says in the *Memoirs of Robert E. Lee*, "They [successful generals] exude the confidence of a gambler holding four aces."

Their audacious actions had a solid foundation build on the same years of study as more recent military leaders like Generals MacArthur and Patton of the 20th century.

Victor Davis in *Between War and Peace: Lessons from Afghanistan to Iraq* persuasively argues that Patton's audacious solution to war with Islamic fascists is to defeat, humiliate, and then help. Only by such humiliation will supporters of terrorism understand the cost of support for the terrorist cause. Patton frequently used Kipling's phrase "the unforgiving minute" to describe times in war when the collective will of a people can collapse. When these times occur, they must be capitalized upon. Davis argues that an audacious Commander today could create favorable diplomatic conditions impossible to achieve by politicians in places like Fallujah and Najaf. Because that is not likely to happen, the perseverance addressed in Gunfighting Leadership Lesson 7 is our best option for victory.

The great professional/leader /statesman has the courage born of audacity to make decisions when serious outcomes hang in the balance. In battle, commanders' decisions take on life and death intensity. In business, senior executives' decisions take on considerable quality of life and resource consequences. In either case, boldness and audacity normally trump a perfect plan.

In today's corporate environment, Michael Dell exemplifies one of the key elements of being audacious—persevering on offense over the long haul until succeeding. Similar to entrepreneurs like Fred Smith at Federal Express, he started his company from scratch in a market that seemed impenetrable with giants like IBM, HP, and Compaq. You have to be audacious to even believe you can succeed against huge odds. The will to persist over years, even decades, helped Dell become the leading PC maker largely because Dell combined that offensive mindset with insights into what the customer wanted (built to order PCs, rapidly delivered). They, and other giants of military or corporate legend, never lost audacity. They developed, through preparation, the confidence to take decisiveness and aggressiveness to a level of boldness that overwhelmed their doubters and competitors.

Napoleon Hill spent 20 years studying hundreds of the world's most prolific people like Andrew Carnegie and Thomas Edison. He found that because of their higher level of study and preparation over time they developed honed instincts that helped them acquire unexplained hunches leading to exceptional results.

Decisiveness and audacity are not born of reckless boldness or juvenile "cockiness." True audaciousness is earned through preparation and action that develops habits and instincts.

Be Clear and Simplify

These concepts clearly have application in any occupation. Being decisive has little value unless the messages conveyed are clear and understood. Developing the habit of a direct communication style, with an aim to simplify, dramatically increases the chances that individuals will be clearly and completely understood.

Any intelligent fool can make things more complex.
It takes a touch of genius to move in the opposite direction.
-Albert Einstein-

Combat is complex enough without adding muddled communication to the "fog of war." The greater the number of people involved and the greater the separation between them, the greater the effort needed to state intent clearly and simply in any type communication.

My father always spoke in a straightforward, uncompromising manner, never making it personal, simply shooting straight. He was intolerant of polite, confusing prose, unflinchingly dismissive of those who failed to keep it simple and straightforward. His "hero for clarity" was President Reagan. He had the privilege of meeting with our Commander-in-Chief to appreciate first hand his famous way of communicating.

My "clarity hero" is General Colin Powell. While assigned as a Chief of Staff Army Fellow and attending the Army War College, I had several occasions to hear or speak with General Powell. He has an extraordinary ability to simplify. No matter what the subject or how complex, he spoke in clear, concise language. Whether one agreed with his position or not, one understood his message. His ability to express intent and the parameters that set the stage for initiative was unparalleled. The best way to develop such a skill is through practice and diligence. Your speech may lack flowery flourishes, but people will appreciate that you are clear and unambiguous.

Every profession develops a second language, a way to help internal communication be understood. Sometimes the language is "colorful," but nevertheless serves its purpose. In the military "Hooah," the all-purpose motivational expression meaning "gung-ho" and being held to a standard, is an example of short-cut military jargon. Radiotelephone procedures have an array of short codes: "Roger" means *I understand*; "Wilco" means *I will comply*; "Over" means *I expect a reply*; "Out" means the *end of the conversation*. Such shortened speech makes for fast, accurate communication and, because it is a habit, is instinctively available under stress. The tone of voice one uses can add clarity without adding unneeded language.

> *There are tones of voice that mean more than words.*
> -Robert Frost-

Such profession-peculiar expressions, acronyms, jargon, hand signals, or other mannerisms add to simplicity for those in the particular profession, but lock out those who are not privy to the language. Therefore, as one's circle of influence broadens to extend beyond those who are "in the know," the use of straightforward, generally understood language is necessary. Nonstandard language has its place, especially in close combat, but it should progressively disappear from common usage once outside the family of those who use it professionally. In the military, a commander of troops from a single service leverages the advantage of common lexicon. A commander of several services faces different lexicons, and a combined operations commander (which includes allies), also deals with differences in culture, language, and historical nuances.

A recent example of the language challenge faced when a myriad of entities are joined for a common purpose is in the formation of the Office of Homeland Security. Since it was founded, language has been a barrier. Different agencies have differing understandings for terms such as "cover" or "clear the building." To keep terms straight, their advisory council recommended they hire a professional lexicographer to maintain and update a common terminology. Until that is done, more explanation and undesirable complexity must be used to achieve the essential clarity needed.

So it is in civilian life that as a person enlarges his circle of influence, the art of simplifying communication becomes more complex. Decisiveness and clarity take on different styles dependent on leadership level. It is doubtful General Patton's abrupt communication style would have been successful in Eisenhower's position as Supreme Allied Commander. However, Eisenhower's more collegial, direct style was appropriate for his position. Likewise, General Schwarzkopf's well-known temper quelled inter-service squabbles, yet he was also accommodating to allies.

Strategic leadership positions in combat, whether military or corporate, demand a complex set of communication skills that are aggressive and direct, yet understood. This is one reason leadership in war has been called "the most baffling of arts.

Gunfighting Lesson 7

Put your personal affairs in order. Those who love their families will honor them by preparing for the possibility of not returning. Preparing a plan for the end of life is sound for all adults, especially those in high-risk professions.

Final Act of Accountability

The military services provide thorough checklists for preparing for deployment in war. They help the service member have a detailed Family Care Plan, which brings medical records up to date, leaves instruction for funeral arrangements, and helps put legal and financial affairs in order. Should the soldier not return, the plan serves as a final act of true professionalism for those left behind.

When a soldier is killed, the services assign a survival assistance officer to help the family. Any responsible adult should choose someone to assist his family in case of unexpected death. Identifying a family assistance individual and executor is not an idle choice. These are difficult, time-consuming tasks. Anyone who has served as the executor on an estate will appreciate the blessing or burden depending on the state of the deceased's personal affairs. The tasks to do so can be obtained from reputable estate planners, attorneys, and financial advisors.

Unfortunately, many people take an "I'll do it someday" approach, not reaping the benefits of reduced stress and peace of mind that come from making such plans. This lesson clearly applies to every responsible adult. Having a goal to assure your personal affairs are in order as part of your plan for life is an ultimate act of being accountable.

Flight Requires Both Wings

An engineer friend of mine, Bill Veltrop, had a full career with a major oil company. His introspection led him to offer some insightful advice for those inclined to "share their soul." The American military and business models, and large Western culture organizations in general, tend to be "yang-centric." Recalling the "yin-yang" concept of wholeness, yang organizations are characterized as competitive, exclusive, achievement-oriented, end-focused, assertive, spirited, and rational. A "yin-centered" culture is collaborative, inclusive, soulful, and intuitive. Excelling in both aspects of wholeness yields the best chance of thriving as an organization or person. As Bill puts it, "to learn to fly requires a yin-yang strength; we cannot just flap our yang-wing and expect to get off the ground."

The gunfighting lessons we offer are predominately yang-centered. This idea of flying with both wings encourages more aliveness through an appreciation of the yin perspective as well. Worthy leaders who fly with both wings leave an enriched legacy, leading even after death. Balanced flight helps keep momentum of causes alive and impacts social good for generations.

Leaving a Legacy

Perhaps some of you will find an extra measure of reward in speaking through the arts as a means of living a legacy for those you love by sharing a part of your soul. Leaving a legacy should include more than tangible assets.

Many senior American warriors have focused on their trade and not explored the world of the arts with passion. My intent here is not to suggest such a "distraction" is essential, but to point out the interesting fact that military captains of some societies have been expected to be more than battlefield victors.

General Vo Nguyen Giap was the architect of the Viet Minh victory over the French prior to defeating the United States in Vietnam. This master strategist put his personal affairs in order before going into battle. He wrote a poem as an emotional expression of longing and yearning for reunion while asserting the need to fulfill his warrior duties. In recent years, an increasing number of people have been adding to their last will and testaments "ethical" or *legacy wills* that include messages for loved ones. This is what I believe General Giap sought to accomplish in his poem, "The Kiss."

The Kiss

The earth bore you here
To bring beauty.
The earth bore me here
To love you deeply.

In love people kiss.
The sweetness they would not miss.
My heart is passionate for you
Still I must go to battle.

My love, it is possible
That I may die in combat
The lips torn there by bullets
Might never be kissed [again] by yours.

Even if I die, my love,
I love you, though I am unable
To kiss you with the lips
Of a slave.

-General Vo Nguyen Giap-

Cecil B. Curry, author of *An Officer and a Gentleman: General Vo Nguyen Giap as Military Man and Poet*, translated by Ho Thi Xuan Hong, Nguyen Hai Quoc, and Nguyen Khac Niem.

Lessons for Gunfighting Leaders

7 Lessons for Gunfighting Leaders

1. Make gunfighting a last resort. When conflict is necessary, make it part of our nation's fiber.

2. Make sure the best leaders do the leading while troublesome "leaders" are removed.

3. State intent, expectations, and parameters directly and simply to encourage clarity and initiative. Aim for a *triple-win* balancing stewardship of mission, people, and resources.

4. Lead by actions, not just position or personality; demonstrate humility with character and competence.

5. Prepare yourself and your unit for suffering, disfigurement, and death; carry out death notification with dignity.

6. Keep the memory of loss and sacrifice alive; memorials and remembrances matter.

7. Persevere—resolve to succeed—leadership provides the glue that keeps the fabric and psyche of organizations and society intact until victory is achieved.

Gunfighting Leadership Lesson 1

Make gunfighting a last resort. When conflict is a necessity, make it a part of our nation's fiber. Gunfighting, in battle or the boardroom, should be a last resort. Whether real or metaphorical, it is not a video game—war is indeed "hell" and should never be romanticized. Do everything possible to maintain peace, and choose conflict only when gunfighting/battle/conflict is the *least-worst* option. When war is waged, mobilizing National Guard, Reserve units, and private sector contractors is essential policy. Widespread use of private-sector resources for engineering, logistics, and weapons system support enables the military to make the best use of troops to fight the battle. Strategic military and civilian thinkers must continually shape the roles and relationships of both sectors for maximum cooperation and mutual benefit for the good of the country in both peace and war. Thus, America's military remains relevant in peace and prepared for war. The corollary of this lesson for businesses at "war" is to enlist the widest possible support for your organization's goals— make your supply chain from supplier to consumer a part of the tapestry providing the product or service.

No great dependence is to be placed on the eagerness
of young soldiers for action for the prospect of fighting
is agreeable only to those who are strangers to it.
-Vegetius 4th Century AD-

War is not to be desired or sought, but is to be respected. There
is no circumstance where killing other human beings should be
celebrated. Nevertheless, in our current war on apocalyptic
terrorists, killing them all is essential. The apocalyptic terrorist
violates the laws of war by refusing to wear a uniform and
purposely targeting civilians. He is by definition a war
criminal. Like a cancer, removing only part of the tumor will
provide only marginal gain. Killing for liberation or freedom is
drastically different from killing for conquest. A detailed
justification of our current war on terror is not within the scope
of this book. I invite you to read Ralph Peter's book *When
Devils Walk the Earth* for an articulate argument to support the
case for the extinction of our current enemy. The history of
Rome is the nearest model to our current conflict. The Romans'
utter destruction of Carthage brought centuries of peace, while
their later attempts to appease barbarians consistently failed.

Soldiers (or others in professions where gunfighting is a
potential event) are the ones best prepared to carry out the act
and the strongest advocates for restraining violence. When a
democratically-elected civilian leadership decides conflict is
necessary, it should be executed with all the force and savvy
military professionals can muster, with the goal of
accomplishing the mission with the least possible loss of life
and destruction. War will result not only in death but also in
considerable added cost in physical and emotional wounds.
There are many casualties who will need lifelong treatment of
their wounds. Almost no one returns from battle unscathed.
Using war as a metaphor in business is useful provided the
limits of the meaning are clearly understood. In civilian
occupations other than law enforcement, where the parallel to

soldiering is obvious, the intent is to convey the same spirit of decisiveness and boldness without the actual loss of life or physical carnage. A "boardroom gunfighter spirit" is needed to compete in global markets. The business leader must use all the tools, tactics, and talents necessary to assure victory and protect his employees' and shareholders' vital interests, especially competing against unethical firms without character and competence worthy of noble competition.

In war, mobilization of the National Guard, Reserve units, and private-sector contractors is strategically essential to our nation's welfare. They relate to the fundamental way in which the wars we fight are entwined in our nation's present and future prosperity. One of the major lessons learned from Vietnam was that the politicians' unwillingness to mobilize the National Guard and Reserve units left the active military isolated from the psyche of the American people. Having learned that lesson, there is a different challenge faced by the conflict in Iraq. While every soldier and his/her family will undergo strain, the quandary facing Reserve and National Guard personnel is especially severe. These personnel signed up to fight when called, without strings attached. Most are professionals who rarely complain. However, they do have a career that must be put on hold. As of Spring 2004, more than 200,000 Reservists and Guard members had been called to active duty, many for a year or more. With their duties come sacrifices and stressors, often in every area of their lives simultaneously. Our lessons apply to them in a special way.

Widespread use of private-sector resources to assist the war effort further engages our citizens in the fight. In Vietnam, the shortage of engineer troops led to the first large-scale use of contractors and civilian workers in an active theater of operations. Today, we see that same phenomenon. In Iraq, thousands of civilian contractor personnel have been deployed to the Middle East to help rebuild Iraq's infrastructure and train Iraqi personnel. In addition, the services employ thousands of Department of the Army, Navy, and Air Force civilians who work in war as well as in times of peace. Many are deployed to the combat zone. Though not combatants, these personnel are subject to considerable risk. Their fortitude to sustain losses and continue to complete their tasks is vital to overall mission success. They too must be recognized as contributors to the national psyche. This practice is so ingrained that the military has even published guidelines to address how to integrate civilians into the battlefield [Field Manual 3-100.21].

Global business has taken on some of the same aspects of interdependence. An isolationist business strategy is doomed to sub-optimal results. Likewise, businesses should enlist every group in their supply chain—from suppliers to consumers—as part of the tapestry providing the products or services. There will still be bumps in the road as drastically different cultures, agendas, and ambitions clash for power, influence, and profit, but the alternative in a world economy is failure to compete at the highest levels.

Gunfighting Leadership Lesson 2

Make sure the best leaders do the leading while troublesome "leaders" are removed. Holding a title that indicates a position of leadership does not make a leader. In battle, as well as in business and life, ineffective leaders can be almost as dangerous as the enemy. Both actual war and metaphorical war requires tough battlefield policies, one of the most important being that the best should lead. While some may find it unfair that the most talented and dedicated should bear the most risk, the reality is that nothing important is gained without risk, and the best leaders are most equipped to deal with it—both in terms of completion of the mission and caring for those they lead.

The American soldier, marine, airman, sailor and coastguardsman is America's true "human shield." To qualify as a *best* leader of combatants, the candidate must learn to win the hearts and minds of those they lead. Most new members of the military services are young, from varied educational backgrounds. For the most part, they view their leaders as heads of a family. The former Sergeant Major of the Army Jack Tilley said it well, "what soldiers do starts in their hearts." Winning their hearts starts with their leaders being a soldier first, then a leader of character.

Put Character First

Followers "to the gates of hell" must believe in the competence and integrity of their leaders. The best soldier-leaders study character-grounded leadership, internalize the values of the profession, and come to terms with why they chose the profession of soldiering. *Once an Eagle*, the 1968 bestseller by Anton Myrer (a World War I Marine), is a must-read leadership primer for professional soldiers and should be on the reading list of serious students of leadership. The hero is Sam Damon, a deeply moral and courageous officer who struggles to make decisions for the good of the mission and the troops, even when those decisions hurt his career. Damon's antagonist is another officer, a brilliant but self-serving careerist. The reason the book is widely read by those in uniform is not only because it embodies the ideals of morally-grounded leadership in the character of Damon, but also because it depicts the struggle leaders feel within themselves for decisions that can hurt their career. This is not to say that the best leaders must be without flaw, and it is certainly not to say that a leader should attempt to project a false image of perfection. The distinction is that a leader deals with himself honestly and rigorously, which gives his followers the assurance that he will do so with them as well.

Leadership is earned by mastering a defined set of skills and earning every day the trust of your followers, peers, chain of command or bosses, and the stakeholders who depend on you. Along the way, character-grounded leadership results in bumps and bruises that impact one's career, but more often such leadership is recognized for what it is and given the value it deserves. Putting character first is just as applicable to civilian occupations.

Internalize the Values of the Profession

The best soldier-leaders internalize the values of the military profession. For the military professional, it means: *Loyalty, Duty, Respect, Selfless Service, Honor, Integrity, and Personal Courage* must become an integral part of who you are. When those values are yours, you are worthy of the trust this nation and the American soldier have placed in you. There is merit in these values to those in civilian professions. With the layoffs experienced by some, a debate about loyalty is likely. The degree of selfless service expected of those in the profession of arms is clearly different. Even so, the idea of internalizing a personal value set as a foundation for leadership of others is solid.

Be Devoted to Those You Lead

The English language seems insufficient in offering words that adequately express the connection between a battlefield commander and his troops. The best career military leaders have been able to find a way to connect with their men in a bond that defies easy explanation. Napoleon observed, "You cannot get men to offer their lives for a few pence, instead you must speak to their souls." General of the Army Douglas MacArthur, in his farewell address at West Point in 1962, eulogized the American man-at-arms as one of the world's noblest figures. In reality, they are men and women with human frailties, not super beings, yet the battlefield leader inspires them, at least for a time, to be the best examples of successful patriotism. Any worthy U.S. battlefield commander I have ever known has "carved his [soldiers'] stature in the hearts of the American people. From one end of the world to the other he has drained deep the chalice of courage [author unknown]." I simply lack the eloquence to express all that needs to be said here; words truly are inadequate to express the depth of relationship between a commander and his troops — the word "devotion" must suffice.

The expression of devotion for those led also applies to civilian organizational leadership. In most civilian professions, a leader's caring and love for his/her subordinates can be just as real, but manifested in more subtle ways. With human life at stake, a military commander can, and at times should, be direct in telling and showing his soldiers how much he cares. Civilian culture more clearly separates one's personal and social life from one's work. Civilian employees do not normally appreciate encroachment into their private or social realms by their work bosses. As Robert Kaplan and David Norton observed in their book, *The Strategy Focused Organization*, knowing what it takes to win the hearts and minds of employees is something military professionals can apply in any context. While achieving this goal begins with internalizing the aforementioned values, they must be explicitly expressed through strong eye contact, overt appreciation and recognition, and fair, constructive reprimands. They write, "Military officers are stereotyped as command and control managers, but the best recognize that in the heat of battle the intangible assets that the troops can draw upon win their hearts and minds." The best corporate leaders embody this as well.

Frequent, timely feedback — on goal setting, performance, and areas of improvement — are leader behaviors that show employees respect and encourage them to seek empowerment. Without a deep imbedded sense of caring and devotion to followers, they will not follow you "to the gates of hell" in actual or corporate combat, nor are they likely to be loyal under stress. The best leader's actions, demeanor, and behaviors all shout *caring* even if, at times, it is "tough love."

Remember the Setting

Defining who the best leaders are mandates that one consider the setting. Task-oriented leaders are most effective when there is a good relation with followers and the tasks are clear (highly favorable setting) or conditions are the opposite (highly unfavorable). When the setting is a total disaster, the best leader takes charge, overlooking interpersonal issues, and gets the job done. The best leader exhibits a relationship-oriented style when there are problems to deal with but conditions are not awful. In such a case, the democratic approach is generally more productive. Leaders influence by being hard—getting angry or threatening; soft—being nice or flattering, or being rational—presenting facts and using reasoning. In general, hard tactics tend to alienate, soft tactics tend to produce less work, and rational tactics tend to work best.

Removing Poor Leaders

The military's pragmatic, performance-based approach to whomever is put in charge and allowed to stay in command has application in corporate America, although it frequently can be more difficult in the latter to relieve poor leaders. Too often, the best technicians or managers are given organizational leadership positions though they lack the character, competencies, or passion to succeed at serving those they lead. Former General Electric CEO Jack Welch only allowed senior line managers who met their earnings and profitability goals to remain in charge, regardless of seniority. He had no qualms about removing those who failed to meet performance goals. This may seem cruel, but it is not only pragmatic in battle or business, but also in the end it best serves the greater good— the family of employees or soldiers and the stakeholders.

Leadership as a Calling

Finally, the best soldier-leaders internalize why they are soldiers (or civilian professionals) and see their choice as a calling. The pleasure of military leadership lies in selfless service for a cause in which you believe. Financial wealth or even public esteem is not the end game. For the soldier leader, this is not an idle decision. Not only are the financial rewards while serving less than for civilians with similar training, education, and experience, but also the financial benefits to loved ones, if killed in action, are modest.

As the military reassesses its global role, the officer facing a career in the service considers there have been twenty-seven deployments in the past ten years compared with only ten in the forty-five previous years. For the "lifer," this is definitely not a sort of outward-bound experience or adventure camp—this is serious commitment. Simply be honest with yourself and ask why you have chosen to be a leader in your profession of choice. If it is not for the right reasons—a profession you have a passion for—you may not have the tenacity to be a true professional, one of the "best" leaders in your chosen profession.

Resolve to be a *best leader* or do not jump into the fray of leadership of others. The increased conflict and difficulty one attracts as he or she climbs the ladder of responsibility and gains increased power is not for the faint of heart. Make sure you are called to serve as a leader and *wired* for the increased complexity and conflict.

Gunfighting Leadership
Lesson 3

State intent, expectations, and parameters directly and simply to encourage clarity and initiative. Directions, boundaries, and rules boost initiative instead of restricting it—an often misunderstood paradox—as they provide a framework to *go for it your way*. Without clarity, many avoid risk and wait for direction. Tell people your expectations and why they can and should succeed, which will increase commitment, confidence, and action. Listen as others restate their understanding to make sure the message is accurately received. The greater the number of people involved and greater the separation from them, the greater the effort needed to state simply, clearly, and consistently.

By communicating intent and expectations, a leader casts a vision and sets boundaries within which soldiers or employees can exercise initiative and judgment, and develop habits and instincts. This is especially important when a leader seeks to make significant changes in the organization's culture and when the average level of empowerment and maturity is low.

People get comfortable in old habits. The company culture, good or bad, gets ingrained. Some responses to a change in habits are irrational based on anger, fear, or laziness. Others resist with good reason: the need is unclear, the direction is not understood, or confidence in the leader, team, or individual is lacking. Without a sense of direction and a framework to work within, many people "freeze in place" — victim to risk-averse tendencies and low-level commitment.

The military seeks to prevent such risk-averse behavior and encourage initiative by clearly stating the commander's intent and expectations while having well understood procedures to establish boundaries. By instilling such clear guidelines, soldiers are free to execute initiative to complete the mission. Such a culture of discipline is not tyrannical. Self-disciplined people who understand the intent and parameters within which they should operate will go to extremes to fulfill their duties. Setting clear standards of performance with simplicity leads to increased commitment and empowerment to fulfill expectations. In simplicity is elegance.

In *Who Really Matters: the Core Group Theory of Power, Privilege, and Success*, Art Kleiner provides his explanation for why organizations act as they do. He states, "It is the perceived interests of the core group that drives most decision-making. What people think they are to do…depends on the perceived needs of the core group." In the military structure, the leaders (both commissioned and noncommissioned officers) are the core group that defines the path to be taken, the objective, and the boundaries.

In many civilian organizations, the core group can be both those with legitimate positional authority and those in staff positions, which increases chances of confusion unless people in the organization know who is in the actual core group and, therefore, to whom to listen for direction.

Civilian CEOs like Jack Welch made sure there was no confusion as to who made up the core group. Under his leadership, only line managers who were tops in their market sectors made the important decisions as to direction and parameters. Any organization or unit needs clear statement of intent and direction from its core group to attain and sustain excellence in its field. That intent comes, not from clichés like "the customer comes first" or "we serve the people of this nation," but from the words and behaviors of the core group.

When words and behavior are consistent, people tend to follow. Even those who disagree would rather follow a leader they can count on to be clear and consistent.

Set High Standards

*It has been my experience that superior people
are attracted only by challenge. By setting our
standard low and making our life soft, we have,
quite automatically and unconsciously,
assured ourselves of mediocre people.*
The Ugly American
-Burdick and Lederer-

In my senior leadership opportunities, I state intent for reaching appropriate standards by having a mindset and plans aimed at achieving what I call a "triple win." Normally this was balancing stewardship of mission, stakeholders, and resources. In my civilian profession, I worked with a company that designed and built projects. There, the "triple win" was cost, speed, and quality. The conventional wisdom is that a client could only have two of the three. However, my experience in benchmarking capital projects revealed that about 3% of all projects were world class—hitting that "sweet spot" in achieving high standards in all three. The remainder obeyed the rules of conventional wisdom. True world-class performance in any profession is truly rare, though comes more often through balancing high standards in all triple win areas than seeking perfection in only one or two areas at the expense of another area.

Clear Intent and Expectations Can Inspire

Great leaders are almost always great simplifiers,
who can cut through argument, debate and doubt
to offer a solution everybody can understand.
-General Colin Powell-

Intent statements take many forms, but the best are expressed in straightforward, simple terms. Three examples illustrate this point.

The Combined Chief's of Staff's order to General Eisenhower in World War II read:

"You will enter Europe and, in conjunction with other Allied Nations, undertake operations aimed at the heart of Germany and the destruction of her Armed Forces."
-U.S. Army Field Manual 1-1, page 42-

My son-in-law has a creative way of communicating his intent. As a school assistant principal, he advises new teachers to exercise "turtle leadership." This means you tackle challenges at a slow yet steady pace, be willing to stick your neck out, and have tough skin because not everyone will agree with you.

The last example comes from the war in Iraq.

The 1st Marine Division Commander's message to his troops just before they launched their attack into Iraq is a strong example of using a letter to inspire and state intent. He clearly states the goal, "end Saddam's reign of terror," and places parameters on the fight, reinforcing what he expects from the troops—"keep your honor clean."

March 2003

1ˢᵗ Marine Division (REIN)

Commanding General's Message to All Hands

For decades, Saddam Hussein has tortured, imprisoned, raped and murdered the Iraqi people; invaded neighboring countries without provocation; and threatened the world with weapons of mass destruction. The time has come to end his reign of terror. On your young shoulders rest the hopes of mankind.

When I give you the word, together we will cross the Line of Departure, close with those forces that choose to fight, and destroy them. Our fight is not with the Iraqi people, nor is it with members of the Iraqi army who choose to surrender. While we will move swiftly and aggressively against those who resist, we will treat all others with decency, demonstrating chivalry and soldierly compassion for people who have endured a lifetime under Saddam's oppression.

Chemical attack, treachery, and use of the innocent as human shields can be expected, as can other unethical tactics. Take it all in stride. Be the hunter, not the hunted: never allow your unit to be caught with its guard down. Use good judgement and act in best interests of our Nation.

You are part of the world's most feared and trusted force. Engage your brain before you engage your weapon. Share your courage with each other as we enter the uncertain terrain north of the Line of Departure. Keep faith in your comrades on your left and right and Marine Air overhead. Fight with a happy heart and strong spirit.

For the mission's sake, our country's sake, and the sake of the men who carried the Division's colors in past battles-who fought for life and never lost their nerve-carry out your mission and keep your honor clean. Demonstrate to the world there is "No Better Friend, No Worse Enemy" than a U.S. Marine.

J.N. Mattis
Major General, U.S. Marines
Commanding

Gunfighting Leadership
Lesson 4

Lead by actions, not merely by position or personality; demonstrate humility with character and competence. A substantial portion of ability to influence others to meet exceptional standards stems from a leader's presence, demeanor, and charisma. However, the most effective leaders demonstrate humility motivated by mission and service to others rather than excessive personal ego or ambition for personal gain. Combining a healthy ambition with humility differentiates truly great leaders from the good ones. Your abilities will be challenged most in times of major change and as you move to organizational and societal leadership.

My father rose to a high rank in both military and civilian hierarchies, yet he remained a humble man. He was the epitome of a professional and leader who could forge diverse interests, differing views, and people of different ethnic backgrounds and countries into an executable plan leading to accomplishment of the task.

When I was to be married he gave me only three key pieces of fatherly advice:

- Make your mother proud.

- Never let any rank or title go to your head—serving is a privilege, so fulfilling one's duty is not about ego and the ambition of a title. Be a servant of those you lead and they will serve you.

- Learn to lead by decisively engaging others in examining alternatives and selecting the one that makes the most sense in your mind and gut.

The person who relies almost exclusively on his title or rank is not a true professional. The rewards received by a professional frequently include rank or title, but when acquired, they are built on trust and merit earned from the contributions of many. As my father used to say, "When you give more than you get you get more than you give."

When energetic young leaders have early success, there is a danger of becoming arrogant. If they are promoted to be a senior executive or official, they often find such positions laden with "land mines." The skill set that got them to this point needs severe adjustments if they are to succeed beyond it. One of those adjustments is ego. The cliché, "It is lonely at the top" is true. Once there, information is mysteriously filtered before you receive it. Many of your former professional peer group, a personnel network you nourished for so many years, behave differently. One is much more capable of adjusting to these new demands if the journey to senior leadership is built on a foundation of trust in character and competence earned through humility aimed at servant leadership. Humble service aimed at a common calling breeds strong bonds of loyalty to a just cause rather than to the individual. The most effective, influential leaders leave their egos at the door. Some of the greatest leadership disasters we witness come from individuals whose ambition gets out of hand. The biggest successes usually come from those who appreciate that a great deal of their power comes from trust and teamwork from others. True leaders seek to serve and develop perceptions of competence as well as less tangible qualities such as demeanor, presence, and humility.

Many senior leaders have difficulty delegating—it doesn't come naturally. However, achieving complex goals in fast-moving, unpredictable environments has a way of humbling those who try. No matter what a senior leader does to reduce risks associated with integrating complex tasks, he can't cover all the bases. He can continue to be frustrated, delegate and hope, or create a culture where those closest to the action earn empowerment. This last course of action is the only sane strategy. This calls for humility in the way the leader behaves.

Power and Conflict

Power and influence are the "horsepower" of leading others. As you climb the ladder in the leadership of others, you increase your circle of influence as well as both positional and personal power. The greater a leader's power, the more conflict he will encounter, no matter how much he seeks to align with stakeholders. As one moves through the levels of leadership, the degree of conflict increases proportionally since players frequently have diverse agendas, ideologies, and beliefs. Therefore, if you are an aspiring leader, we suggest you assess your tolerance for conflict—and whether your calling is strong enough to merit the added stress—as you continue to rise in responsibility, power, and influence.

I hope I shall always possess firmness and virtue enough to maintain what I consider the most in noble of all titles, the character of an honest man.

-President George Washington-

Gunfighting Leadership
Lesson 5

Prepare yourself and your unit for suffering, disfigurement, and death. Carry out death notification with dignity. A corporate version for this could be *prepare yourself and your organization for setbacks and losses*. In either the military or corporate arena, be ready to assume more responsibility and groom others to be leaders in case of losses. Accomplish the mission first; mourn later. Conveying the loss of a loved one is one of the leader's most solemn duties. Death notification by the commander who was there helps assure accuracy in reporting and prevents the unit leader from becoming callous or losing sight of the price paid in blood for freedom. Deal with loss thoroughly, with compassion and dignity.

In battle, people inevitably are wounded, killed, or missing in action. The human spirit wants to immediately mourn the loss, yet battle leaders must complete the mission first. A combat leader must defer mourning. The horror of battle need not be dwelled upon, but I include one excerpt from the movie, *We Were Soldiers*, to reinforce the sense of loss and the need to defer mourning until after the battle is won, no matter what transpires.

The movie is principally about Lt. Colonel Harold Moore (played by Mel Gibson), the Battalion Commander of the U.S. 7th Cavalry Unit, and the battle he and his men fought early in the Vietnam War. With thousands of North Vietnamese soldiers attacking a few hundred U.S. soldiers, Lt. Colonel Moore's leadership and professionalism under almost unimaginable stress avoided a massacre. His leadership prepared his unit, as much as is possible, for the carnage of war, losses of leaders, and losses due to "friendly fire." As a result, Moore's battalion suffered about half the casualties of its sister battalion and less than one-tenth the casualties of the North Vietnamese Army forces. As Lt. Colonel Moore put it, "Once one has trusted another with their life, everything else is small change." At the end of the battle, Moore's unit suffered 79 American soldiers dead and 121 wounded. Yet, mistakes were made in the invariable "fog of war"—at one point; napalm in the command post area engulfed several soldiers in flames. Yet, Charlie Hastings, his Forward Air Controller, and his buddies saved the day for Lt. Colonel Moore's Battalion in that horrible battle in the Ia Drang Valley in November 1965.

You may die. Your unit must prepare for the possible death of its leaders; therefore, you and your subordinate leaders must be ready to move up and take more responsibility if needed. Combat changes the mental state of a leader and followers because fear complicates the ability to act appropriately. The earning of empowerment is critical when the stakes are this high. A more direct leadership style is often required to minimize fatal mistakes or recover from those made. Your investment in preparation for leadership and true professionalism enables you to empower to the degree appropriate, to have the instincts to respond correctly, and the toughness to persevere through it all.

After the battle is the time to feel grief for the loss of soldiers in one's command. To the extent it is possible, the knowledge that you made the commitment to prepare and made the tough decisions based on the best information available will help you live with that sadness. Remember the dead with honor, and never forget their sacrifice.

Toughness through setbacks and losses comes from prior knowledge that they will occur even if the exact nature or timing is uncertain. Succession planning is a must, in battle or business. That said, the preparation and growth of emerging leaders is one of the preeminent responsibilities of senior leadership. Too often, it is neglected until too late.

With the Internet and global instantaneous communication it is possible that loved ones will learn of the loss of a soldier in battle before the unit leader can complete this solemn task. Even so, the commander must take the time to make the notification personal so loved ones will have an accurate, personalized account written with the care the deceased deserves. The military's support system does a great deal to preserve the dignity of the fallen and offer the respect deserved through burial. Our companion book, *Patriotism in Action*, gives an account of the traditions kept alive in a funeral with full military honors.

The loss of employees also will likely be a part of corporate experience. When a senior colleague of mine passed away from a heart attack, the company I worked for fully embraced the same philosophy of survival assistance and honor in burial that

I had experienced in the service. Hopefully, most organizations are this way.

Several gunfighting lessons have considered death from different vantage points:

- Put your personal affairs in order as a final act of professionalism and accountability;
- Prepare yourself and your unit for death;
- Carry out death notification with dignity;
- Memorials and remembrances matter.

The intent is not to be morbid; rather it is to serve as a strong incentive for a commitment to be a *true professional*, and to take with seriousness the devotion and discipline needed to be a *best leader* under stress.

The military shares the above lessons with first responders, rescuers, and law enforcement personnel. This is a brotherhood, imperfect as all are in living our lives, yet bound with the same sense of the value of sacrifice for all for the greater good.

Gunfighting Leadership
Lesson 6

Keep the memory of loss and sacrifice alive—memorials and remembrances matter.
Arlington Cemetery, "The Wall," the Arizona memorial in Hawaii, the Korean and World War II memorials, the Iwo Jima monument, these and other memorials offer links to fallen warriors and reminders of the price paid for freedom by America's "human shields." While in combat, soldiers must postpone dealing with grief. Memorials are an agent for cleansing and healing, as well as fuel for perseverance in trying times. While keeping the memory alive, they can help those remaining move forward. The same lesson applies to those lost in any profession charged with protecting others or single individuals giving their life for another.

Years after I left Vietnam, I visited the Vietnam Memorial—
"The Wall," as it is known by so many—to see the names of
those I had lost. When it rains, tears seem to glow on the
marble. This monument provides a personal and ongoing
connection to fallen warriors and a sanctuary for grief for their
comrades, friends, and family.

Stretch visits
"The Wall" and
the engraved
name of his friend
from high school
and West Point,
Tommy Hayes.

When a soldier is in combat, he must postpone dealing with
grief until the battle is over. There is no shame in grief, and
memorials serve as agents for cleansing it. We cannot undo the
past. The conventional wisdom is that one cannot move
forward by looking back. However, I have found that keeping
a tie to those who sacrificed for others helps heal the wounds
from loss and enables me to move ahead with resolve.

In his recordings called "Reflections on Albany" Vietnam
veteran Jim Lawrence offers vignettes that make the agony of
battle and loss of a comrade real. He reflects both the sorrow

and guilt of the survivor who returned and the need to turn that into renewed sense of purpose to remain a vibrant patriot. Quietly listen to "Conversations with a Tombstone, a Voice from the Wall, and The Gold Star Kid," and remember.

World War II Veterans Memorial

Korean Veterans Memorial

Other monuments provide similar meaning and motivation for veterans of other generations. They should carry the same message for all Americans: their fellow warrior citizens have fought for all that is good about America—for the idea of freedom—and that together, with sustained vigilance and perseverance, we can assure the continuation of that ideal for generations to come.

Meaningful celebrations of patriotic holidays help our people stay focused and committed in the fight for safety and security.

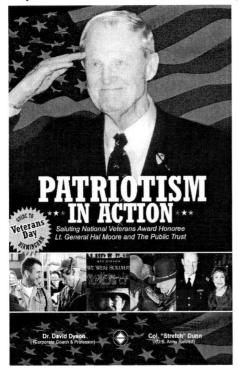

In our companion book, *Patriotism in Action,* we offer examples of how citizens remember the sacrifice needed to persevere until the victory is won (as in today's war against terrorists). A patriotic guide provides insights into the meaning of patriotic holidays and ceremonies that engender patriotism and respect for the flag. We conclude the book with Call to Action ideas you can choose from to demonstrate patriotism.

Gunfighting Leadership
Lesson 7

Persevere. Resolve to succeed. Leadership is the *glue* that keeps the fabric and psyche of organizations or nations steadfast until victory is achieved.

Perseverance, steadfastness, not giving way—all convey a sense of staying with the task until the desired end is achieved. This lesson applies to war, business, organizations, families, or individuals. In the context of this book, perseverance refers to the ability of leaders to make sure followers "press on" until the desired end is achieved. Leaders keep the mission and values alive, especially when things get tough and some want to quit, assuring they are embraced by the next generation if necessary. Leaders are the "psyche custodians" for their organization's collective thinking and actions just as the Commander in Chief, Congress, and senior military leaders are responsible for shaping our national psyche in times of war. "Press on" until the people are protected, the mission complete. The enemies of America include in their strategic assumptions that our people will grow impatient. They know we cannot be defeated if our will remains strong, so they try to cause enough pain for us to grow impatient and quit. This lesson uses Vietnam as a backdrop for the greatest external threat America is faced with today—the war against terrorism, but the lesson applies to other worthy causes as well.

Nothing in the world can take the place of persistence.
Talent will not, genius will not, education alone will not—
persistence and determination alone are omnipotent.
"Press on" has solved and will solve
the problems of the human race.
-President Calvin Coolidge-

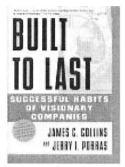 *Built to Last,* by James Collins and Jerry Porras, takes a detailed look at secrets to enduring companies—those that outlive their founders and prosper through tough economic cycles and times of considerable change. One secret is that leaders of such organizations pay close attention to the art of preserving the purpose and values—the core ideology or their reason for existence—and aggressively changing the rest to continue to prosper. We call this secret *the glue that keeps the fabric and psyche of the organization together.*

Two stories follow. They represent my experience with providing leadership to keep the fabric and psyche intact until the "battle is won." The first is a mini-review of a large organization I headed from 1985 to 1987, which needed to change to assure its legitimacy and prosperity. The second illustrates the need for perseverance on a much broader scale— the nation's (and Western culture's) war on terrorism. Together, they illustrate the greatest challenge senior leaders have—that of keeping their organizations and causes relevant and preserved in the minds and hearts of their stakeholders— the core reason for doing so is to achieve "victory."

Changing an Organization to Assure Its Prosperity

Thanks to the considerable efforts of historians in documenting the life and times of the U.S. Army Corps of Engineers Mobile District, 1815 - 2003, I am able to share observations about how that organization underwent accelerated cultural changes to meet the demands of its many stakeholders. The District is an organization of about 3,000 employees spread throughout forty field offices in the southeast United States and Latin America. Its primary mission is providing engineering studies and construction projects for both military and civil authorities. My role was to take the leadership mantle, do my part, then hand it off to my successor, thus keeping the prosperity process moving. The details of meeting that challenge are beyond the scope of this book, but the lessons I learned from that experience are relevant. My most difficult task was achieving "buy-in" from the varied subcultures concerning the organization's future. Accomplishing that required nurturing a climate of trust based on candor and respect, shedding entrenched beliefs—among them that sharing power is a sign of weakness, and fostering a belief in my employees that the commander's motives for change were for the sake of their future success instead of self-serving. Caring leadership, teamwork, mutual trust, clarity in communications, and values-based decisions made constructive change possible. These changes were made more difficult because of the mixed public and private sector nature of the work and involved stakeholders who based decisions on political expediency, election-year priorities, interest-group pressures, and congressional budget cycles. The continued success of that organization today speaks to the collective ability of a succession of commanders to be the glue that keeps the fabric of that organization together. The challenge of perseverance becomes even more acute at the national and global levels.

The National Case for Perseverance in War

A basic thread that runs through this second story is that our nation has historically engaged in major conflict at intervals that roughly align with each generation. Clearly, there are cycles of conflict versus relative peace. In times of peace, America has made a habit of compressing its military and sacrificing a degree of preparedness to address other priorities.

For a historical review of this phenomenon, read *America's First Battles 1776-1965* by Brigadier General William Stoff and Charles Heller. America's military serves at the pleasure of its people, and they are the last to seek the conflicts that seem to inevitably come their way. Therefore, this lesson on perseverance grew from a belief that there are some causes or wars that require a long period of time to be won but are no less worthy of the effort. In our nation's past, the Civil Rights Movement and Women's Suffrage were examples of such causes. This story is told to illustrate the need for the same type of tenacity in our current conflict, the War on Terrorism.

In an American culture where many are raised on and addicted to sound bites and immediate gratification, perseverance is at a premium. In truth, worthy causes require a sustained will to overcome the inevitable losses of momentum. Leaders are the keepers of the faith in this regard, ultimately accountable for helping followers endure for the long haul to find success.

A look at the Vietnam War experience and its aftermath will serve us well in our war against terrorism. We failed to apply the perseverance lesson 40 years ago and cannot, as a nation, afford to fail again. What follows is a blend of facts and opinion on my part. Some of my views will not be shared by all readers, but hopefully the general case for perseverance over decades will be a point of mutual agreement.

This lesson focuses on perseverance *once a decision to go to war is made.* Whether Vietnam was a "just war" or not is not addressed. Inevitably, there seldom will be unity in what constitutes a "just war" and Vietnam in retrospect was certainly questionable. It is always difficult to assess the full consequences of actions, so war, when executed is a good example of a *least-worst* choice (recall Gunfighting Professionals Lesson 5). Once a decision to go to war has been made, then follow through — adjusting to the unforeseen consequences — is paramount.

Those of you younger than 50 have not experienced a prolonged war and its impact on either our military or our nation's psyche, so I take you on a short journey back in time. In the late 1960s and early1970s, the military felt a crisis in confidence—the country was severely divided in its view of the war effort. In Vietnam, our enemy discovered that while they could not defeat us militarily, persistence could defeat us when the tide of internal dissention in America took hold. North Vietnamese General Vo Nguyen Giap said, "The United States will be caught in a dilemma; he has to drag out the war in order to win it and does not posses the psychological and political means to fight a long-drawn-out war." Unfortunately, he was right. We were not willing to engage in "attrition warfare," where one side decides to wear down the other to the point of losing patience and quitting.

General Giap possessed one of the finest military minds of the last century. His strategy to vanquish a militarily superior opponent was to undermine our resolve by inflicting political defeats. He launched a major surprise offensive against U.S. and South Vietnamese forces on the eve of the Lunar New Year. The cost in North Vietnamese casualties was tremendous, but the move was pivotal in galvanizing U.S. sentiment against President Lyndon Johnson and the war. *It broke the will of the American public to persevere.* Giap was perfectly aware of the peace movement and used this gambit to maintain a firm stance in the Paris negotiations and fracture the American will. I think his aggressive move, combined with the peace protests, prevented a U.S. victory. It is my belief that another year of U.S. pressure would have damaged the North Vietnamese capability to the point that the South Vietnamese forces could have secured a victory on their own despite the other constraints imposed on our forces. In addition, politically imposed orders prohibited us from pursuing the enemy into Cambodia, even in instances of hot pursuit to finish a battle. Therefore, North Vietnam used Cambodia as a sanctuary.

Initiative was sacrificed for the diplomatic fiction that Cambodia was neutral. In addition, President Johnson refused to activate the National Guard and reserve units; therefore, war was not a part of the fabric of the nation. Even though we fought with one arm tied behind our back, we won almost every tactical battle. Yet, we lost the war. We lacked the perseverance to win. The Army and the nation retreated in the 1970s for some serious introspection and soul searching.

In the 1980s, discipline, hard work, and resources restored the Armed Services' competence and confidence. The Gulf Conflict in the early 1990s proved that the quality of leadership and competence in the military had largely been restored. However, the post-Gulf conflict period of the 1990s saw the drastic weakening of the military's infrastructure, as we let our defenses down and allowed a depletion of the human intelligence component of our intelligence-gathering capability. It was clear, following the Cold War, that the military services needed to transform to a lighter, faster, more mobile force with new operational concepts, yet that path has been a rocky one.

Some downsizing in personnel was inevitable and appropriate. The services shrank in numbers from about 2 million personnel in 1991 to about 1.4 million in 2003. Downsizing while simultaneously increasing overseas commitments resulted in extended stays of more military personnel in hostile areas. Today, with 130,000 troops in Iraq and almost 80,000 more in Korea, Kuwait, Afghanistan, and the Balkans, the services are stressed during clean-up and rebuilding operations. The soundness of our ability to plan and execute battle has again been proven, but post-conflict operations put considerable stress on our remaining military capabilities. In the active Army, the service most employed to remain, peacekeeping operations has been reduced to 485,000; 65 percent are married. Of the 370,000 Army soldiers (Active, Reserve and National Guard) overseas in 120 countries, 215,000 are without their families. More needs to be done to help our soldiers.

In addition to the increased stress on personnel, our armaments have been strained. Many weapons systems and platforms have been allowed to age without appropriate replacement (e.g. the B-52 bomber is more than four decades old, air refueling platforms are rusting out, etc.). Not so readily evident, but equally important, is the loss of intellectual capability from cuts in education funds. As a result, the intellectual products derived from education suffer.

The cost of procrastination and 1990s downsizing will be high. Former President Clinton's disdain for the importance and traditions of the military strained relationships between the services and the administration and led to cuts in the bone marrow of the services—its people, their education, and programs aimed at family cohesiveness. The perseverance required will place stress on the ability to retain the best and the brightest of those remaining in the wake of such cuts.

Private military companies (PMCs) have a long history of providing support to the military in times of war. An added consequence of belt tightening is the continued pressure to increase the use of PMCs to handle more essential high-tech systems and support functions for the military. The increasingly contractor-dependent military raises the risk that at any time civilian employees from PMCs could refuse to deploy or refuse to return to a high-risk location, and in doing so threaten a critical military operation. A PMCs' ultimate duty is to its shareholders, yet many of the highly complex weapons systems we now use are so complex the military must depend on expert civilians to maintain and, in some cases, operate them. The Global Hawk drone, M1A1 tank, Patriot missile, etc., are all heavily contractor-dependent. Contractor support is a working partner of our military, but not a proxy for it. The military is still "the glue" in leading the perseverance cause.

While the services tightened their belts in the 1990s, the drums of war continued to beat in foreign lands, and we pretended not to hear. We made a lot of money, focused on entertainment, and became an easy target. With the 9/11 terrorist attacks, the pendulum swung back up again with a rebirth of national fervor for the common defense. While awakened, it remains a challenge to stay awake. The ebb and flow of the current Iraq situation shows the delicate nature of "national fervor."

Our preparedness comes in cycles—almost by decade. We have entered an up cycle as the challenge of Al-Qaeda (and other terrorist groups) remains before us. In our war on terror, our senior civilian and military leaders must be *the glue* that keeps the fabric of our armed services and nation together throughout the up-and-down cycles of this protracted conflict.

For the Army, West Point serves as the "leadership glue factory." David Lipsky, author of *Absolute American*, was raised to dislike the military. His father promised "to have his legs broken" if he pursued the military profession. As an adult writer for *Rolling Stones* magazine, he became a specialist in the college generation. After covering 35 colleges, he was given an assignment to cover cadets at the United States Military Academy. He spent four years studying the way cadets unlearn many of the habits and instincts they brought with them and graduate with a new set of professional skills, habits, and instincts to serve as *glue soldiers*—the keepers of the flame for the Army institution. He gained an appreciation for graduates and the role they play in keeping the fabric of the Army together. The challenge now is to have enough graduates make the military a career and thus help keep the professional ethos of the Army together through this protracted conflict. The same role holds true for the other service academies.

Why will this war against terror take so long? Because this war is between two ways of thinking and action. It won't end with an armistice or peace treaty. In the mind of the Jihadist, Islam is in mortal danger of western corruption and cleansing requires defeating us—their hatred is consuming. They will fight until all infidels are destroyed. They are committed to spectacular violence without limits—they have no regard for civilized rules of warfare. Their "weapons system" is religious dedication where dying for the cause is heroism. According to a recent Rand Corporation study, "their brand of religion justifies a protracted war and gives them the moral basis under the guise of the will of Allah." Western thinking relies on reason and logic—rational ways of knowing and acting. Born of reason, America, through its intellectual, economic, and military might, is the world capital of this type philosophy. Therefore, in this war our enemy's target is anything and everyone that is American. Unfortunately, the only way for Americans and democracy to win is with "the spirit of the bayonet" and all the actionable intelligence and firepower we can concentrate against each individual terrorist cell. This terrorism war should not be measured in months, but in years. It is a war of continuance. Until Vietnam, our nations' wars did not last over four years. This war on terrorism will last much longer. With a strategy like General Giap's in Vietnam, it is prudent to bet that terrorists believe that a few casualties a day will, in time, wear on the nation's psyche. To compound the challenge, local tribal customs perpetuate the conflict. For example, some Arabs believe in the "rule of five" that requires that if something is done to someone, then five of his bloodlines are obligated to attack in response. Such ancient customs make the fight continue through generations. Our people and our Army will have to weather the ups and downs of cycles of preparedness and impatience and stay the course—probably for generations. Only true professional leaders who have earned our trust can keep the nation awake and committed to do that.

You don't defeat the enemy, you defeat the enemy's will.
-Sun Tzu-

While battles are won by soldiers well led, wars are won with a shared perseverance of the American people to go the distance. War requires almost infinite patience. It tends to play out in agonizing slowness. Wars are not able to be choreographed to end at a certain point. There is much darkness before the dawn. But there is a sign of light. Judge Don Walters was part of a 12-man team in Iraq evaluating the justice system. Upon his return, he extolled the rapid resurgence of sanity and services in Iraq at an unprecedented rate compared to the post-war recoveries of Germany and Japan.

Whether in a prolonged war or a prolonged "battle" with competitors for market share, perseverance—the will to go the long haul—is a key to victory. In the war on terror, our senior leaders, regardless of political affiliation, must be able to keep the psyche of our people intact. Americans can learn a great deal from Israel in this regard. Their seemingly unending conflict continually acts to drain their national spirit and needs constant nourishment. We simply have to follow their lead, and not give terrorists the same strategic advantage we gave General Giap over three decades ago. As a people, we must display to the world the capacity for debate but use only one voice when it comes to a willingness to win and protect our people—however many years or generations that takes.

No matter how long it may take us to overcome this premeditated invasion, the American people, in their righteous might, will win through to absolute victory.
-President Franklin D. Roosevelt-
(after Pearl Harbor, December 7, 1941)

The above story shows that the perseverance lesson is most dramatically illustrated at the strategic/societal level of leadership. The statesman leader exerts influence in a global, competitive setting where conflict and fiercely competitive ideologies interact to impact generations. Even so, this lesson applies to every professional and leader regardless of level. President Coolidge's charge to "press on" is a requisite for victory—in war, in life. As a nation, we cannot afford to set a snooze alarm—we must stay constantly awake and vigilant.

After the Call to Action, in which we summarize the core lessons for your internalization, you will find Tools for Assessment and Action. A separate workbook with a Capstone Exercise to help you complete an assessment and develop a strategy for stress is available by ordering from Dyson Institute or attending a seminar.

Summary of Lessons and Call to Action

7 Lessons for True Professionals

These lessons and actions can complement strategy and best practices for your professional life—to use and teach.

1. **Prepare character and competence to develop disciplined habits and instincts to do the right things well, even under stress, thus earning trust in self and from others.** Identify areas of improvement and change as priorities in plans and invest in learning and development to expand capacities. True leaders develop personal leadership and serve others first, then lead where they can to fulfill their callings and do the most good.

2. **Earn empowerment rather than wait for it**. Admit that you are more responsible for your performance and growth than is your supervisor. Accept that your responsibilities, results, and rewards come from you, first, and partners second. Identify desired results, improvements, and actions in your professional plan. Anticipate what your supervisory leader needs to trust you have earned empowerment. Help your "manager" serve more like a mentor by presenting your plan with stated intent and seeking coaching, putting callings and stewardship before ego. Proactively seek to develop higher levels of trust in your competence and character for the seven levels of empowerment: (1) Tell, (2) Teach, (3) Direct, (4) Coach, (5) Support, (6) Delegate, (7) Empower.

3. **Practice "no excuses" accountability.** Own it! Focus on solutions and results as well as efforts, taking responsibility for the mission and your part. Mitigating circumstances often affect an outcome, but one person is ultimately accountable.

4. **Develop ethical fitness and decision-making from the start.** Loss of trust in character is harder to restore than well-intentioned mistakes or under-developed competencies. People are more willing to forgive failure

through valiant effort than intentional violations of trust. Have personal and organizational training to reinforce how to make tough ethical decisions and choose *the harder right*. Stay aware that good "intent" does not always equal good "impact" and perception and truth do not always match.

5. **Decide to think with positive expectancy and make the best of situations.** People face many disappointments and paradoxes in professional and other areas of life, especially when the stakes get high and stressful. Learn to make peace with them, persist, and "bounce high" when you fall.

6. **Fulfill your calling and live a legacy to find meaning.** Money is like oxygen; you need it, but it does not give meaning to life. Design your life to be a masterpiece. Write and internalize your mission, vision, and legacy.

7. **Be a champion for your calling, your profession, people you serve, and your organization.** Choose to develop a world-class "A" level attitude with commitment and courage toward seeking mastery in your competence. Work on your plan for life until getting to an "A" level of believing you have discerned your callings and written your choices. Identify and describe your desired legacy, then persist with commitment to fulfill it. Demonstrate character to keep promises and do the right things, even under stress. Develop confidence as you take action rather than waiting for confidence before you take action. Grow in your sense of connection to projects and the people working on them, matching on mission and values more than on personality. Develop from the inside-out genuine charisma based on character and competence that attracts people who want to work with you on common goals. Serve as a champion for people and organizations of good intent, helping them identify and fulfill their callings, gifts, and talents toward stewardship and with distinction.

7 Lessons for Stress

The lessons help people prepare for normal and intense stress, such as emergencies, being or feeling ambushed, ethical dilemmas, and other unanticipated challenges. Responses to stress can start before it happens—prepare, act, and then react.

1. **Develop your *Fitness Package* for the 7 areas of life.** Be good at the basics. *Physical:* start with the basics of sleep, breathing, nutrition, and exercise—avoiding addictive substances and behavior—to create an energy platform needed for resiliency. *Financial:* living within your means helps your attitude, health, and relationships, minimizing stress over money. *Professional:* a plan with direction and priorities leading you to desired results boosts inspiration, performance and rewards. *Personal:* a plan for life to fulfill your callings and care for your needs. *Social:* handling stress positively helps build positive relationships and minimizes self-inflicted conflicts from reacting to painful stress and broken trusts negatively. *Philanthropical:* taking time to contribute beyond ourselves gives an extra sense of meaning and joy. *Spiritual:* identifying, developing, and fulfilling callings, gifts, and talents is at the heart of significant living when done in obedience, love, and service. Purpose, fitness, and balance help you *feel in the flow of living instead of feeling dragged along by the current.*

2. **Identify sources of stress.** Ask and answer what causes stress for you–and why—so you can prioritize ways to leverage good stress and mitigate bad stress.

3. **Distinguish between good and bad stress.** Good stress can provide a positive edge that leads to motivation, focus, and energy to act on priorities. Bad stress often comes from feeling unprepared, unsatisfied with actions and/or results, and unsure if competencies or resources will meet demands. Assess your stressors as good or bad to help you develop strategies for stress.

4. **Develop a strategy for normal and intense stress.**
Anticipate stress; feeling pressure is inevitable, especially if
you seek to serve in significant ways. Decide in advance
how you will behave as your best-self to leverage good
stress and mitigate negative pressure. Discern if the
solution is greater immediate investment of time and
energy working on priorities or improving your "fitness
package" to prepare for and respond to stressful pressures.
5. **Use stress to help you achieve peak performance.** Stress
from challenging goals and pressure to perform can boost
success if you have mastered actions through mental and
physical rehearsal and are prepared and focused on
priorities. Use these experiences to improve your
capabilities and capacity to absorb stress.
6. **Practice *safe stress* in advance.** Seek simulations and other
opportunities to practice and test yourself—expand your
comfort zones—before the stakes get high. Example in the
military: war games that simulate real conditions. Example
in civilian life: set up advance deadlines to put pressure on
yourself to deliver on a project early, giving you time to
improve instead of waiting until the stress turns negative.
Feeling prepared reduces stress and improves performance.
7. **Create structures, rituals, and habits to proactively
leverage positive stress and mitigate negative stress.**
Create appointments with yourself and others to invest the
time and effort needed to fulfill priorities. Identify honestly
what you need to break through barriers to go to the next
level of character and competence, plus service and
achievement. Until you develop your personal integrity to
levels of maturity in which you virtually always keep
promises, invite accountability partners to help you take
action. Start rituals that become habits consistent with
where you want to go and who you want to be. While
God's natural law is ultimately in control, people prepare,
take action, and handle life stressors.

7 Lessons for Gunfighting Professionals

The lessons focus primarily on soldiers, first-responders, and others in life-endangering professions. They also apply in other areas of civilian life, with simple and creative adaptations.

1. **Develop a "soldier's heart" through spiritual centeredness.** Prayerfully internalize your purpose through sincere introspection to know the reasons you fight. Reconcile suffering and killing before going into combat. Internalize the warrior ethos. Believe in yourself and the cause you serve. The noble warrior is an instrument of his people with a honed sense of civilized equilibrium in a harsh profession.

2. **Anticipate feeling absolute fear under stress and prepare your instincts so you can trust them.** Fear freezes. The ability to maintain control starts with one's frame of mind. Successful outcomes to stressful engagements are often dependent on "pucker factor" (functioning well under stress). Fear often comes from the unknown. Learn in advance as much as you can about the realities of what you are likely to face. Train your mind in advance under realistic conditions using simulations and drills to hone reasoning and decision-making skills with absolute trust in your instincts as your goal. Once confronted, you only have time to execute!

3. **Find seasoned Noncommissioned Officers (NCOs) to serve as mentors and teachers.** Seasoned veterans help you move from "book smarts" to "street smarts" in learning the profession. They provide a bridge to learning the meaning of caring for others.

4. **Be tough. Experience extreme physical and mental stressors like prolonged intensity of focus and sleep deprivation to develop habits, instincts, and endurance to function effectively for long periods under tough conditions.** If in the military, attend Army Ranger School, Navy SEAL Course, Marine Recon, Air Force Special

Operations School, or other training that prepares your mind and body for real conditions. If a first-responder, seek SWAT training or the equivalent. The public can attend conditioning, sports, and other training camps. Reputable similar experiences work to help you supercompensate through systematic exposure to greater stress followed by recovery. Develop discipline to self-start, stretch capacities, and maintain your fitness package. Short-term "pain" pushing your comfort zones is a prerequisite to prepare for intense stress, though the experience yields lifetime benefit.

5. **Prepare for paradoxes and having to choose the *least–worst* option.** Many times in battle and in life there are no desirable options—all have negative consequences. In war, tough decisions have to be made under extraordinary circumstances, such as when the enemy has no regard for non-combatants. Innocent people are sometimes casualties, clearly an undesirable option, but sometimes the "least-worst" choice available. Noble soldiers will go to any length to protect their own and other innocents, yet the "fog of war" sometimes means losses through "friendly fire." Soldiers of honor detest loss of life, yet must anticipate and prepare for the possibility. Most civilian professions have their own harsh paradoxes to face, such as budget cuts affecting good people and projects for the greater good.

6. **Be decisive, aggressive, even audacious—indecisiveness is a fatal flaw.** Visualize and prepare for taking decisive action in anticipated scenarios. Audacious, daring action can help "rally the troops" and turn a battle in your favor. To assure understanding, communicate with simplicity and clarity.

7. **Put your personal affairs in order.** Those who love their families will honor them by preparing for the possibility of not returning. Preparing a plan for the end of life is sound for all adults, especially those in high-risk professions.

7 Lessons for Gunfighting Leaders

1. **Make gunfighting a last resort. When conflict is a necessity, make it a part of our nation's fiber.**
Gunfighting, in battle or the boardroom, should be a last resort—only when the "least-worst" option. Whether real or metaphorical, gunfighting is not a video game—war is indeed "hell" and should never be romanticized. When war is waged, mobilizing National Guard, Reserve units, and private-sector contractors is essential policy. Strategic military and civilian thinkers must continually shape the roles and relationships of both sectors for maximum cooperation and mutual benefit for the good of the country in both peace and war. Thus, America's military remains relevant in peace and prepared for war.

2. **Make sure the best leaders do the leading while troublesome "leaders" are removed.** Holding a title that indicates a position of leadership does not make a leader. In battle, as well as in business and life, ill-prepared leaders can be almost as dangerous as the enemy. War requires tough battlefield policies, one of the most important being that the best should lead. While some may find it unfair that the most talented to lead may bear the most risk, the best leaders are best equipped to deal with it—in terms of completing the mission and caring for those they lead.

3. **State intent, expectations, and parameters directly and simply to encourage clarity and initiative.** Direction, boundaries, and rules boost initiative instead of restrict it—an often-misunderstood paradox—as they provide a framework to "go for it your way." Without clarity, many avoid risk and wait for direction. Tell people your expectations and why they can and should succeed, which can increase commitment, confidence, and action. The greater the number of people involved and greater the separation from them, the greater the effort needed to state simply, clearly, and consistently.

4. **Lead by actions, not just position or personality; demonstrate humility with character and competence.** A substantial portion of ability to influence others to meet exceptional standards stems from a leader's action, presence, demeanor, and charisma. The most effective leaders demonstrate humility motivated by mission and service to others instead of excessive ego or ambition for personal gain.

5. **Prepare yourself and your unit for suffering and death; carry out death notification with dignity.** In either the military or corporate arena, be ready to assume more responsibility and prepare leader replacements for losses. Accomplish the mission first; mourn later. Conveying the loss of a loved one is a solemn duty. Deal with loss thoroughly with compassion.

6. **Keep the memory of loss and sacrifice alive; memorials and remembrances matter.** Memorials offer links to fallen warriors and reminders of the price paid for freedom by America's "human shields." While in combat, soldiers must postpone dealing with grief. Memorials are an agent for cleansing and healing, as well as fuel for perseverance in trying times. While keeping the memory alive, they help those remaining move forward. This lesson applies to those lost in any profession charged with protecting others or individuals giving their lives for others.

7. **Persevere. Resolve to succeed. Leadership is the *glue* that keeps the fabric and psyche of organizations or nations steadfast until victory is achieved.** Leaders keep the mission, values, and vision alive, especially when times get tough and some want to quit. Leaders are the "psychic custodians" for their organization's collective thinking and actions.

Call to Action

We summarize the four sets of seven lessons into seven summary actions to help you internalize and implement. Living as your best-self—capable of meeting life's normal and acutely stressful situations—requires learning lessons and implementing a personal and professional life plan.

Philosophy

To be a true professional and leader in life often requires changing our ways of thinking—our paradigms, beliefs, and expectations—that govern our instincts and actions.

1. **Decide to develop personal leadership and serve as a true professional.** Choose to prepare your character and competence to develop thinking, plans, habits, and instincts to expand your capacity to do the right things well, automatically, even under stress. This prepares you for growth in the leadership of others from team through organizational and even societal leadership.

2. **Earn empowerment** rather than wait for it, practicing *no excuse accountability* for your promises.

3. **Think with positive expectancy and persevere.** Anticipate how you will make peace with paradoxes, least-worst decisions, and disappointments so you can react positively to them. Develop your attitude of commitment and confidence along with your skills and knowledge.

Plan

Leaders in life as well as in organizations invest in *design before construction.* Even if spending only minutes per day identifying and writing callings and plans, this habit must get action. Only an estimated 5% of people put this principle into practice, yet this is both scriptural and common sense truth. When our systems, social traditions, and habits include plans that inspire and guide, quality of thinking and behavior will increase and crimes of ethics, waste, and violence will decrease.

4. **PLAN and LEAD in LIFE and your called profession.** Pray. Listen. Act. Now. (PLAN) to choose your calling. Design the life you are called to lead and the legacy you want to live. Write your plan for life and read it regularly. Include in your plan a vision of what living as your best-self looks like; develop in advance a quick response strategy for acute stress, challenge, and disappointment.

Practice

5. **Prepare your instincts** in advance so you can trust them. **Practice safe stress** before the stakes get too high. Share your plans with stakeholders to **state intent, expectations, and parameters**—for yourself and others—and to **help managers operate more like mentors**.

6. **Develop a fitness package for the 7 areas of life** to help you renew, improve, and consistently live your priorities as your best-self, even under stress.

7. Use assessment tools to **identify sources of stress and strategies for stress**. Plan and implement proactive strategy to leverage good stress and mitigate bad stress.

Assessment and Action Plan Tools

We offer those who embrace the essence of our ideas tools that capture the spirit of the lessons. We provide these templates and tools to help you take action:

- Professionalism Assessment and Action Plan
- Professional Plan Template
- Personal Life Plan Template
- Wheel of Balance and Action Plan
- Fitness Package Assessment and Action Plan
- T.I.M.E. Checkup and Action Plan
- Gunfighting Assessment and Action Plan
- Abstracts of Capstone Workbook and Companion Book

Professionalism Assessment

Purpose: to assess your level of trust in self, and commitment/confidence in your team/organization.

Instructions: Assess where you are **Now** and the level **Desired**.

Scale: Circle A-F (A=excellent, B=good, C=satisfactory, D=poor, F=failure).

Trust in Myself for the 7 Components of Attitude/Character	Now	Desired
1. **Choices**—I have identified my callings and written plans for my life that inspire and guide me.	ABCDF	ABCDF
2. **Commitment**—I am dedicated to my callings/priorities, and pursue them…	ABCDF	ABCDF
3. **Character**—I do what I say I will… keeping promises to myself and others.	ABCDF	ABCDF
4. **Courage**—I act on what is important, even before feeling totally confident.	ABCDF	ABCDF
5. **Confidence**—I believe in my character/competence—attitude/ability.	ABCDF	ABCDF
6. **Connection**—I feel connected to the people and projects I serve.	ABCDF	ABCDF
7. **Charisma**—I attract, inspire and encourage like-minded people who match on goals and values to work with me.	ABCDF	ABCDF
Trust in Myself for the 7 Components of Ability/Competence	**Now**	**Desired**
Skills		
1. **Experience**—I have good first-hand skills for my responsibilities.	ABCDF	ABCDF
2. **Practice**—I prepare in advance for performing important actions.	ABCDF	ABCDF
3. **Habits/Instincts**—I have designed and follow good habits that develop instincts to do the right things well, automatically, even under stress.	ABCDF	ABCDF
Knowledge		
4. **Education**—I have academic preparation…for my profession/other areas.	ABCDF	ABCDF
5. **Training**—I invest in instruction/coaching related to core purposes…	ABCDF	ABCDF
6. **Self-study**—I continuously learn and improve knowledge about key areas related to my callings and capacities, as well as people I wish to emulate.	ABCDF	ABCDF
7. **Observation**—I watch others who are masters to emulate their inspiration, actions, and results.	ABCDF	ABCDF
Trust in Myself for 7 Lessons of Professionalism	**Now**	**Desired**
1. **Professionalism**—I earn trust by developing my character and competence.	ABCDF	ABCDF
2. **Empowerment**—I earn empowerment rather than wait for it to add value and responsibility.	ABCDF	ABCDF
3. **Accountability**—I own my responsibilities, efforts, and results; when things do not go as planned I seek solutions.	ABCDF	ABCDF
4. **Ethical fitness**—I have identified my desired beliefs/values that lead to ethical behavior, even when tempted, under stress, or "ambushed."	ABCDF	ABCDF
5. **Positive expectancy**—I envision success with hope and bounce back from disappointments.	ABCDF	ABCDF
6. **Legacy**—I have written the legacy I seek to leave, which motivates and guides my priorities.	ABCDF	ABCDF
7. **Champion**—I am a *champion* for my profession, people and organizations.	ABCDF	ABCDF
Trust in My Team and Me	**Now**	**Desired**
Commitment—I am loyal to my position, roles, goals…people and projects.	ABCDF	ABCDF
Confidence—I believe in our collective ability to serve and succeed.	ABCDF	ABCDF
Trust in My Organization and Me	**Now**	**Desire**
Commitment—I am loyal to the organization, its mission, and my accountability to my part in our success.	ABCDF	ABCDF
Confidence—I believe in our organization, plan, systems, leadership, and our ability to succeed.	ABCDF	ABCDF

Professionalism Action Plan

Purpose: tool to help you identify areas of priority, concern, and barriers, then develop solutions to achieve higher levels of attitude/character and ability/competence.

Admit the truth about the person you feel called to be—where you are and where you desire to be—and the barriers.

Accept the impact if you stay the same and envision the results if you take action.

Act to identify how you could do your best, what you should do and what you need from others.

List the top areas that merit development to build your capacity to be your best-self. What key **actions and habits** could help you get to your goal?

List **barriers** that keep you from improving and threaten your ability to retain your capacities/opportunities. List **actions and rituals** you could start to form habits and develop yourself to overcome these barriers.

List what you need from others to succeed. Admit what you need from your **supervisory leader or team** to succeed at a higher level or overcome a barrier. State what information or assistance you **need from your organization**.

Input for Stress Assessment: As a result of this assessment, list specific areas that cause you stress. Focus on what matters most where the greatest grade difference lies. For example, my stress is: *My "empowerment" current grade level is "D" and I seek "A" but my boss is not receptive to the concept. I am unable to convince my boss that I should be empowered to fulfill my primary responsibilities.*

Professional Plan Summary

Mission of my Position
(purpose/main reason...)

To...

My Vision for Impact on others
(legacy / desired results from my service on my colleagues, company, community...)

Colleagues: I...
Clients:
Company:
Community:

Contributions (the most important things I do)

7 Diamonds of Excellence	Key services & benefits	Empowerment level
1. Opportunity/Business Dev.		
2. Client Service/Promises		
3. Financial Results/Admin.		
4. Personal/Prof. Dev.		
5. People Dev.		
6. Organizational Dev.		
7. Association/Community		

Goals and Important Activities

7 Diamonds of Excellence	Results Desired	Action
1. Opportunity/Business Dev.		
2. Client Service		
3. Financial Results/Admin.		
4. Personal/Prof. Dev.		
5. People Dev.		
6. Organizational Dev.		
7. Association/Community		

Time Priorities—Hours / Week

7 Diamonds of Excellence	Now	Vision	Action
1. Opportunity/Business Dev.			
2. Client Service			
3. Financial Results/Admin.			
4. Personal/Prof. Dev.			
5. People Dev.			
6. Organizational Dev.			
7. Association/Community			

Professional Constitution and Capabilities

Mission
(Calling or purpose)

To...

Vision for Impact on others / Desired Results
(Legacy / results from my service on my…)

Clients

Colleagues

Company

Community

Core Capabilities
(Roles / areas and key contributions / benefits to others)

Professional Distinctions
(1-7 differentiators of you, your services, or your organization you want people to know when choosing or advocating you)

Preparation and Experience

Education / Training

Service / Experience

Personal
(Family/Personal Interests/Volunteer)

Contact
(Phone, fax, email, web site, address…)

Call to Action   269

Personal Constitution

Mission
(my life purpose)

To:

Vision Summary
(person I am called to be / life I want to lead—affirmations...)

I...

Physical

Financial

Professional

Personal

Social

Philanthropical

Spiritual

Callings, Gifts and Talents

Callings
(Passions, likes, loves..., I have always wanted to ..., I feel God wants me to ...)

Gifts and Talents
(Spiritual gifts such as Leadership, Teaching, Administration, Mercy...)
(Specific talents/things I do well such as computers, speaking...)

Roles, Goals, & Important Actions

(IMPACT) Summary for 7 Areas of Life

Area of Life / Role	Goal / Desired Result	Activity / Action
Physical		
Financial		
Professional		
Personal		
Social		
Philanthropical		
Spiritual		

Professionalism Under Stress / Dunn and Dyson

7 Steps to Achieve a Priority Resolution

To Achieve, Improve, Change, Transform, or "Master a Goliath"…

Plan

1. Resolution purpose / area to improve or change / area of transformation / Goliath to master (mission):

2. Describe what results you want (vision).

3. Answer why you should succeed—the reasons to follow through (motivation).

4. Consider how you could accomplish the goal—the major steps on your journey—actions, time—how many hours and when, money, assistance needed, accountability, systems, structures… (plans & assessment).

Decision

5. Decide if you are willing to follow through to fulfill the resolution (choice), if you place higher value on these results and activities than the ones you must replace or reduce time for (priorities). If no, accept. If yes, I will follow my plan enthusiastically, adjusting as needed, until ❏ this date _____ ❏ assess and decide to change ❏ I succeed

_____   _____
Resolved   Accountability partner

Action

6. Read and affirm your resolution daily, preferably aloud, to focus your thoughts, renew your motivation, internalize your mission, and strengthen your commitment needed to create and sustain momentum (conditioning).

7. Increase probability of success by making the right actions automatic—target times for appointments with yourself and others for action to insure investing the time needed (structure) until you form habits and instincts. Compare efforts of TIME (Time. Inspiration. Money. Energy) and effectiveness with vision and results (assessment); adjust as needed to close gaps(personal integrity); Set up positive and negative rewards (system); share your resolution with a trusted accountability partner and ask for specific support such as listening, encouraging, reminding, coaching… (accountability).

Wheel of Balance Assessment

Assess your grade on each spoke at this time. Then, connect the dots to see how balanced your wheels are for life. As you assess, admit the truth about imbalances and stressors though also consider that no one is completely fulfilled in all areas.

The goal should be relatively equal balance based on values and circumstances not equal time, inspiration, money, and energy invested in each. The possibility of fulfilling good results in one area might take 50 hours and only five in another.

Your view of balance may vary with stage in life. Significant imbalance in any area normally will increase stress. Use the information from this simple tool to assist in the development of your stress strategy.

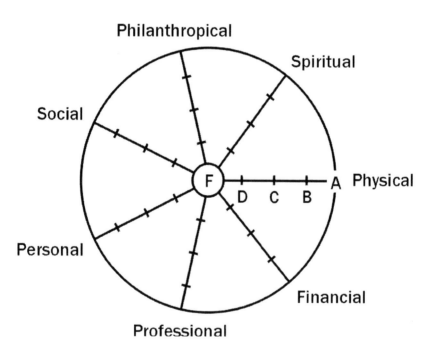

Wheel of Balance Action Plan

List areas of greatest importance and imbalance. **Prioritize** by numbering 1…

For each important area of imbalance, what **"bite size" actions** can I take to meaningfully move me in a positive direction?

Input for Stress Assessment: As a result of this assessment, list specific areas that cause you stress. Focus on what matters most where the greatest grade difference lies. For example, my stress is: *My wheel clearly shows that my physical and spiritual areas are grossly imbalanced. I lack the drive to live a healthy lifestyle and seek a sense of spiritual calmness.*

Fitness Package Assessment

Purpose: to assess your levels of fitness the 7 areas of life.

Instructions: Read each statement and assess where you are **Now** and level **Desired**.

Scale: Circle A-F (A=excellent, B=good, C=satisfactory, D=poor, F=failure)

Physical Fitness—The Energy Platform	Now	Desired
I **exercise** regularly (at least three times per week) for a minimum of thirty minutes each time	ABCDF	ABCDF
I **eat** nutritious foods most of the time and "fun" foods in moderation.	ABCDF	ABCDF
I **sleep** well and feel rested when I awake.	ABCDF	ABCDF
I know my **natural rhythms** and use them to my advantage to work at peak capacity	ABCDF	ABCDF
I build more **sustained capacity** through supercompensation [Challenging one's physical, emotional, and spiritual "muscle" past its current limits to build more sustained capacity].	ABCDF	ABCDF
I do the **basics** like drink at least 6-10 glasses of water and breath deeply several times each day.	ABCDF	ABCDF
I am generally healthy with minimal suffering from sinus/allergy, headaches, mood swings, fatigue, indigestion, or other problems caused by stress.	ABCDF	ABCDF
Financial Fitness	Now	Desired
I am living within my means.	ABCDF	ABCDF
I am investing to satisfy future **financial security** needs.	ABCDF	ABCDF
I have a working knowledge of **budgeting** and **financial planning**.	ABCDF	ABCDF

Professional Fitness (Covered Separately in Professional Assessment)

Personal Fitness	Now	Desired
My **fitness rating** in the following areas is:		
Ethical Fitness	ABCDF	ABCDF
Mental Stability/Sharpness	ABCDF	ABCDF
Emotional Strength	ABCDF	ABCDF
Attitude and Outlook	ABCDF	ABCDF
Judgment	ABCDF	ABCDF
Cultural Awareness	ABCDF	ABCDF
Inquisitiveness	ABCDF	ABCDF
Social Fitness	Now	Desire
I reunite with **family and friends** in a positive, enjoyable manner regularly.	ABCDF	ABCDF
I have **others** for whom I care deeply.	ABCDF	ABCDF
I have **fun** regularly.	ABCDF	ABCDF
I am "enjoying life's journey."	ABCDF	ABCDF
Philanthropical Fitness	Now	Desire
I volunteer in civic/educational organizations or charitable causes.	ABCDF	ABCDF
I give financially to civic/educational organizations or charitable causes.	ABCDF	ABCDF
My written legacy includes plans to contribute meaningfully to others.	ABCDF	ABCDF
Spiritual Fitness	Now	Desire
I believe in a higher power from which I draw strength and comfort.	ABCDF	ABCDF
I feel a sense of spiritual centeredness, a calmness of heart.	ABCDF	ABCDF
I invest in prayer, study, and service in a spiritual organization.	ABCDF	ABCDF

Fitness Package Action Plan

Purpose: to provide a simple tool to help you take "bite size" action steps to regain or maintain a sense of balance.

Admit the truth about where you are and desire to be

Accept the impact if you stay the same or if you take action.

Act to identify how you could move in a positive direction in areas that need work.

For each area of greatest grade difference, what "**bite size**" actions can I take in each to meaningfully move in a positive direction? For example: *Area—I don't live within my means; Action—sell 2nd car and consolidate and pay off credit card debt.*

Input for Stress Assessment: As a result of this assessment, list specific areas that cause you stress. Normally these will be those where the greatest grade difference lies. For example, my stress is: *My physical fitness grades are bad and I am unable to break a cycle of fatigue, low energy, and sleeplessness.*

T.I.M.E. Checkup

Scale: Circle appropriate grade for where you are now and desire to be (A=excellent to F=failure).

Time	Now	Desired
I spend enough *quantity* time on *what* matters most—*personal.*	A B C D F	A B C D F
I spend enough *quantity* time on who and what matters most—*social.*	A B C D F	A B C D F
I spend enough *quantity* time on what is most important—*professional.*	A B C D F	A B C D F
The *quality* of the time I invest is high with focus and energy.	A B C D F	A B C D F
I assess my time use in relation to my priorities regularly.	A B C D F	A B C D F
I have knowledge of time and life leadership principles and practices.	A B C D F	A B C D F
Inspiration	**Now**	**Desired**
I have identified and written my callings, gifts and talents	A B C D F	A B C D F
My plan includes my callings/mission, vision, legacy, goals, priorities…	A B C D F	A B C D F
My plan includes written desired values/beliefs and a vision for them.	A B C D F	A B C D F
I feel a sense of mission in life and for my callings, gifts, talents…	A B C D F	A B C D F
I feel inspired by my desired legacy.	A B C D F	A B C D F
I feel inspired about my life—or at least the potential and direction.	A B C D F	A B C D F
I feel wanted and valued in my *social* relationships.	A B C D F	A B C D F
I feel wanted and valued in my *professional* relationships.	A B C D F	A B C D F
I have the character and commitment…to do most of what is important.	A B C D F	A B C D F
I have the ability/competence to do most of what is important.	A B C D F	A B C D F
Money	**Now**	**Desired**
I understand money gained is a by-product of invested time, inspiration, money, energy.	A B C D F	A B C D F
I understand what results and actions get rewarded in my profession…	A B C D F	A B C D F
I invest enough time and effort in what gets rewarded financially.	A B C D F	A B C D F
I am living within my means.	A B C D F	A B C D F
I am investing to satisfy needs for future fiscal security.	A B C D F	A B C D F
I have knowledge of financial matters—budgeting, purchasing…	A B C D F	A B C D F
Energy	**Now**	**Desired**
My *physical* energy keeps me going at work and home until time to rest.	A B C D F	A B C D F
My *intellectual* energy keeps me interested and focused.	A B C D F	A B C D F
My *emotional* resilience to setbacks is high and I renew quickly.	A B C D F	A B C D F
I can work with focus and enthusiasm for as long as needed.	A B C D F	A B C D F
I have energy for important people and things after my work is done.	A B C D F	A B C D F
I do the basics well like drink 6-10 glasses of water daily.	A B C D F	A B C D F
I sleep well and feel rested when I wake.	A B C D F	A B C D F
I eat nutritious foods most of the time and "fun" foods in moderation.	A B C D F	A B C D F
I breathe deeply at least several times per day.	A B C D F	A B C D F
I do vigorous exercise or physical work 3+ times per week.	A B C D F	A B C D F
I keep good posture and positive facial expressions most of the time.	A B C D F	A B C D F
I know my natural body rhythms and take advantage of them.	A B C D F	A B C D F
I supercompensate to extend my physical/emotional energy.	A B C D F	A B C D F

T.I.M.E. Action Plan

Purpose: to provide a simple tool to help you take "bite size" action steps to improve T.I.M.E.
Admit the truth about where you are and desire to be
Accept the impact if you stay the same or if you take action.
Act to identify how you could move in a positive direction in areas that need work.

Time

Inspiration

Money

Energy

Input for Stress Assessment: As a result of this assessment, list specific areas that cause you stress. Focus on what matters most, what holds you back, and where you could affect change. For example: *I am not living within my means and I can't manage my budget. [Sample action: I will only purchase necessities until I am living within my income.]*

Gunfighting Assessment

Purpose: to assess your levels of satisfaction with your preparation for combat.
All the services offer extensive training to prepare personnel for combat. This assessment supplements that training with questions for young military personnel who seek to enhance their preparation based on our gunfighting lessons. Like our other tools, it provides a way to help identify soft spots in preparation, so actions can be taken to harden them.

Instructions: Read each statement and assess where you are **Now** and level **Desired**.

Scale: Circle A-F (A=excellent, B=good, C=satisfactory, D=poor, F=failure)

I am generally satisfied with steps I have taken to...	Now	Desired
Reconcile the harshness of battle before facing combat.	ABCDF	ABCDF
Practice decision-making under stress with tools such as battle simulations.	ABCDF	ABCDF
Identify and gain seasoned Noncommissioned officers as mentors.	ABCDF	ABCDF
Gain toughness by completing a military school aimed at probing my physical, mental, and emotional limits under stress (Ranger School, Marine recon, SEAL…).	ABCDF	ABCDF
Deal proactively as best I can with the many paradoxes of war (harm to innocents, casualties due to friendly fire…).	ABCDF	ABCDF
Develop my ability to appropriately select between decision-making options from deciding without consultation to deciding based on consensus.	ABCDF	ABCDF
Express myself with clarity in both verbal and written forms.	ABCDF	ABCDF
Put my personal affairs in order, specifically:	ABCDF	ABCDF
Financial (minimize debt, insurance…).	ABCDF	ABCDF
Legal (will, power of attorney…).	ABCDF	ABCDF
Estate (instructions to executor, funeral arrangement decisions…).	ABCDF	ABCDF
Express my deepest self and desired legacy to my loved ones in forms they can treasure (letter, poem, art, music...).	ABCDF	ABCDF
Embrace the warrior ethos of a noble soldier—internalize values of the profession.	ABCDF	ABCDF
Determined if I am called to be a warrior leader of character and servant for the nation?	ABCDF	ABCDF

If I am or expect to be a leader of military personnel, I am generally satisfied with the steps I have taken to...	Now	Desired
Be a follower first and experience the influence, positive or negative, of military leaders.	ABCDF	ABCDF
Apply ethical reasoning in tough decisions affecting my team, unit, or organization.	ABCDF	ABCDF
Identify which of the 23 dimensions of leadership in the Army Model I most need to improve.	ABCDF	ABCDF
Be competent in the "how to's" of the profession at my level of leadership.	ABCDF	ABCDF
State intent, expectations and parameters associated with directions given.	ABCDF	ABCDF
Lead and coach subordinates–praise progress, redirect, or reprimand.	ABCDF	ABCDF
Study military leaders and works of respected authors who share their insights into the profession of arms.	ABCDF	ABCDF
Inspire others through example and encouragement.	ABCDF	ABCDF
Influence others through presence, demeanor, and charisma apart from positional authority.	ABCDF	ABCDF
Understand the grieving process after the loss of a loved one and a leader's role in completing the mission while giving reverence to the deceased.	ABCDF	ABCDF
Visit memorials and cemeteries where veterans are buried to quietly pay homage to the sacrifice.	ABCDF	ABCDF
Persevere at a complex, difficult task until completed.	ABCDF	ABCDF

Gunfighting Action Plan

Purpose: to provide a simple tool to help you take "bite size" action steps between where you are and where you want to be.

Admit the truth about where you are and desire to be.

Accept the impact if you stay the same or if you take action.

Act to identify how you could move in a positive direction in areas that need work.

List the areas of greatest importance. **Prioritize** by numbering 1…

List what barriers keep you from improving in your top priority areas. **What "bite-size" actions** can I take to overcome the barriers and move toward the grade I desire?

Input for Stress Assessment: As a result of this assessment, list specific areas that cause you stress. Focus on those that matter most where the greatest grade difference lies. For example, my stress is: *I do not have my personal affairs in order and I worry about my ability to do the legal, medical, and financial tasks before deployment.*

Abstract of *Professionalism Under Stress Capstone Exercise Workbook*

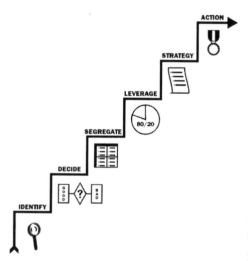

The capstone exercise workbook is available separately from Dyson Institute. The workbook includes the previous suite of tools provided in this book, instructions and templates for you to assess stressors and take lasting action to leverage positive stressors and mitigate negative ones.

The *workbook* also includes a case study, which illustrates how a fictional character, John Ustress, goes from identifying stressors to developing a pragmatic stress strategy.

Abstract of *Patriotism in Action*

Patriotism in Action demonstrates how serving as a true professional is an act of patriotism. It illuminates several lessons from this publication that relates to patriotism and remembrance for the fallen. Through examples and photographs we encourage appreciation for the service of military professionals and the meaning of patriotic holidays. Call to action ideas for how civilian and military professionals can do our part in peace and war enrich the contributions of patriots.

We designed the *Professionalism Under Stress Workbook* and *Patriotism in Action* to complement this *Professionalism Under Stress* book as a set of resources for you to receive knowledge, tools, and inspiration to prepare for living as your best-self. We encourage use of this set as part of your Call to Action.

Closing

If you have read this book, you made a choice to take in information that can add value for you. Now, you have another choice. You can tuck it away as, we hope, informative, interesting, and inspiring. Or, you can do what a true professional would do: decide upon ideas to internalize, write the important actions to take in your plan, and get started.

Whenever we learn new knowledge or gain added inspiration, true professionals typically have a new opportunity to internalize new or expanded ways of thinking and to act on ideas gained. This application distinguishes good stewards from wishful thinkers with good intent who do little.

When Dr. Ken Blanchard came to teach a seminar for us, I remember his advice, which I pass on often: *sometimes it is better to take action on one book than it is to read a second book.* A friend once joked that he needed to start running. He read a book about running. Then, he quipped, instead of starting to run he read another book on something else. Decide which lessons resonate with you and what action you should take—and get started—before you move on to new topics.

Respectfully consider what shall result from your reading about professionalism through the lens of combat and civilian professionals who have offered insights about learning and leaving a legacy. As you consider if and how you might apply the lessons and tools from this book, consider a passage from a commencement speech by Former President Ronald Reagan, as shared by friend and advocate Gerry Casey, fellow member of the Personal Leadership Association.

The character that takes command in moments of crucial choices has already been determined. It has been determined by a thousand other choices made earlier in seemingly unimportant moments. It has been determined by all those "little" choices of years past—by all those times when the voice of conscience was at war with the voice of temptation—whispering that "it doesn't really matter." It has been determined by all the day-to-day decisions made when life seemed easy and crises seemed far away—the decisions that, piece by piece, bit by bit, developed habits of discipline or of laziness; habits of self-sacrifice or self-indulgence; habits of duty and honor and integrity—or dishonor and shame.

-President Ronald Reagan-

Appendices

Glossary

References

Recommended Readings

Genesis for our Book

Appreciation

Dyson Institute Books/Seminars/Services

Glossary

Primary definition sources: *Webster's New Twentieth Century Dictionary*, http://www.Dictionary.com, and *The Dyson Dictionary: Positive Words to Plan and Lead Your Life*. When a word has multiple meanings, we use definitions that apply to context used in this book.

Ability: the quality of being able to do something, especially the physical, mental, emotional, professional, financial, or legal power to accomplish something; a natural or acquired skill or talent.

Accountability: called to account; answerable.

Abet: to incite; normally used in a bad sense like "aiding and abetting the enemy."

Acronym: a word formed from the first letter of several words; a form of simplified vocabulary.

Action: doing something, moving, affecting, influencing; deed, behavior, accomplishment, and performance.

Addiction: to give in habitually or compulsively.

Affirmation: asserting as true; positive declaration; confirmation. Statements in a personal vision that describe and reinforce ideas representing the life one wishes to live.

Ambush: an instantaneous surprise; being or feeling attacked.

Analogy: correspondence in some respects between things otherwise dissimilar; similarity or resemblance.

Arrugah: Navy motivational call. See "Hooah" for Army and Marine motivational call.

Attitude: the manner of acting, feeling, or thinking that shows one's beliefs, values, opinion and disposition; a state of mind or a feeling about a person, event, or thing; a manner of carrying oneself: *stood in a graceful attitude.* Dyson Institute includes in the seven components of attitude: choice, commitment, character, courage, confidence, connection, and charisma—with character representing all of these components.

Attributes: a person's fundamental qualities and characteristics.

Audacious: bold, daring spirit supported by thorough preparation of instincts. [Dyson Institute Definition]

Balance: mental or emotional equilibrium; to compare by estimating the relative importance or value of different things.

Battle Drills: repetitive, rigorous training in how to attack, defend or respond to serious likely threats or situations. Military examples are ambushes or vehicle searches. Law enforcement (SWAT) examples are active shooter, drug bust, vehicle take down, or hostage rescue. First responders have similar intense drills in likely, repetitive situations.

Behavior: conduct; manners; carriage of oneself, with respect to propriety or morals.

Belief: an acceptance of something as true; a strongly held opinion, expectation, judgment; creed.

Benchmarking: a standard or point of reference for measuring.

Best-self: planning and leading your life as a good steward fulfilling your callings, gifts, and talents.

Calling: what we discern as our highest purposes; divine summons; vocation; profession; trade; occupation.

Character: moral or ethical strength; keeping promises; doing what you say you will; displaying an attitude of commitment, courage, and confidence even after initial inspiration has waned. Dyson Institute uses character as virtually synonymous with attitude, an expanded view from traditional thinking.

Champion: has attributes of a winner; an ardent defender or supporter of a cause or another person.

Charisma: ability to attract others, earn the devotion of others; a person with charisma draws others to work with them because of purpose and/or personality.

Choices: responses to our callings; what we decide are our priorities; decisions we make.

Coach: private tutor, trainer, or instructor.

Commitment: the act of pledging or engaging oneself.

Competence: adequate fitness or ability; suitable; capable; fit for the purpose. In the military it links character (doing the right things) and leadership (influencing people to do the right things well).

Confidence: an assurance of mind or firm belief in the trustworthiness of another; reliance on one's own abilities; belief in one's own competency; self-reliance; assurance.

Contented Achiever: one who is fulfilled and materially successful; they do what they enjoy and are paid well for it. [Crouch, et al, *The Contented Achiever*]

Courage: the attitude or response of facing and dealing with anything recognized as dangerous; difficult, or painful, instead of withdrawing from it; spirit; desire; bravery; boldness; resolution; heroism, gallantry.

Covenant: a binding and solemn agreement by two or more persons; contract, bargain, stipulation, promise, engagement.

Creative: inventive; productive; power to create.

Creed: a statement of belief[s], principles, or opinions.

Creed (Organizational): a statement of beliefs, principles, philosophies, affirmations, or desired behaviors that steer the decisions and actions of the group.

Creed (Personal): a collection of favorite statements of beliefs, principles, and affirmations that help define how a person desires to live; when read regularly, these statements condition the mind to seek fulfillment.

Decision: act of choosing, making up one's mind; conclusion; resolution; determination; opinion.

Defilade: to arrange so the terrain or structure will protect from direct fire.

Destiny: ultimate fate; destination.

Determination: the mental habit of settling upon some line of action with a fixed purpose; adherence to aims or purposes; resoluteness.

Disappointment: feeling from failing to satisfy a hope, desire, or expectation.

Discern: to perceive, detect, recognize.

Discipline: the result of training that develops self-control, character, etc.

Distress: extreme pain; anguish of body or mind; unhappiness.

Earn: to acquire or deserve as a result of effort or action.

Edge: keenness of senses, as of desire or enjoyment; zest.

Education: knowledge or skill developed by a learning process.

Empower: to give power or authority; to give ability; to enable.

Esteem: valuation; estimation of worth; respect.

Ethical Fitness: doing the *harder right* or possessing character and competence to be able to make the right ethical choice even under extreme stress. [author definition]

Ethos: fundamental values, habits, customs peculiar to a specific people, as in the soldiers' "warrior ethos."

Excellence: possessing good qualities in an unusual degree; highly laudable, meritorious, or virtuous in persons, or valuable and esteemed in things.

Excuse: an attempted justification for not keeping a promise; a pretended reason.

Experience: all that has happened to one; undergoing or observing something; individual reaction to events, feelings; activity that includes training, observation, or practice.

Faith: unquestioning belief; trust; confidence; conviction.

Fear: feeling of anxiety; timidity; uneasiness; apprehension; dread.

Financial: budget, purchase, invest to satisfy needs for fiscal security, hope, freedom to pursue callings; pertaining to finance—resources, money, revenue, and wealth.

Financial Fitness: living within one's means; able to take care of basic security and personal/family needs, knowledge of planning, budgeting, principles and practices. [Dyson Institute]

Fitness Package: developing fitness and balance in the 7 areas of life—a major negative stress reducer. [author definition]

Flow: the essence of the most enjoyable, satisfying moments in our lives; condition in which you get so involved in something that you forget yourself. "Performing at your best and loving it." [Csikszentmihalyi, *Flow*]

Freedom: able to choose action freely; liberty; independence.

Fulfill (Fulfillment): to realize one's ambitions, potential.

Gunfight: a duel or battle with firearms. Here we use gunfighting as a metaphor for acute stressful situations. Although the corporate world is not literally a war, "conflicts of human interest" occur in almost every profession and, at times, result in acute stress.

Gunfighting: a fight between persons using pistols or revolvers. "The brotherhood of the close fight" (Gen. Keane).

Goal: the end or final purpose a person aims to reach or accomplish.

Habit: an automatic behavior done often and hence, usually, done easily; an act that is acquired; a practice or custom.

Harder Right: decision that most positively affects the widest circle of people for the greater good, even if requiring sacrifice.

Harmony: agreement in feeling, action, ideas, interests.

Health: physical and mental well-being.

Honesty: truthful, trustworthy, or upright.

Honor: esteem due or paid to worth; a sense of what is right, just, and true; gesture of respect or distinction, earned achievement, code of integrity.

Hooah: Army and Marine jargon which has evolved to have several meanings but generally it is an all purpose expression for gung-ho for the military and being held to a standard; a motivational call. [Al Pacino rode the expression to an Oscar in *Scent of a Woman.*] See "Arrugah" for Navy motivational call.

Impact: making a strong impression; making a significant difference.

Initiative: characteristic of originating new ideas; ability to think and act without urging.

Innovation: effecting change in the established order; introduction of something new.

Inspiration: inspiring influence; stimulus to creative thought or action; a prompting of something written or said; in theology, a divine influence resulting in writing or action.

Instinct: to make an inherent capability or behavior; a reaction without conscious thought.

Internalize: to take in and make an integral part of one's attitude and beliefs.

Jargon: form of simplified vocabulary peculiar to a group, nonstandard, shop talk, slang...see acronym.

Job Shadowing: matching one person's career interest with a seasoned, caring mentor who works in that career area. It allows the individual to observe the connection between education, marketable skills, and the work place.

Knowledge: information you use to know what to do.

Leader: one who leads or guides; one in charge or in command of others; one who has influence or power. [Dictionary]

Leader: one who seeks to fulfill his callings as his best-self and help others fulfill their callings to serve the greater good. [Dyson Institute]

Leadership: action; guidance; direction; showing the way by going first; position or office of a leader...capacity or ability to lead, influence. [Dictionary]

Leadership: Fulfilling our callings and choices as our best-selves; serving and leading others to live as their best-selves, and wisdom to understand and persistence to fulfill the greater good. [Dyson Institute]

Leadership: "The art of accomplishing more than the science of management says is possible." [General Colin Powell]

Leadership, Combined: leadership of military personnel from countries in addition to our own.

Leadership, Direct: face-to-face, first line leadership of others. Leadership of immediate subordinates.

Leadership, Interpersonal: interacting with and influencing others in society, with accountability but no responsibility such as when we interact with people we do not know. [Dyson Institute]

Leadership, Joint: leadership of military personnel from multiple services, mainly Army, Navy, Marines, Air Force, and Coast Guard.

Leadership, Life: planning and leading our lives in the seven areas of life. [Dyson Institute]

Leadership, Managerial: service to and leadership of leaders of teams and/or programs and groups, as in leadership of a group of teams in a division within an organization. [Dyson Institute]

Leadership, Organizational: providing synergistic strategic direction to an organized community of individuals, teams, divisions, and programs to serve clients, suppliers, and other stakeholders—balancing mission, people, and resources. Ensure design and creation of structures and systems to inspire and guide people to do the right things automatically. Help answer the questions, *what is our mission? How will we provide distinctive service? What do we value? How will we do our best—individually and collectively?* Help lead the way doing that with inspired service and influence. [Dyson Institute]

Leadership, Organizational: leadership of units from company through corps levels (100± - 1000's) and Department of the Army, Navy, or Air Force civilians at directorate through installation levels. The skills required differ from direct leadership in degree, but not in kind. The skill domains are the same but organizational leaders deal with more complexity, greater uncertainty, or unintended consequences and influencing more through policy-making and systems than face-to-face contact. [Military]

Leadership, Personal: understanding and acting on the common denominator principles of doing your best to be your best-self. [Dyson Institute]

Leadership, Societal: Visionary influence transcending and connecting individual, group, organizational, and cultural interests, as in social, economic and environmental considerations to serve the greater good at a community, regional, national, or international level. [Dyson Institute]

Leadership, Strategic: leaders at the major command through Department of Defense levels; includes global, regional, national, societal levels. [Military]

Least-worst: situations requiring a decision where no course of action is ideal and all have down-side consequences. [author definition]

Legacy: something handed down; a gift, a tradition.

Lesson: an experience, example, or observation that imparts beneficial knowledge or wisdom and leads to action.

Life: the time a person is alive; one's manner of living; the period of flourishing, usefulness.

Management: serving through the art and science of planning, organizing, directing, and controlling....

Maslow's Hierarchy of Human Needs: a pyramid-shaped model showing five major areas of need a person seeks to satisfy in typical priority order—physiological, safety/security, belongingness, esteem, and self-actualization. [See Dyson Hierarchy of Motivating Values with expanded seven levels.]

Mastermind Alliance: a group of persons who work together in harmony toward a common purpose.

Mastery: expert knowledge; eminent skill.

Meaning: has significance; having purpose; understood by acts or language.

Mentor: a wise and faithful counselor.

Metaphor: transfer from object it ordinarily designates to one it designates by implicit comparison or analogy. Metaphors often lead to models but the difference is significant. Models represent existing knowledge; metaphors explore new realms.

Mission: the special task or purpose for which a person is destined in life; calling.

Mission: The combat operation assigned an individual or unit. [Military]

Mission (Personal) Statement: a written statement summarizing a person's purpose in life; or statements of personal and professional purposes; the essence or summary of a vision statement; if the vision is the painting, the mission is the title. It usually starts with "To" followed by the purpose. [Dyson Institute]

Model: a schematic description of a system, theory. A person or thing considered as a standard of excellence to be imitated; to form or plan after a model, pattern, or design; conform to a standard of excellence. A models main advantage is that it imitates what works.

Moral: capable of making the distinction between right and wrong in conduct.

Morale: mental condition regarding courage, zeal, confidence, discipline, enthusiasm, and endurance.

Motivate: to furnish with a motive; to give impetus to; to impel.

Motivating Value: values that motivates a person to seek a result or condition. The Dyson Hierarchy identifies seven motivating values: Survival, Safety, Security, Social Connection, Self Esteem, Success, and Significance as the main values that motivate people. [See Maslow's Hierarchy of Human Needs.]

Objective: something aimed at or striven for; the aim or goal..

Officership: practice of being a commissioned leader swearing an oath of loyalty and service to the constitution.

Paradigm: a set of assumptions, concepts, values, and practices that constitutes a way of viewing reality for the community that shares them, especially in an intellectual discipline.

Paradox: a condition in which things tend to be contrary to each other.

Passion: extreme, compelling emotion; intense emotional drive or excitement.

Patriotism: love and loyal support of one's country.

Peak Performance: the psychology and practices of performing as your best-self.

Persistence: enduring continuance; lasting quality; resoluteness; tenacity; endurance.

Personal: belonging to human beings; private; individual; pertaining to character, conduct . . .

Personal Area of Life: plan, read, play, hobbies, listen to music, maintain your home...for emotional, mental, and intellectual health and development... [Dyson Institute]

Philanthropical: charitable; benevolent; generous; humane; contribute service and resources for schools, communities, charities, causes... [Dyson Institute]

Physical Area of Life: eat, sleep, bathe, groom, exercise to survive and care for physiological needs of the body; natural; visible. [Dyson Institute]

Positive Expectancy: state of expecting; focusing desired positive outcomes and solutions rather than worrisome negative possibilities.

Power: in this text, it means influence over others as in "power is the horsepower of leadership." It stems from a combination of position or title and perceptions others have based on the leader's presence, demeanor, and charisma.

Pragmatic Optimist: One who "looks at the bright side" in a practical way. [author definition]

Principle: the ultimate source, origin, or cause of something; a fundamental truth, law, doctrine, or motivating force upon which others are based; a rule of conduct.

Priority Performance: living your priorities through personal leadership principles that include focusing on mission, goals, and time priorities. [Dyson Institute]

Professionalism: professional status, methods, character, or standards. The general public seems to add the label "professional" to someone who has chosen a profession and has experience. We advocate a higher-level expectation for the "true professional."

Professional: engaged in a specified occupation for pay or as a means of livelihood; having much experience and great skill in a specified role. To work, learn, and train to serve while earning a living and enjoying a career.

Professional/True Professional: a person who seeks mastery and *earned empowerment* through *trust in character and competence,* preparing and persisting to develop fitness and habits to do *the harder right* well—even under stress. [authors]

Professional/Master Professional: a professional who knows and does the right things instinctively, with excellence. Like an Olympic athlete, the master professional develops fitness, capabilities, and instincts through preparation and practice over time until excellence comes naturally. [authors]

Rappel: controlled descent by means of a rope; in the military, normally from a helicopter or down a cliff or building.

Remembrance: something serving to celebrate or honor the memory of a person or event; a memorial; a greeting or token expressive of affection.

Ritual: a higher level habit with added meaning performed regularly so as to reinforce a desired end, as in a family tradition or desired habits to fulfill a resolution; a set form or system as in ceremonies.

Root: a primary source; an origin. An essential part or element; the basic core. A progenitor or ancestor from which a person or family is descended. The condition of being settled and of belonging to a particular place or society.

Roots: state of having or establishing an indigenous relationship with or a personal affinity for a particular culture, society, or environment:

Satisficing: doing only the degree of excellence required for the mission or task; not striving for perfection as a standard in everything when that extra effort adds little value. [Herbert Simon]

SEAL: acronym for Sea, Air, And Land; the Navy's combination of frogman/paratrooper/commando.

Significance: transcending success to seek higher level values like stewardship and spirituality.

Simulation: a representation of reality. "Games" or devices used to enhance ability or verify competence.

Skill: ability to do something well; proficiency; expertness.

Social Area of Life: having to do with human beings dealing with one another; share and do for others—through recreation and responsibility—for fun and fulfillment—to belong, care for, love... [Dyson Institute]

Spiritual: spirit or the soul, distinguished from the body; often thought of as the higher or better part of the mind; showing refinement of thought and feeling; sacred. Pray, study, worship, give and serve God to understand and fulfill your highest callings and gain higher level peace and fulfillment.

Spiritual Gift: a capacity such as leadership, teaching, or administration, which often complements your talents or those specific things you can do well.

Stakeholder: one who has a share or an interest, as in owners, team members, suppliers, and family members.

Strategy: the science of planning and directing large-scale military operations, maneuvering forces into the most advantageous position prior to actual engagement with the enemy; a plan or action. A plan created to fulfill a mission, vision, or goal by considering options and choosing satisfactory actions.

Stress: strain; pressure; tension; strained exertion that affects the body and mind; change to which you must adapt.

Stress, Bad: negative feelings often caused by poor preparation or effort and/or aiming at incorrect priorities, which weakens energy, results, and fulfillment—as in falling short on something important because of bad choices or investing time in something you should not be doing. [authors]

Stress, Good: positive pressure to perform and improve aimed at important priorities, which boosts energy, results, and fulfillment—as in working on an important project with limited time or resources and added expectations.

Stress, Intense: excessive changes, strains, or pressures, such as getting ambushed or suffering from trauma.

Stress, Normal: everyday changes, strains, and pressures such as from time demands, financial needs, relationship conflicts, and disappointments.

Stress, Safe: expanding beyond one's comfort zone in a demanding yet safe way with the intent of helping to better handle unexpected or extremely stressful situations. [authors]

Structure: To give form or arrangement; *structure a curriculum; structure one's day.*

Success: living your priorities; achievement of something desired; a favorable outcome; in secular society, the gaining of wealth, fame, rank.

Successful: having a favorable result, as in a successful mission.

Supercompensate: challenging a physical, emotional, or spiritual "muscle" past its current limits to build more sustained capacity.

SWAT: Special Weapons And Tactics.

Sweet Spot: aiming at and hitting a target balancing multiple important priorities like mission, resources, and stakeholders; a "triple-win." [authors]

Talent: a gift committed to one's trust to use and improve; any natural faculty, ability or power; something you do well, such as computers or sports; connected to spiritual gifts or general abilities like teaching or administration.

Teach: to show how to do something; to give instructions; to train; to guide study; to provide with knowledge, insight.

Teacher: one who instructs, trains, educates; provides knowledge, insight, enlightenment.

Toughness: resilience; able to withstand great strain without breaking down; rugged.

Trauma: a very disturbing, stressful experience; emotional shock from a real threat or one's interpretation of circumstances.

Threat: a future obstacle; impending danger; intent to inflict pain; clearly a source of stress, often intense stress.

Triage: A process in which things are ranked based on likely benefit when limited resources must be allocated.

Trust: Firm reliance on the integrity, ability, or character of a person or thing. Something committed into the care of another. The condition and resulting obligation of having confidence placed in on; reliance on something; belief in he honesty and integrity.

The Wall: Vietnam Veterans' Memorial in Washington, D.C.

Values (Motivating): foundational choices that drive behavior; what motivates a person most significantly; desired outcomes that drive goals and time priorities—survival, safety, security, connection, esteem, success, significance [Dyson Hierarchy].

Victory: success in any contest or struggle involving the defeat of an opponent or the overcoming of obstacles; triumph.

Vigor: active physical or mental force or strength; vitality; intensity; energy.

Vision: a mental image; the ability to perceive something not actually visible, as through mental acuteness or keen foresight; force or power of the imagination.

Vision, Personal: self-concept, expectations, affirmations.

Vision Statement: visualizing and describing desired outcomes; if your dreams or plans went like you want, what would happen.

Warrior Ethos: professional attributes and beliefs that characterize a noble soldier—refusal to accept failure, tight fabric of loyalty to other soldiers, leader accountability, will to win battles while living up to military values.

Will: strong purpose, intention, or determination (as, "where there's a will there's a way"); energy or enthusiasm; power of self-direction.

Wisdom: the faculty of making the best use of knowledge, experience, understanding; learning.

References

Books

Barber, Brace E. *Ranger School: No Excuse Leadership.* Patrol Leader Press, 1999.

Barnett, Rebecca. *Winning Without Losing Your Way.* Winning Your Way Inc., 2003.

Beckwith, Carol and Saitoti Tepolot Ole. *Maasai.* Abrams, 1980.

Bell, Ted. *Hawke.* Pocket Books, 2003.

Bennis, Warren and Nanus, Burt. *Leaders: The Strategies for Taking Charge.* New York, Harper & Row, 1985.

Burdick, Eugene, and Lederer, William. *The Ugly American.* W.W. Norton and Company, 1999.

Chapman, J.E. *The Leadership Styles of Generals Lee and Patton.* Birmingham-Southern College, 2003.

Covey, Steven R. *The 7 Habits of Highly Effective People.* Simon and Schuster, 1989.

Covey, Stephen R. and Merrill, A. Roger. *First Things First.* Simon & Schuster, 1994.

Curry, Cecil. *An Officer and a Gentleman: General Vo Nguyen Giap as Military Man and Poet.* March 1994.

Donnithorne, Colonel Larry (Ret.). *The West Point Way of Leadership.* Bantam Doubleday Dell Publishing, 1993.

Drucker, Peter F. *The Effective Executive.* Harper & Rowe, 1996.

Dunn, Lieutenant General Carroll H. *Base Development in South Vietnam 1965-1970.* Washington, DC, Department of the Army, 1991.

Dunn, Stretch, and Dyson, David. *Ethical Decisions and Actions.* Dyson Institute, 2002.

Dyson, David. *Suggestions for Successful Living: Positive Ideas for the 7 Areas of Life.* Leave a Legacy, Dyson Institute, 1994.

Ed Ruggero. *Duty First: West Point and the Making of American Leaders.* New York, Harper Collins, 2001.

Estes, Lieutenant Colonel Kenneth W. (USMC Ret.). *The Marine Officer's Guide.* Naval Institute Press, 1956.

Farrand, Max. *Autobiography of Benjamin Franklin.* Signet, 1949.

Field Manual 22-100. *Army Leadership Be, Know, Do.* Department of the Army, August 1999.

Field Manual 3-100.21. *Contractors on the Battlefield.* Department of the Army, January 2003.

Fisher, E. *Guardians of the Republic: A History of the Noncommissioned Officer Corps of the U.S. Army.* New York: Ballantine. 1994.

Frankl, Victor E. *Man's Search for Meaning.* Washington Square Press, 1946.

Fritz, Robert. *The Path of Least Resistance.* Ballantine, 1989.

Garfield, Charles. *Peak Performers: The New Heroes of American Business.* Avon Books, 1986.

Giles, Doug. *Ruling in Babylon,* Xulon Press, 2003.

Gregory, Jeane and Bruce, Harvey. *A History of the Mobile District Corps of Engineers, 1815-1985.* Prepared by Brockington and Associates, Charleston, SC, 2004.

Hansen, Victor Davis. *Between War and Peace: Lessons from Afghanistan to Iraq.* Random House, 2004.

Heller, Charles and Stoff, Brigadier General William (Ret.). *America's First Battles 1776-1965.* December 1986.

Hill, Napoleon. *Think and Grow Rich.* Fawcett Columbine, 1937.

Holy Bible, Thomas Nelson Publishers.

Hutson, Don; Crouch, Chris; and Lucas, George. *The Contented Achiever*. Black Pants Publishing, 2001.

Keegan, John. *The Face of Battle*. Penguin Group, 1978.

Kennedy, Lieutenant General Claudia J. and McConnell, Malcolm. *Generally Speaking*. Warner Books, 2001.

Kidder, Rushworth, *How Good People Make Tough Choices*, Fireside, 1995.

Kleiner, Art. *Who Really Matters: The Core Group Theory of Power, Privilege, and Success*. Doubleday/Currency, 2003.

Kryzewski, Mike. *Leading with the Heart*. Time Warner, 2000.

Lipski, David. *Absolutely American: Four years at West Point*. Boston, Houghton Mifflin, 2003.

Loehr, Jim and Schwartz, Tony. *The Power of Full Engagement*. Free Press, 2003.

Long, A.L. *Memoirs of Robert E. Lee*. Blue and Grey Press, 1983.

Mackenzie, Ross. *Brief Points*. Naval Institute Press, 1941.

McMahon, Colleen. *The View from Gabbatha*. Church Publishing, 2003.

Moore, Lt. General Harold (Ret.) and Galloway, Joseph. *We Were Soldiers Once...and Young*. Random House, 1992.

Myrer, Anton. *Once an Eagle*. Harper Torch, 1968.

Newman, Major General Aubry S. *What Are Generals Made Of?* Novato, CA: Presidio Press, 1987.

Novak, Michael. *Business as a Calling*. The Free Press, 1996.

Nye, Colonel Roger H. (Ret.). *The Challenge of Command*. Wayne, N.J.: Avery Publishing Group, Inc. 1986.

O'Neill, Robert J. *General Giap; Politician and Strategist*. New York, Praeger, 1969.

Peters, Ralph. *When Devils Walked the Earth*. Pocket Books, 2004.

Powell, General Colin (Ret.). *My American Journey*. Random House, 1995.

Petre, Peter and Schwarzkopf, General Norman H. (Ret.). *It Doesn't Take a Hero*. Bantam Books, 1992.

Scheffler, Israel. *Of Human Potential*. Routledge & Kegan Paul, 1985.

Simon Center for the Professional Military Ethic, United States Military Academy, West Point, NY. Extracts from: *The Army Officer Concept, Criteria for Assessing Self-Reflection* , draft of new edition of *The Armed Forces Officer*, 2004.

Smith, Hyrum W. *The 10 Natural Laws of Successful Time and Life Management*. Warner Books, 1994.

Smith, Major General Perry M (Ret.). *Taking Charge: A Practical Guide for Leaders*. Washington, D.C.: National Defense University Press, 1986.

Shaara, Michael. *The Killer Angels*. Ballantine, 1974.

Stoner, A. E. James and Freeman, R. Edward. *Management*. Prentice Hall, 1992.

Tucker-Ladd, Clayton E. *Psychology and Self-Help*. Mental Health Net, 1996.

Tzu, Sun. *The Art of War*. Dover Publications, 2002.

United States of America Federal Flag Code. 2001.

Walker, Paul K., Chief Historian. *Engineer Memoirs of Lieutenant General Carroll H. Dunn*. U.S. Army, Office of History U.S. Army Corps of Engineers, Alexandria, Va., 1968.

Warren, Rick. *The Purpose-Driven Life*. Zondervan, 2002.

Webster's New Twentieth Century Dictionary. Second Edition, Simon and Schuster, 1983.

Wooden, John with Jamison, Steve. *Wooden: A Lifetime of Observations and Reflections On and Off the Court.* Contemporary Books, 1997.

Wright, Evan. *Generation Kill.* G.P. Putnam's Sons, 2004.

Journals/Magazines/Articles/Reports/Letters/Messages

Biance, Anthony and Forest, Stephanie. "Outsourcing War," *Business Week,* September 9, 2003.

De Atkine, Tex. "Preliminary Report on Conditions in Iraq," Baghdad, December, 2003.

Dunn, Major C. Hilton (Stretch). "Terrain Boards as Tactical Instructional Aids," *Military Review Magazine, Professional Journal of the U.S. Army,* October 1975.

Fohn, Rosanne. "Move it, Move it," *USAA Magazine,* Oct. 2003.

Holley, Dr. I.B. "Reflections on Leadership for Would-Be Commanders," US Air War College, Air Univ. Press, circa 2000.

Iraq After Action Report, "Convoy and AT/FP Info," Dec. 2003.

Iraq, Letter home from Company Commander in 24th Engineer Battalion, "Another busy week in Baghdad," November 2003.

Johnson, Dr. Dewey. "Leadership: Some Thoughts after Twenty-Five Years," U.S. Air War College, Air University Press, circa 2000.

Loehr, James and Groppel, Jack. "Energy Management," *Chief Learning Officer,* December 2003.

Lawrence, Jim. *Reflections on Albany—The Agony of Vietnam.* Recorded at Boutwell Studios, Birmingham, A, 2005.

Mattis, Major General J.N. "1st Marine Division Message," 2003.

New York Times. Editorials Section A., March 29, 2003.

Schinnerer, John, PhD. "The ROI of an Effective Ethics Program." HR.com.

Veith, Gene. Article without title relating exploits of CPT Zan Hornbuckle during Iraq conflict, provided by Steven Dvorchak, January 6, 2004.

Waddell III, Colonel Donald (ret.). "A Situational Leadership Model for Military Leaders," *Aerospace Power Journal*, Fall, 1994.

Washington Post. "Homeland Security Trips Over Language," April 24, 2004.

Web Sites

http://www.activelivingleadership.org/costcalc.htm

http://www.army.mil

http://www.armyranger.com

http://www.civitaninternational.com

http://www.Dictionary.com

http://www.DysonInstitute.org

http://www.girlscouts.org/program/gs_central/promise_law

http://jaxmed.com/booras/FP_creed.htm

http://www.kiwanis.org/about/objects.asp

http://www.lzxray.com/battle.htm

http://www.NewsMax.com

http:/www.nps.gov/wamo/history/contents.htm

http://www.nspe.org/ethics/eh1-cred.asp

http://www.optimist.org/default.cfm?content=Vistors/Visitors

http://www.rdrop.com/~cary/html/creed.html#troop

http://www.rotary.org/aboutrotary/4way.html

http://www.scouting.org

Photographs

Dyson, David. Stretch Dunn at War Eagle Battalion Military Ball at Auburn University, 2003.

Kristian, Tech Sergeant (U.S. Air Force Ret.). Soldiers in Iraq.

Latoff, Rick. WWII Memorial.

Cover photos: Brady Parks primary photo. NSPE photo of two engineers. Rights to remaining photos are either from authors' library, Institute Library, or purchased by Dyson Institute.

Lectures/Interviews/Briefings

Gerber, Michael. "The E-Myth," TPN TV broadcast, circa 1995.

Jenkins, Brian M. "The Operational Code of the Jihadist," Rand Corporation briefing for Army Science Board, April 2004.

Lang, Enrique. Professional Football player, January 10, 2004.

Tilley, Jack. Sergeant Major of the Army. "Farewell Remarks," January 15, 2004.

Walters, Judge Don. "A Shreveport Judge's Report on Iraq," lecture, September 2003.

Audiotapes

Fanning, P., McKay, M. and Sonenberg, N. *Applied Relaxation Training*. New Harbinger Publications, 1991.

Davis, Martha, Ph.D., Eshelman, E. R., and McKay, M., Ph.D. *The Relaxation and Stress Reduction Workbook*. MJF Books, 2000.

Recommended Reading

Additional publications we have found beneficial that may have influenced our thinking though are not cited as references are provided to include a more extensive list of resources:

Allen, James. *As a Man Thinketh*. DeVorss & Company, 1983.

Blanchard, Ken and Bowles, Sheldon. *Gung Ho!* William Morrow and Company, 1998.

Blanchard, Ken and Hybels, Bill. *Leadership by the Book*. William Morrow, 1999.

Covey, Stephen R. and Merrill, A. Roger. *First Things First.* Simon & Schuster, 1994.

Crouch, Chris. *Getting Organized: Learning How to Focus, Organize and Prioritize.* Dawson Publishing, 2005.

Dyson, David. *Suggestions for Successful Living: Positive Ideas for the 7 Areas of Life. Leave A Legacy Publishing, 1994.*

Maslow, Abraham. *Motivation and Personality.* Addison-Wesley, 1987.

Maxwell, John. *The 21 Irrefutable Laws of Leadership.* Thomas Nelson, 1998.

National Institute of Science and Technology, *National Baldrige Quality Program Criteria for Performance Excellence*, 2005.

Peters, Thomas J. and Waterman, Robert H. *In Search of Excellence.* HarperCollins, 1982.

Pitino, Rick. *Success is a Choice.* Broadway Books, 1997.

Genesis of our Books

Colonel C.H. "Stretch" Dunn (U.S. Army Retired) speaks to cadets, cadre and guests of the War Eagle Battalion Military Ball at Auburn University to educate and inspire America's future soldiers.

The War Eagle Battalion at Auburn University invited Stretch to present the keynote speech at their Military Ball. His message focused on the cadets and included how they should prepare, what others expect of them, stories and lessons from his combat experiences, preparation that saved his life, plus his views on the roles of the soldier and our military in the United States of America.

Feelings of patriotism and need for professionalism remained extra high because of the "9/11" attacks by terrorists on the World Trade Center, the Pentagon, and a jetliner that missed a target thanks to heroic acts of civilian passengers. Stretch's speech included more than emotion—he was prepared with specific suggestions for preparation and action.

I felt inspired by the unfortunate though realistic need to fight terrorists. Further, I saw immediately applications for civilian professionals as well as our military. That was the genesis of what started as a booklet and has grown to co-authoring this book as well as our companion book, *Patriotism in Action*.

Within weeks, Stretch's dad passed away. The ensuing trip from Birmingham to Arlington National Cemetery at our nation's capital for the full military honors funeral inspired photographs and writings leading to development of *Patriotism in Action* and strengthened commitment to this book. The collective journey pursued to offer both books to you has fueled preparation to provide lessons, examples, and actions that can help you—and us—develop higher-level capacities.

My callings include learning, organizing, and teaching common denominator principles and practices of doing our best—personally as well as in families and organizations. That calling drives my writing, teaching, and serving as it did in founding Dyson Institute as an organization to support professionals to help people PLAN and LEAD in LIFE. I feel fortunate to work with Stretch and others who understand the important role of the military and its methods of preparing people to "be, know, and do" to serve with honor under intense stress and sacrificial circumstances.

We feel a calling to share with you principles and practices we believe add value in combat and civilian life—corporate, college, and church—as well as personal and family life. We are honored to serve you through these words and hope to continue with you the journey toward living as our best-selves.

David Hilton Dyson
Dyson Leadership Institute
Birmingham, Alabama USA

Appreciation

It is difficult to adequately thank all who helped this book come to life—either in providing inspiration for its content or through direct aid in its production. We will try.

My thanks to...

My wife, Joan, for her love, boundless energy, and support.

My mom, for helping us edit the first edition as she did for thirty-three books edited for her husband of sixty-three years.

My dad, for helping to teach me what it means to be a true professional and a soldier-leader.

Captains Tomas J. Hayes and Boyd (Mack) Harris, two classmates long deceased though always remembered as exceptional role models of leadership and professionalism.

Dr. Rita Oberle and Dr. Joyce Shields for years of mentoring.

Mo Faber, Norm Cooney, and Joe Oberle, great friends whose flow of e-mails provided tidbits of insights and inspiration.

Brady Parks for infinite patience in making many of the photographs and designing the cover.

Tom Wofford, Roman Szymberski, and Rick Swain for editing advice.

Barbara Dryden, Bob Nelson, and Mike Theus for assistance with editorial changes, desktop publishing, and printing.

Auburn University—The War Eagle Battalion for inviting me to speak to their Military Ball—preparation and presentation of that speech inspired this book. And, The Pi Kappa Alpha Fraternity Chapter for hosting us during our trip and for making my visit to a fraternity house a positive experience.

Stretch

And thanks to...

My mom, who gives copies to her church members and affirms how students can benefit from our books.

My dad, who gives copies to his "coffee buddies" and military friends.

Kyle Crider, for much needed desktop publishing and loyal service beyond the expectations of his graduate internship.

Hack Sain, who gave us opportunity to develop some of our lessons in helping him "leave a legacy of leaders" in Sain Associates—and became one of our trustees.

Dwight Wiggins, who gives books to his children and clients, plus serves as trustee and chairman of our advocates council.

Faculty of Dyson Institute who demonstrate professionalism and leadership through preparation and inspired service.

Members of the Personal Leadership Association for listening to our ideas and reading drafts at our monthly seminars.

Owners and executives in our Leadership Education briefings for verifying our concepts and applications.

Participants in our Professional Development Education seminars for learning what it takes to be true professionals.

Our PLAN for LIFE workshop seminar students who identify and take action on ideas that inspire and guide them.

Sponsors and clients who give us opportunities to serve.

Troyce, Brandon, and Nick Brunson for persevering with us to get it right in printed form.

Roy Williams at *The Birmingham News*, Michael Hart at *Success Radio Network*, and Lauren Bishop Cooper at *Birmingham Business Journal* for helping us tell our story to more people.

David

Dyson Leadership Institute

…provides research and publication, teaching, and service designed to learn, teach, and help people and organizations PLAN and LEAD in LIFE. We teach and coach principles and best practices, plus systems to help individuals, teams, and organizations to succeed with significance over time.

We applaud your effort to prepare and serve as a patriot in action and true professional. We invite you to:

- ◆ Join our e-list to receive announcements and invitations regarding publications, educational programs, and faculty.
- ◆ Enroll for seminars and services to help you develop and serve at higher levels in life, profession, and leadership.
- ◆ Let us know how we can help you to PLAN and LEAD in LIFE, plus leave a legacy through common callings. If your mission matches ours, we invite you to also consider offering volunteer service and/or sponsorship support so we can succeed with greater significance together than we can separately.

David@DysonInstitute.org or CHDStretch@DysonInstitute.org

205.969.Dyson (3976)
205.968.Fax1 (3291)
www.DysonInstitute.org
www.ProfessionalismUnderStress.com

Mission

To help people and organizations
PLAN and LEAD in LIFE
to fulfill their callings.

Vision

1. Individuals understand their callings, gifts, and talents—and make choices to fulfill them—designing and using a PLAN for LIFE that inspires and guides them to learn and LEAD their lives, leaving a legacy.
2. Organizations and teams succeed and distinguish themselves with improved design of mission, vision, values, goals, strategies, structures, systems, and best practices that support and reward people to do the right habits automatically.
3. We serve our state and nation to benefit colleges, corporations, professional societies, churches, and other organizations who seek to serve as "champions" of individual, family, and organizational development.

Beliefs

1. People can continually improve and empower themselves if educated, enlightened, and encouraged with principles and practices that help them lead significant lives as their best-selves.
2. Systems should be designed to support individual development and empowerment to support organizational values and goals aimed at helping people do the right habits automatically.
3. If we the people improve ourselves and systems that support the common denominators of personal and organizational excellence, we can love and serve others more meaningfully, thus improving our world.

Dyson Institute Resources

Books

- ❏ *Professionalism Under Stress: 7 Lessons for Professionalism, Stress, and Gunfighting in Military and Civilian Life.* Stretch Dunn and David Dyson.
- ❏ *Professionalism Under Stress* on CD to read.
- ❏ *Patriotism in Action.* David Dyson and Stretch Dunn.
- ❏ *Patriotism in Action* on CD to read.

Get copies for personal use, gifts, and training

- ❏ For a list of booksellers and our most recent list of resources, call or write to Bookstore@DysonInstitute.org.
- ❏ Purchase online at www.ProfessionalismUnderStress.com or DysonInstitute.org.
- ❏ Bulk orders for organizations/courses: executives and training/learning leaders, please call or provide contact.
- ❏ Bookstores and suppliers: please call or provide contact.
- ❏ Add me to your e-mail list for invitations/announcements.

Name_____

Phone_____

Email_____

Ask your favorite bookseller to provide you with our books
or call us
205. 969.Dyson (3976)
www.DysonInstitute.org

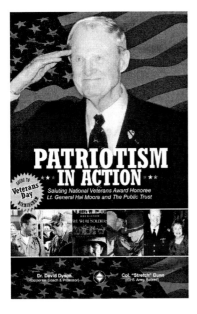

Patriotism In Action

Saluting National Veterans
Award Honoree Lt. General Hal
Moore and The Public Trust
Dr. David Dyson and
Col. Stretch Dunn
190 pages, 100+ photographs,
interesting for students and
adults.

Selected Contents

Full Military Honors Funeral,
Riderless Horse, 21-gun Salute
"Taps" —Lyrics and Story
Gen. Douglas MacArthur: A
Patriot's Farewell
Memorials: Washington Monument, World War I, WW II,
    Iwo Jima, Korean War, Vietnam
The Pledge of Allegiance to the United States of America
Patriotic Songs: The National Anthem, America The Beautiful
    God Bless America, America, Proud to be an American…
Patriotic Holidays: Memorial Day, Independence Day, Veterans
    Day, and Guide to Veterans Day Birmingham
Medal of Honor Heroes with ties to Alabama
Lt. General Hal Moore: National Veterans Award Honoree
    We Were Soldiers: book and movie, This I Believe Message for
    America, Patriot in Action Legacy: The National Endowment
    for the Public Trust, Home of the Brave, and Character-
    Based Leadership Program for Youth
Tomb of the Unknown Soldier
U.S. Flag: President and Children Pledging Allegiance,
    Astronaut Neil Armstrong Places U.S. Flag on the Moon…
U.S. Soldiers Praying in Iraq
USS Birmingham
Call to Action for a Patriot, Patriotic State

www.PatriotismInAction.us

"Stretch" Dunn

Col. C.H. "Stretch" Dunn, Jr. (U.S. Army Retired), PE, is a 1966 honor graduate of the U.S. Military Academy (West Point), a distinguished graduate of the Command and General Staff College, Army War College Fellow, and a professional engineer.

Col. Dunn served in three infantry divisions, earned the Expert Infantryman Badge and four awards for bravery, including the Silver Star in Vietnam. He co-invented the Dunn-Kempf war game used to teach a generation of small unit leaders war fighting techniques. Later, he headed a 1,000-soldier combat unit and a 3,000-person engineering and construction management organization with 40 field offices in the Southeast United States and in Latin America.

Following retirement after 26 years in America's Army, Stretch served 10 years in corporate America with BE&K, an international engineering and construction company based in Birmingham. After his second retirement, he joined Dyson Leadership Institute as president to advise, write, and teach on leadership and ethics, including faculty for the Personal Leadership Association. He directs the *Professionalism Under Stress* and *Hack Sain Leadership in Engineering* programs. He serves as vice chairman of the Character-Based Leadership for Youth and The Home of the Brave Task Force and is a founding fellow for The National Endowment for The Public Trust.

Stretch serves on the board for his West Point class and several organizations in the Birmingham Area, including the Norton Board at BSC, and sings in the choir of his church. He received the Johnny Johnson Loyalty Award for long-term volunteerism to Dyson Institute, primarily through the Personal Leadership Association.

Stretch lives in the Birmingham Area with his wife, Joan, and cat, Jasmine. He has two children, Steve and Cheryl, and four grandchildren.

David Dyson

Dr. David Dyson attended schools in the Birmingham Area, then earned the Bachelor's Degree in Business at Auburn University, Masters in Management at Birmingham-Southern College, and the Doctoral Degree in the Department of Educational Leadership at Vanderbilt University. He completed the Institute for Educational Management at Harvard University and the College Management Program at Carnegie-Mellon University.

David served college students and alumni as an educational and leadership consultant on the national staff of Pi Kappa Alpha Fraternity and associate vice president and adjunct professor at Birmingham-Southern College before starting Dyson Leadership Institute. He serves as an author, executive and life coach, leadership and management consultant, professor and trainer with the professional mission: *to help people and organizations PLAN and LEAD in LIFE.* He has served as president of five volunteer organizations. In 1992, David founded the Personal Leadership Association with Johnny Johnson. He is a founding fellow for The National Endowment for The Public Trust and serves the Principled Leadership Committee.

Awards for servant leadership: 10 Outstanding Young Citizens of Alabama; 10 Outstanding Senior Students, Auburn University; Outstanding Undergraduate Member (1975) and Outstanding Alumnus (1984), Pi Kappa Alpha Fraternity at Auburn; #1 Region and #7 National First-year student businessman and "The Diamond Award" for effort from The Varsity Company of Thomas Nelson Publishers; honor graduate, BSC Masters in Management; in Birmingham, Outstanding Young Educator and Top 40 Under 40.

David is the son of Eb and Joan Dyson, brother to Pam Bryant and Patty Thompson, "Uncle Dave" to Lea, John, Noah, Joshua, and Hannah, and pet parent to Samson.

Notes and Ideas